Getting to The Motley Fool Online!

David and Tom Gardner are cofounders of The Motley Fool, an online forum that can be found on the Web at www.Fool.com and on America Online at Keyword: FOOL.

Whether you're looking for additional research on the stocks in your portfolio, new investment ideas, information about your 401(k) plan, daily news updates on the world's most dynamic companies, minute-by-minute stock quotes, or just a place to talk to other investors, Fool.com has all of that and more—available twenty-four hours a day.

You can enjoy additional benefits of being a Fool by registering (for free!) at Fool.com. These benefits include:

- Special discounts on Foolish products
- Your own personalized Fool home page
- The ability to track your portfolio online and compare its performance with the S&P 500
- The opportunity to post messages on our popular discussion boards
- Alerts when there are Fool appearances or events in your neighborhood

Check it all out at www.register.Fool.com.
Get Foolish!

THE
MOTLEY FOOL
YOU HAVE
MORE THAN
YOU THINK

THE FOOLISH
GUIDE TO
PERSONAL FINANCE

Completely Revised
and Expanded

DAVID and
TOM GARDNER

A FIRESIDE BOOK
PUBLISHED BY SIMON & SCHUSTER
NEW YORK LONDON TORONTO SYDNEY

For Mom

FIRESIDE
Rockefeller Center
1230 Avenue of the Americas
New York, NY 10020

FIRESIDE and colophon are registered trademarks
of Simon & Schuster, Inc.

Designed by Irving Perkins Associates

Manufactured in the United States of America

9   10

Library of Congress Cataloging-in-Publication Data

Gardner, David, date.
The Motley Fool you have more than you think : the foolish guide to personal finance /
David and Tom Gardner.
p. cm.
Includes index.
1. Portfolio management.   2. Investment analysis.   3. Finance, Personal.
I. Gardner, Tom, date.   II. Motley Fool, Inc.

HG4529.5.G3728 2001
332.6—dc21
00-046328
ISBN-13: 978-0-7432-0174-2
ISBN-10:   0-7432-0174-4

Contents

Introduction

Our Fairy-Tale World

ONCE UPON A TIME there was a prosperous country called the United States of America. America had fertile land, sunstruck coasts, purple mountains, and a happy people. She sported free public education, expensive but effective health care, and high-speed data networks anyone could tap into with a computer and a modem. In America more than any other place ever, you could do and say what you wanted, and your destiny was largely—to an almost disturbing degree—in your own hands. In fact, despite the protestations of whichever political party happened to be out of power at the time, America was the envy of the world.

But there was one thing that Americans lacked. Despite their comparatively rich status, Americans had very little understanding of what to *do* with their money. Most would just spend it, all of it—and in many cases, even more than that. In fact, 70 percent of Americans carried around monthly debt on misunderstood little plastic devices called credit cards. Even those not seduced by these devices had a problem. Their instincts might have been right: Save the money and make it grow. But how to save it, *how* to make it grow, was something no one ever taught them.

It must have had something to do with their educational system. Their schools, particularly the best ones, focused on the liberal arts: languages, literature, history, philosophy, plus a little science and mathematics. But while some Americans were taught calculus before college, few were taught any of the elementary personal finance and investing terms that would make their lives so much easier *after* college. Easy-to-understand concepts—price-to-earnings ratios, discount brokers, index funds, depreciation, balloon payments—became instead terrifying (or terrifyingly boring) shadowy beasts whose names were to be spoken in whispers if they must be spoken at all. Pent up in their cages, the beasts remained forever inaccessible. It wasn't just the bars that kept these concepts caged—there was no formal education of any kind about money!

But what was it that most United States citizens worked the better part of their adult lives to obtain? What would enable them to buy the house, the car . . . or to retire, or to put *their* children through school? The irony was inescapable: Due to an oversight of the educational system, one of the few truly universal, commonplace, and important subjects—money—became the stuff of an exclusive ruling class of "financial professionals."

And most of these "professionals" had for decades clothed the subject in expensive garments: overlong and extravagant words, weighty tones, an air of exclusivity. The implication was that only a Wise man could make sense of it all. But should that have been surprising? Most of the establishment made its money by managing that of *others*. That was the whole business. Thus, the less that the United States knew about its money, the greater the business for its car salesmen, banks, insurance salesmen, stockbrokers, and financial planners. Indeed, the establishment had little incentive to teach anyone anything at all! As history had occasionally and unfortunately demonstrated, the greatest money was made off the greatest ignorance. Future historians needed to look no further than the government itself for proof, as one state government after another sponsored daily lotteries preying on the widespread lack of financial understanding.

Capitalizing on ignorance was all the rage, short-term game that it was. And the game's top players would indeed have been long-term winners if it hadn't been for one tiny little plot twist we intentionally haven't yet mentioned—the birth of online mass communication.

The birth of the Internet.

In July of 1993, from a small shack on the back of a nondescript residential property far removed from Wall Street, a little publication printed its first issue, bearing the improbable title *The Motley Fool*. Its goal was to educate, to amuse, and to enrich. Its name, alluding to Shakespeare's Fools, arose from the belief that truth often lay outside the bounds of conventional wisdom. The publication had its shtick, it had some decent ideas, and it had a terribly small audience . . . mainly family friends.

A year later, that same publication emerged from that same shack in newly hatched electronic form on America Online (AOL), and a small subversive movement had begun. Within a year, The Motley Fool became AOL's best-known site. At the close of 1995, Foolishness spread to an additional site, on the World Wide Web (www.Fool.com), whose audience and community of participants now number several million. We know the story so well because we were the guys who, way back when, were hacking away all night at our keyboards in that small shack.

But hey, *what* the heck was going on here?!

The answer was easy, but you had to know where to look. You had to look at medieval Europe, five centuries earlier.

At that time, it was another universal, commonplace, and important subject—religion (here, Christianity)—that had become an exclusive province. For centuries, a tiny but powerful elite clergy had been the exclusive interpreter of biblical stories and truths for the illiterate masses. And as is the case with our modern-day financial world, language then also served as a control. The medieval church wrote its documents and celebrated its Masses exclusively in Latin, a foreign language to most of its adherents, who spoke only their own local dialects.

That condition persisted until the development of the first great mass medium for publishing, in the 1430s: the Internet's truest technological ancestor, the printing press. Over the next century, Johannes Gutenberg's movable metal type ushered in a period of technological innovation, intellectual ferment, and social revolution of a type the world hadn't seen for more than a thousand years. Martin Luther translated the Bible into German; John Calvin and others did the same in French. Their efforts opened up new understanding and education for the populace, giving birth to what we today call the Reformation. The result? A new, open publishing standard diminished the church's power, following the democratization of its subject. The Bible found its way to the bedside table.

This should all be sounding very familiar, because the Internet is serving the same benign purpose today that the hand press did in the fifteenth century. (If the analogy interests you, flip to "Appendix I, Scribes? Meet Printers!", for some humorous further elaboration.) And don't expect any nice comments from the giants that the Internet is slaying, either! It's called revolution, dear reader. Let's fast-forward a few centuries and look a little deeper.

The French Revolution kicked off on July 14, 1789, when a Parisian mob stormed the now famous (and demolished) prison La Bastille. That day, a shocked King Louis XVI (who would lose his head three and a half years later) turned to his trusted Duke La Rochefoucauld-Liancourt and asked, "Is it a revolt?" The duke answered bluntly—and quite accurately—"No, sire, it is a revolution." Indeed it was, and is today as much as ever.

The world is changing rapidly, and as in the past, these changes favor *you,* the individual, not the entrenched establishment. That accords with the opinion of another Frenchman, the renowned student of America Alexis de Tocqueville, who asserted more than 150 years ago that America gets more democratic and egalitarian with every passing day.

So we are today perched at a crossroads between the Old World—where average people were kept in the dark about their finances—and a New World, in which we each now have the means to manage our money effectively. What's cleared the way toward this New World is a bulldozer of contributing factors that include greater distribution of educational materials, universality of corporate retirement plans, ubiquity of mutual funds, accessibility of investment information via the Internet, the popularity of investment clubs, the success of the discount brokerage industry, ongoing price reductions and improvements in personal finance software, and an increasing expectation among our younger generations that they'll receive nothing from (government-managed) Social Security. And about fifteen or twenty other reasons as well.

As Rabbi Hillel charged us, so we charge you with regard to managing your money: "If not now, when?" To which we add, *if not us, who?* In this un-Wise tome we'll have occasion to mention many people who'd *like* to manage or otherwise relieve you of your money. Unfortunately, in most cases they bring with them some basic conflicts of interest that put them at odds with your own greatest good. In fact, if you sometimes just stare long enough at the warm and fuzzy television ads put out by the financial services industry, you may begin to glimpse a huge gape-jawed monster lurking behind. "MONEY!" it roars, meaning yours.

Tocqueville was fond of pointing out that we Americans care a good deal about our money: "I know of no country, indeed, where the love of money has taken a stronger hold on the affections of men and where a profounder contempt is expressed for the theory of the permanent equality of property." So it's not just our voracious financial services industry that cares so much . . . it's all of us. OK, so if we do care so much about our money—which is often made to sound wrong or bad, when it needn't be—then it makes even more sense that we should be stewards of *our own* wealth.

Given the historical trends, the Internet's game-changing new rules, and the revolution that's occurring as we write, managing your own money is now easier and more rewarding than ever before. Indeed, we expect that the fairy-tale world depicted at the opening will increasingly look like most fairy tales—drawing off images of an antiquated past. America is waking and will never be the same.

In the tradition of all Motley Fool scribblings, what you now hold in your hands provides practical, simply worded, and systematic advice for creating your own successful approach to saving, spending, and investing money. No preexisting financial knowledge necessary. (It might even be a detriment.)

$20 Million Patience

The prologue ended, the music subsiding, the crowd in its seats and now becoming hushed, we begin our show with one simple premise. As it is with your life, so too with your money: *You have more than you think.*

Every dollar that you've saved, every penny in the pig, has a potential value far greater than you think. You might live in a worn-out shanty a stone's throw from railroad tracks, with no more than $250 to your name, but we're telling you that those savings hold more possibility than you think.

And maybe you'd say you don't know anything about—nor have any interest in—your money. Maybe attending to your credit card, bank account, or broker seems simultaneously daunting and petty. All those calculations of percentage points, interest payments, and growth rates leave your heart feeling cold, your mind in a dizzy somersault, your soul empty. Most Americans feel the same way—outmatched and thoroughly uninspired by the world of personal finance and investing. You'd be no different from the rest.

But even then, or particularly then, *you have more than you think.* For instance, you will derive far greater pleasure from understanding your finances than you might currently imagine. Take a second to ponder on something you really love in this world. Surfing? Mystery books? Ping-Pong? French wine? Long-distance running? The disciplines in each of these actually mimic those of basic money management. The joy associated with one can naturally transfer over to the other.

In the few hundred pages you have before you, we offer plain language, a smattering of basic mathematics, a few dozen gags, and the occasional random burst of common sense. These things compose the palette and brush we'll use to illustrate that you can succeed in achieving true wealth whether you're starting out today with $57 in your savings account, $500,000 in your brokerage account, or $77,200 in mortgage debt. True wealth isn't just about money, of course, though your money will be expanding, secure, supportive of your ideals, and probably more than you need. True wealth comprises also family happiness, cultural enrichment, the satisfaction of a job well done, and copious extra time to pursue your hobbies and interests. We'd be fools (small *f*) to promise you all these things here. But what we can state emphatically is that a secure financial situation makes each of these far easier to come by. And we do promise that this book will transform the toilsome, tormenting task of mastering your money into good, clean, energizing fun.

In fact, if by the end of *The Motley Fool You Have More Than You Think* you find that this is *not* the case—that we've bored you or confused you, or just generally let you down—we'll fall back on our standard Foolish recommendation, which is to encourage you to sue our multibillion-dollar litigating powerhouse of a publisher.

As mastery is our end, let us begin by studying the best. If you'd like to be the best softball hitter in your neighborhood, watch how Ted Williams swatted at a pitched baseball. If you want to be a filmmaker, Hitchcock's numerous classics await you at the corner store—why not start there? Today's great pianists grew up playing Chopin, Mozart, Brahms, and Beethoven *for years*. Fools that we are, we propose that this is the exact approach to take with your money.

In our search for a model, we stumbled upon a rather unlikely character. Our Chopin of finance wasn't a full-service broker, wasn't a big-name money manager on Wall Street, wasn't a self-proclaimed financial expert inking columns in the daily paper. She wasn't a man, either. And she was uncelebrated—no magazine covers, certainly, and in fact not even a single appearance on any of today's superabundant financial shows on cable TV. She was nobody, really. She was just an individual investor. In a financial world where Wisdom and celebrity are so closely associated, she was just a darn Fool. The notion that she, quietly investing on her own, might be the *most* expert would undermine all that America believes to be true about money. Here too, Pythagoras was right: To find truths, we must invert.

So, who is she?

Ladies, gentlemen, and Fools, meet Anne Scheiber, a New Yorker whose initial $5,000 investment in common stocks in 1944 steadily grew into $22 million by the time of her death in 1995. The only reason we ever heard of her is that in her estate she deeded all of her money to Yeshiva University in New York, creating a splash media event at her death. As the story unraveled, investors at The Motley Fool online tried to figure just how she could have ended life with a treasure chest befitting royalty. The answer lay in simple thinking and the power of compounded numbers.

Anne Scheiber's investment portfolio grew at an annual rate of 18.3 percent. Some years, she lost a bundle—between 1972 and 1974, her portfolio lost nearly half its value. In other years, she nearly doubled her money. But, all told, her money grew at that average yearly rate of 18.3 percent. Let's artificially apply a steady rate of 18.3 percent annual growth to her $5,000 investment, just to see what it looks like after one, ten, thirty, and fifty years:

$5,000 Portfolio Growing at 18.3 Percent per Year

Initial Investment	After 1 Year	After 10 Years	After 30 Years	After 50 Years
$5,000	$5,915	$26,842	$773,593	$22.3 million

The inquisitive reader may be wondering just what it took to grow Ms. Scheiber's money at that swift annual rate of 18.3 percent. Was she mixing in some casino betting? Did she take Trump-like risks, borrowing unthinkable sums of money? Was she seen down at the dog tracks on Wednesday evenings with large bills and a bagged jar of whiskey? Did she rely heavily on expensive advice from the marbled mansions in Manhattan's downtown?

Not exactly.

Ms. Scheiber did not play her money in real estate, bonds, options, gold coins, derivatives, or ostrich farms. She wasn't a gambler. And she never bought a single mutual fund. Though she had an account with a full-service broker, she eschewed that industry's accustomed approach to investing, which involves frequent trading using up-to-the-second information. If Anne Scheiber were writing this introduction, she'd be leaning over our keyboard right now typing in that her profits were achieved in an unremarkable fashion, by a method that anyone in America—regardless of gender or race or all those other largely artificial distinctions that the media is always foisting upon us—could have used to turn $5,000 into $22 million.

How did she do it?

She invested her long-term savings in the stock market—an arena that many Americans considered highly speculative at the time, just as they do now. Scheiber used that money to become part owner in a handful of well-known businesses. She recognized that millions of people drink Coca-Cola and Pepsi every day, that millions treat themselves with medicine from Schering-Plough and Pfizer, that millions drive Chrysler automobiles. And so, after some basic financial analysis, she bought some stock in each of these and held on for decades.

We don't want to oversimplify here. Holding on to the same stocks *for decades* isn't something of which we're all instinctively capable. It took patience above all, particularly during bad market years. Hand in hand with that patience was the resolve to ignore the sometimes loud and panicky headlines splashed across the covers of our nation's glossy news and financial magazines. And not everyone is born with Ms. Scheiber's awareness that active trading in and out of different investments leads to three things, all bad for the average investor: (1) anxiety, (2) high commissions for the brokerage firm, and (3) stiff yearly capital gains taxes. We're not saying everyone can be Anne Scheiber, but it seems a good deal easier and more enjoyable to take her road to riches than most of the others we've come across. Anne Scheiber inverted the conventional Wisdom to find the truth.

It is this conventional Wisdom that we'll be assailing throughout these pages. After all, common thinking says you'd need huge sums of capital to buy stocks, that the stock market is *big* and indecipherable, and that you shouldn't invest without the expensive assistance of a professional. Applesauce! That nonsense comes from the industry itself, which makes money off of your ignorance. Theirs is a philosophy of material convenience; they make a lot of money when you can't do it yourself.

As new as our *roll-up-your-sleeves-and-do-it-yourself* mantra may sound, it's as old as the public markets. Many of history's great investors and financiers—Rothschild, Getty, and Buffett among them—have held that common Fools with a bit of discipline and persistence can turn paper into platinum. Those ideas were effectively iterated once again recently by an unlikely source—one of our nation's great mutual fund managers, a darling on Wall Street, Peter Lynch. Lynch spent his career among the Wise as he managed Fidelity's largest fund, Magellan. From 1977 to 1990, he sweetened the lives of his investors by earning them annual returns of over 29 percent. A $10,000 investment in Magellan grew to $274,000 during his thirteen-year tenure. One might expect Mr. Lynch, upon retirement, to have toured the country in regal attire, championing "professional" money management. After all, he must have used unusually sophisticated strategies and exposed his investors to substantial risk in the process, right?

Nope. Like Anne Scheiber's, Lynch's approach is straightforward and accessible. And rather than pumping up Wall Street and the mutual fund industry, upon retirement he sat down and wrote a number of investment books that, more than any before, promote the idea that "amateur" investors can best manage their own money. To support this highly un-Wise position, Lynch tells the story of a group of seventh-graders at St. Agnes School in Boston who, by using nothing more than horse sense, consistently outperformed 95 percent of our nation's richly rewarded fund managers and financial advisors.

Kids were beating up all over the starched shirts.

Given what we've already written, you probably won't be surprised by their method. They bought companies like the Gap, Disney, Nike, Tootsie Roll, Pepsi, Topps, and NYNEX. They looked for household names with strong future prospects. Finding these companies took little more than focusing on excellence among strong long-term consumer businesses, an approach we'll teach in this book. Importantly, their approach avoided the greatest mistake that most people make with their investing, which is buying stuff they don't understand. The seventh-graders started small, bought what they knew, and did it all themselves.

So here you have it. Five thousand dollars standing pat for fifty years on its way to becoming $22 million. Seventh-graders trampling Wall Street. And in the face of it, a financial services industry whose expensive marketing and overpriced advisors are hell-bent on saying it can't be done. Given this milieu, you just know it's time for some multicolored caps to tumble across the stage. It was the Fool in Elizabethan theater who played to the people while speaking simple truths to the king and queen. Hundreds of years later, Folly is alive and well, and the truths to be told in today's financial world are that

• You can do much better managing your own money than giving it over to someone else

- You can quickly and painlessly learn how to save thousands of dollars on a house, a car and other major purchases
- Planning and executing your financial decisions needn't take more than a few hours each month
- You will actually enjoy this work, if it's framed Foolishly
- The only math you'll need is straight out of your fifth-grade textbook
- Being rational about these matters is both crucial and fun

Unfortunately, this simple message of regular savings, sensible spending, and self-directed investment in stocks hasn't yet reached everyone. We live in a nation where approximately 70 percent of the individual ownership of public companies remains in the hands of 10 percent of the people. This is *not* because only rich people can buy stocks: it simply speaks to a broad lack of education about finances.

Unfortunately, too, even when people *have* started investing, of late they've been socking their futures away into mutual funds. Americans have poured over $4 trillion into stock funds, in most cases not realizing that these funds have consistently underperformed the market. Of course, this is better than dropping it on the greyhound in lane six. But over the past five years more than 80 percent of stock mutual funds have underperformed the stock market's average return. With these and other missteps, the gap between the haves and the have-nots is widening; it's as much the result of poor math skills as anything. Later in this book, we'll present an extreme and show how, over time, the investor who starts with just $500 in common stock will demolish the wealthy lottery player or casino bettor starting with $15 million. This Fool will also outrun the steady investor with a good deal of money in underperforming mutual funds.

In simple mathematics lies your financial success. That Foolish truth was never more important than it is today. The mathematical misreads that damage so many savings accounts in America are now beginning to create nearly insurmountable problems. As of this writing, consumer debt tips the scales at $550 billion. The average household in the United States that carries a credit card balance has more than $7,000 worth of credit card debt. And recently, scarily, over half of those surveyed in a poll on success chose the state lottery as the only way to get ahead financially. Imagine that. Financial dependency and numerical ignorance are sharing the same bed, and the child born of that unfortunate coupling is not going to win any beauty contests. One need look no further than the nearly $3.7 billion spent on lottery tickets in the state of New York in 1998 and 1999 to see as much.

Much of our ongoing work involves a concerted effort to terminate this cozy relationship between bad math and financial servitude. (When we use "we" in this regard, we're referring inclusively to ourselves and our entire Foolish troupe—of which you are now a part, so take up the belled cap with us!) Probably our single best weapon is the spread of ideas made possible by the Internet. The digital network, which enables a simultaneous, mass conversation around the globe, is radically redefining how we gather and process information. Your schools, libraries, and business competitors have already made the Internet core to their undertakings, so if you somehow haven't already, it's high time you did too.

The new public dialogue about finance and investing will continue to force changes in the way entire industries operate. For instance, beyond Wall Street, the networked world forces car and insurance salesmen to alter their traditional approaches to the consumer. They don't so easily run a dozen fast-talking salesmen at you with rotating deals, long contracts, and unnecessary charges. They can't expect that, before signing on the dotted line, you won't sign in to Fool.com and ask thousands of people what they think of whole life insurance, car warranties, leasing deals, and the like. They will have to expect the opposite, since from now on you needn't make a single important financial decision in isolation.

And this move to mass conversation is also rewriting what Wall Street is. Over the next decade, the compensation system in the financial world is going to be almost completely scrapped and rebuilt to support its customers' interests. Electronic transactions are bringing costs down throughout the industry, and the Internet is spreading the word about better service and better prices. While the average commission for a trade executed by a full-service broker still hovers around $150, the average trade through a discount broker runs about $15. And there are numerous accounts which now allow you to execute trades for free. How long will these inequities last? Even less time than you'd probably think, given the existence of the Internet. Likewise, actively managed mutual funds charging 1.50 percent management fees are now having to compete with electronically managed index funds charging 0.18 percent management fees. For a $50,000 account, that's a difference of $660 per year. And the index fund is beating more than 80 percent of those higher-priced managed funds! Did someone just nail a coffin shut? Is that a death knell we hear playing?

Everywhere in the money world, plus is becoming minus, theirs is becoming yours, and the folly of Wisdom is giving way to the wisdom of Folly.

It is in this environment that *The Motley Fool You Have More Than You Think* has found its way to your fingertips. The main reason you need this book is to learn the useful personal finance information that will help you spend less, save more, turn your own profits, and teach and encourage others to do the same—and to share in a couple of good laughs. If you help us revolutionize the financial world along the way, even better.

We at Fool Global Headquarters are fully aware that the enjoyment one gets from buying a car or speaking with a financial advisor ranks right up there with the pleasurable act of sticking one's hand in a blender set on puree. If you're like most people, you just want to get it all over with, praying that you got an OK deal. So you stumble through life half valuing the car, the house, the term life insurance, the stockbroker, and half rushing to get to the end of the process. This hurriedness and mass disenchantment with personal finance creates a financial services industry that benefits lucratively from a titanic amount of societal ignorance. In their ideal world you fall asleep over the contract, they shake you awake, and you sign the document.

This disenchantment stems largely from a collective belief that financial decisions all just seem too big and complicated. But the people who succeed at investing have never thought of it as a big "financial" thing, disconnected from the rest of their lives, but rather as a series of simple purchase decisions, much like price shopping at the grocery store. Yes, we'll soon take a death-defying ride through the analysis of everything from slot machines and the state lottery to credit cards, insurance plans, mutual funds, the stock market, and much, much more. But the simple and numerical truths will become evident, and the "numerical" tasks will never get more difficult than the addition, subtraction, multiplication, and division chalked on your grade-school blackboard. Maybe we should have titled this book *Easy Numbers, Easy Money*—it would probably have sold more copies.

As we prepare to begin, we should probably let you know up front what this book will *not* do. That way, no hard feelings, no questions asked, no sense of having been misled. If you're browsing at Borders or Barnes & Noble, read this section *right now* to figure out whether or not to place this book back on the shelf. (With the cover *facing out,* please, and, in fact, if you could just adjust the bookshelf so that our other books also have their covers facing out, that would be great.)

Although we'll concentrate on personal savings early in the book, do *not* expect us to dawdle too long on how to live frugally, perhaps saving $10 by not sending birthday cards this year. Even if you live to the ripe old age of ninety-five, life's too short to trade away happiness for halfpennies. Though the Fool.com Web site has a dedicated circle of "Living Below Your Means" enthusiasts, *The Motley Fool You Have More Than You Think* will not teach you how to budget out the joys of being.

When we begin concentrating on investing, we will not show you how to trade stocks for a living. Further, we'll neither teach you all the latest Wall Street jargon nor put you down into the pits with Manhattan's energetic commissioned traders. If you are disappointed by this, let us know with a letter or e-mail, and if we get enough of such messages (say, 1 to 2 million), we'll consider following up this book with the sequel *We're Wise Now: The New Foolish Tune Plucked from Our Market Research.*

Next, on a more serious note, this book will not spend much time teaching advanced stock-research techniques. We've done some of that in the second and third books of our Motley trilogy, *The Motley Fool Investment Guide* and *The Motley Fool's Rule Breakers, Rule Makers,* and offer additional help in that direction in *The Motley Fool Investment Workbook.* Further, our online site, Fool.com (available also at America Online at keyword: FOOL), has additional fresh information pumping out twenty-four hours a day, making it a veritable treasure trove for active students of investing. The amount of information moving through our online areas *each day* is currently the equivalent of seventy-five full-length books, give or take a score.

Like any Fool book, this one is written for everyone—to inform the novice and to amuse the sophisticate. If you're a serious investor, we hope you'll find numerous investment suggestions, ideas, and pointers throughout this un-Wise tome, and you might also be interested in *The Motley Fool Investment Guide* or *The Motley Fool's Rule Breakers, Rule Makers.*

Finally, because we lack expertise in these, as well as the necessary space to go after them, this work will also fail to teach the basic sailing knots, how to make candles, where to fish for pike or perch, or anything about Zulu war tactics. Each would open up new worlds, but each is a subject that—without exception—we know very little about. *Que será, será.*

To close, simple thinking and public conversation about money today are discharging lightning bolts of new knowledge and understanding across the country, scorching conventional wisdom in all its forms. In belled caps and colored slippers, Fools are actually getting paid (through improved investment returns) to peek in on the downfall of unnecessary kings.

The message swirling around our corner of cyberspace today is that money management ain't as hard as these kings have it cracked up to be. Starting with very little, Warren Buffett has in his lifetime created $28 billion of wealth. With characteristic humility—but even, we think, with some accuracy—Buffett recently called his achievement "remarkably unremarkable." Peter Lynch beat everyone on Wall Street, then wrote two books about how overrated the fund manager, the stockbroker, and the financial advisor are. And starting with little money and lots of patience, Anne Scheiber accumulated more wealth on her own than most of us could ever need.

Lest you think that not everyone can make that sort of money, please understand, dear Fool, what is happening over at Yahoo! these days. According to Matt Richey, the Fool's director of investment strategies, on the day this sentence was inked, Yahoo!'s stock rose $4 per share, earning its cofounder and chief yahoo Jerry Yang $181.5 million in profit *in a single day*. Mr. Yang is human. This is a guy who has a clause in his contract that permits him to work barefoot. What you'll find if you look closely is that his achievements are far more mathematical than magical, more natural than preternatural. And best news of all for you and us is that the stock market has made it possible for a whole bunch of other people to own his stock, earning the very same returns, if not in quite the same amounts. This is part of the miracle of America, though a very pedestrian sort of miracle it is. It's high time you understood and shared in it, if you haven't already.

Before shutting down our little introduction, permit us to say once again that this book is for people who don't read financial books. Financial books are terribly dull and use complicated language. What you have here in your hands is a naughty little time-saver written by English majors, laced with jokes about the establishment for no reason other than that the establishment has proven so unwilling to make any jokes about—or explain—itself!

PART I

YOU HAVE MORE THAN YOU THINK

You Have More Than You Think

Brain

The revelation of thought takes men out of servitude into freedom.

—Emerson

W E HAVE NO intention of insulting anyone by leading off this chapter with a section simply titled "Brain." Let's face it . . . we pretty much all know we have brains, and while we could always be smarter, few of us feel *too* cerebrally bilked.

That said, many people seem quite willing to dismiss the exercise of reason when confronted with situations that smack in any way of the financial. Take the huge popularity of credit card debt, for instance. Like horses wearing blinders, a whole generation of Americans has grown up focused only on meeting that "minimum monthly payment" line, failing to recognize the implications of paying annual interest rates *in excess of 15 percent.* Observations like that inspire us to lead off this crucial chapter by stating unapologetically that you have more than you think: *You have a brain.*

"All men by nature desire knowledge," wrote Aristotle, but many have disavowed their nature when it comes to finance because no one ever taught them anything about the stock market, or explained how a retirement plan works. Once we are freed from classrooms and textbooks, the subject becomes completely off-putting, as are many of the other subjects we didn't study in school, like quantum physics or Babylonian history. But finance isn't at all like quarks or ancient kings. You deal with it every day. Really now, how often do you handle money and spend it, and how many people spend *how many hours* dreaming about it? If we can understand our dreams, we *should* understand our money.

That time for you, dear reader, is at hand.

Speaking of brains, the old cliché runs that we actually use only 10 percent of our brain cells. You probably won't even need to use half that much to read, understand, and use the book before you. Let's begin proving that by returning to our earlier example of credit card debt, a subject that—perhaps more than any other—we simply cannot harp on enough.

For every dollar that remains unpaid on their credit cards, many people are paying sixteen to eighteen cents over the course of a year. It doesn't take a graduate degree in anything to discover that 16 to 18 percent is well above what you pay for most loans (at last look, 8 percent for cars, 8 percent for homes, and 14 percent for personal loans). Additionally and importantly, this rate is way beyond the annual investment *gains* you should expect from any standard form of investment. The stock market, the best-performing investment vehicle of this century, has posted average annual gains of 11 percent. Ask yourself what would happen if you were consistently to borrow money on your credit card to invest in the stock market (which some people actually do). How long would you be in business? And remember, stocks outperform everything else!

We'll get into credit and debt later. For now, it's enough to point out that your average ten-year-old should find nothing difficult about reading about and understanding the credit card problem presented here. But it's clear that few people really do understand this; you can see it in the way they run their day-to-day lives. And the credit card industry is taking direct advantage of this, playing us for dumb.

You have a brain. But most people think they don't when it comes to anything financial. Additional examples abound. Do you have friends with money in the stock market? Or in a mutual fund? Ask them to explain exactly what they're invested in. Chances are *very* good that they'll be able to tell you little more than the name of the company or the fund. This is the direct result of someone else having sold them investments that they know nothing about. Most people with savings have their money in mutual funds but don't really know what the funds are or how they work. Some Americans own stocks without recognizing that stocks simply represent their part ownership in a given company. And how many people own shares of oil-and-gas, gold-mining, or high-technology companies without really having the faintest idea how those businesses work or what the companies' products are? Come on, now . . . you're better than this, and you have more than you may think.

In his delightful book *One Up on Wall Street,* Peter Lynch points out the irony that most of us Americans spend a great deal more time and care making home appliances purchases (like refrigerators) than we do on our investments. The irony couldn't be stronger: Consumer electronics cost hundreds of dollars and lose value over time starting the very minute you walk out of the store. For some reason, however, we'll roll up our sleeves, check prices, read and compare the long lists of features, do a bit of "test-driving," and haggle with the salesman before we buy a Walkman.

By contrast, our investments often involve *thousands* of dollars and will *appreciate* in value over time! But we've made up our minds that investments are complicated or boring, or really just "gambling" at heart, so we just don't think much about them.

What do we do, then? We employ a financial services company to manage investments for us, be that a brokerage firm, mutual fund, financial planner, whatever. Amazingly, once again we fail to ask our financial professional the simple and revealing question "How do *you* make money?" A follow-up, which should always be asked, is simply "How do you make *more* money than that?" If you walk away with nothing else about investing from these Foolish pages, walk away with a simple understanding that

- Brokers earn commissions for each trade made on your account—and they make *more* money by trading your account in and out of more investments
- Mutual funds take a portion of the money you give them to manage— and they make *more* money by attracting as many other people's money as possible
- Financial newsletters make money through subscription fees—and they make *more* money by enticing larger numbers of subscribers

"Nothing astonishes men more than common sense and plain dealing," wrote Ralph Waldo Emerson. Astonish yourself by applying some of this common sense and you'll find that each of the ways that the entities listed above make *more* money is ultimately detrimental to their customers' interests. (Please note that your name tag reads "customer.")

Brokers make money when they move you in and out of different investments—even very good ones. They get an additional lick off your ice cream cone every time. Each of these moves also adds to your annual tax burden. Further, this frenetic activity tends conveniently to suggest to many customers that "Geez, only my broker can keep up with this stuff . . . I just can't do this on my own." *Au contraire!*

Mutual funds spend additional monies (your money) advertising themselves so they can attract more money to manage. Plus, every additional customer they bring to their beachfront makes it that much less enjoyable for existing customers who have already laid out the towels and put on the tanning lotion. To put that in financial terms, the bigger the fund gets, the more dollars it has to spread around; the more dollars in play, the less nimble it becomes; the clumsier it is, the less likely it is to outperform the stock market.

Finally, financial newsletters end up having to show you pumped-up numbers to attract subscriptions. Some of them obtain such numbers through creative accounting, and they possess more gadgets in their bag of tricks than you'd find in a Swiss toy maker's shop. A host of best-selling financial newsletters and books are marketed on the basis of illusory or impossible-to-achieve big-sounding returns.

The easiest way to understand things is to ask very simple questions about them. Unfortunately, many of us are afraid to ask basic questions because we think it might make us look stupid. Actually, you look stupid only when you hide your lack of understanding behind a presumed knowledge. To return to the theme: We have more than we think. We can bring the power of reason to bear on this subject. Reason's most basic tool is just asking questions. And asking questions is the very thing that many financial professionals today do *not* want you to do.

Don't cooperate. Wait for your answers.

Finally, the very act of your sitting down to read this book already demonstrates that you've decided to move from servitude to freedom (in Emerson's felicitous phrase, which led off this chapter). The heart of our work on money is a fundamental belief in rationalism, in the idea that we can and should bring our powers of reason to bear on financial matters. The application of reason is in fact the *only* natural way to succeed with finances. If you're not using your brain, you're using something else: somebody else's advice, the daily horoscope, or blind luck. Your brain is the more powerful instrument.

Time

You also happen to have more time than you think. "Time" here refers both to mundane daily time and to your overall lifetime.

We needn't belabor the point; a few examples should suffice. Let's start with educating yourself about saving, spending, and investing. You have more time than you think. Sure, the financial world is all about getting you to act quickly, since you're more likely not to use your brain (see previous section) if you're convinced you don't have the time to. That's part of the game.

Ever been cold called? Your phone rings in the midst of a dinner party, you pick it up, and some guy from "First Mutual" is pitching you an Argentine bond or shares in a "wireless company" (with no real explanation of what doesn't have wires attached to it). What's his goal? To sell you on the idea, regardless of its merit, and *to make the sale NOW*. What's your goal? In most cases, it should be to hang up immediately, or, at the very least to ask about the SuperTaco.

Whenever a cold-caller rings, insist that if there's a way to get you a SuperTaco, there's a guaranteed sale in it for the caller. If the stunned broker attempts to return to his spiel, repeat that you were under the clear impression that this call was going to revolve around SuperTacos, and that unless SuperTacos are going to be discussed promptly, there's a real chance that the police are going to have to be brought into the equation. If the broker continues to discuss non-SuperTaco-related matters, burst into tears. This is sure to prevent your ever receiving another such call again.

Time is your greatest ally in many ways. At Fool.com, we frequently hear from new investors who have been cold called. They come online to ask questions about how they should respond to the guy at First Mutual. Regardless of whether they take our advice never to return the call, these readers of ours have already won. Why? They took time; they *used* time to their advantage. They didn't allow anyone to pressure them.

The same thing happens in a softer-edged way between many investors and their full-service brokers. Your broker calls you to pitch a new investment idea. She'd be very happy if you just said, "OK, you're the pro, go for it, Debbie." But you really shouldn't, *ever*. Even if Debbie is the greatest broker in the world, you should still take the *time* to think about her idea, maybe make a few calls, learn something on your own about the suggestion. Debbie may not intend to be pressuring you at all, but you'll still often feel pressured regardless. The temptation will be to relieve the pressure by saying, "Just go ahead with it." But you have more *time* than you think.

One of the effects of our earliest efforts to encourage people to think about the stock market was that a whole bunch of people who'd never invested before jumped right into the market. Which is great, because that has always been our primary point. But one thing we can't control is how a reader actually puts into play the principles we write about, whether online or in any of our books. It's probably inevitable that at least a few people somewhere have jumped right into the market with aggressive stocks and big gambles, figuring they could go out and make a killing now that they knew the stock market was the place to be. For all we know, some of them did make killings, but more often than not impatience gets you killed.

That's why we continue to teach people to "do it on paper" for a while. Practice investing by playing the hypothetical game of I Would Do This Now. Write it down, follow it, see how you do, and see what you can learn from that. Take a year or more to do this. You have years and years to invest (and we say this even if you're seventy-five years old), so don't get caught up in thinking that if you don't act now, the rocket's leaving the launchpad. You have more time than you think.

Don't be in a hurry to invest.

If you already are an investor, you probably already know how great an ally time really is. The stock market has returned an average annualized rate of approximately 11 percent since 1926. If you'd just plinked down $1,000 into the stock market seventy years ago and forgotten about it, you'd have $1,488,000 today. In the seventy-first year, assuming it's average (11 percent), you would net another $163,700 on top of that—just one year's returns—more than 163 times the whole amount you socked into the market seventy-one years ago

Can numbers speak more eloquently?

Those seventy-one years have had their share of scary moments. Over a two-year period from January 1973 to December 1974, the market declined a horrendous 45 percent from peak to trough. Then in October 1987, the market dropped 26 percent of its value in *two days*. Worse than that, the market lost 67.6 percent from 1928 to 1932, during the market crash that began the Great Depression. But despite these and many other poor periods, there were and are so many good periods for the stock market that if you just buy and hold tenaciously, you'll be become rich. Seriously.

Always remember Anne Scheiber, who patiently and systematically bided her time with a handful of core holdings and died half a century later with $22 million. Reminds us of the ending to one of our favorite flicks, when the Wizard of Oz asks the Scarecrow, the Tin Man, and the Cowardly Lion the simple question "What do *they* have that *you* don't have?" He went on to give gifts to each of them that represented that one thing (a diploma, a ticking heart, a badge of honor).

What Anne Scheiber had that many of us lack is patience. Another way of putting it? *She* knew how much time she had.

Finally, in an age of market research and demographics and targeted products, we're not playing that game. The points we're making apply to everyone. Even if you're seventy-five years old, you probably do have more time than you think. But regardless of the date and time of your final hour, you should be thinking not just about saving for yourself but about building and leaving a legacy to those coming after. So even those who would not appear to have more time than they think in most cases actually do, and they should generally act under that assumption.

Other People

As with our brains and the time we have, so too the value of other people is often lost on us.

Sad but true, not all people are valuable all the time. You've told your children four times in the past week not to take food out of the kitchen, and they just fumbled a bowl of tomato soup on the living-room carpet. Or was it that your college roommate borrowed your car without asking and drove it into a river? He's fine, but the car's gone, and once the news has settled, his value to you may have declined fairly dramatically. And what, you ask, is the value of that broker who pitched you $5,000 worth of restaurant stock that is now trading at twenty-five cents a share? Sometimes people so hurt your financial standing that you think about swearing them off, living in a hole in the tree next to Howard Hughes.

But don't.

Look in the right places and you will discover invaluable insights from other people. In the money world, you just can't get enough input. Even the bad stuff helps. Some out there have grandparents who, right now, are picking up quarters out of white plastic buckets and discarding them into slot machines. Still others have siblings who somewhat systematically call for a loaner. (We each claim the other brother does this wantonly, and we're trying separately to get our sister to back us up on this.) Fifty bucks here, another fifty there. Learn from their mistaken approach to money. Eschew righteous moralizing and show them some of the numbers from this book.

On the other side of the coin, as it were, most of us have at least one or two family members to whom we can turn for lessons and help in thinking about money. Surely your father has gone through the dreary car-buying scenario enough times to give guidance. And maybe one of your cousins just bought a house; it might be useful to see how she managed that process. Hey, you say that your aunt is a money manager? We hope you've recently taken her out to a superb lunch to query her about investing (if only to learn all her mistakes—*ba-da-boom*). Your ideal financial confidants date all the way back to your first little red wagon, your first broken bone, your first big mistake, and your first date. (It occurs to us briefly that in some rare instances—we'll hope not yours—all four of these could even have been part of the same incident.)

It's your family.

For some people, family isn't a suitable option. Maybe you were kicked out of the clan for marrying the wrong guy or for not following the slew of your ancestors to Princeton. Families can occasionally be a nuisance. So, fine already, because you can find people in other places. Those close friends all around you make perfect checkpoints as you step out into the world with a walletful of cash. In our upcoming section on how to buy a car, perhaps our most useful suggestion is that you never travel down to a dealership all by yourself. Though many of us have done just that, including *both* of the authors of this book, it makes no sense. Why sit all alone as six different negotiators present you various (often equally unfavorable) deals and slam in front of you an overlong contract flooded with legalese? Being alone at a car dealership isn't much fun, and it also isn't very *safe*.

Entire corporate armies have formed for the purpose of loosening a few hundred extra dollars out of your wallet each year. You're putting yourself at a miserable disadvantage by not working together with your friends. Maybe a dinner club of five that meets once a month to talk about money strategies is a good idea. If you'd like to use a name like The Motley Fool Dinner Club™, we're always looking to spin profits from licensing.

An alternative to TMFDC is to start your own investment club consisting of friends, neighbors, business associates, and very smart pets who invest a certain amount of money into a portfolio containing stocks that the group has selected. In fact, you might check out one of our other books, *Investment Clubs: How to Start and Run One the Motley Fool Way,* for some guidance on this. (An interesting fact that we'll offer up to stoke the fires of the ongoing but, we hope, ever-friendly battle of the sexes: According to a study by the National Association of Investors Corporation, of the all-men, all-women, and mixed-gender investment clubs, the all-women clubs have the best average performance record.)

We now move from what has sounded like a telephone advertisement (friends and family) to the next group of people who can add tremendous value to your bank account: the authors of financial books. No, not all of them. If the cover of the book portrays a dandy in a sleek suit with a toothy grin directing his index finger your way, stay the heck away. You also may not find much use for the equally frightening nine-hundred-page financial books inked by dusty-headed academics with a fetish for binomials and unreadable charts. Combine these two extremes and you may have found the catalyst behind our entire nation turning away from its banking and brokerage accounts and crying uncle on all money matters.

Ah, but in between the two dreadful extremes are some absolutely wonderful books. John Kenneth Galbraith, Philip Fisher, Peter Lynch, and, more recently, Guy Kawasaki, all are responsible for some of the better contributions to American letters this century. Before you tear open the covers of that next sensational crime novel, give a book dedicated to business or investment a chance. (For some of our favorites, check "Appendix II, Books You Should Like.") The world of money features all the stories you could want about honor and disgrace, despair and joy.

Remember that the financial world does not want you to educate yourself; it hates the idea that you might actually read this stuff. Picture the grimace of the mediocre fund manager when he spots some Fool on the train reading about Warren Buffett. The CEOs of full-priced brokerage firms are horrified that you might learn enough about your money to manage it quietly yourself—at one-tenth the cost of having them do it for you! And imagine the rattled expression of the commissioned insurance salesman when he realizes that you actually know what you're doing. Browse the business section next time you're in a bookstore. There are gems to be unearthed.

Finally, this wouldn't be a Fool book if we didn't mention here the relative values of the Internet. Our global network attracts tens of millions of people to it every day, and the majority of adults in America are signing on to the Internet regularly. They're already e-mailing relatives and friends, and researching and following conversations on every subject imaginable: overcast-stitch sewing, candlepin bowling, ice sailing, otolaryngology, hothouse flowers, Southeastern Conference college basketball, and the miserable underperformance of most managed mutual funds.

In truth, every topic imaginable is being considered on the Internet and examined in detail. By this point the mass media has more or less embraced the Internet, and though there are frequent scare pieces citing crime, pornography, anonymity, mass suicide, and the dreaded computer virus, the reality is that 99 percent of the activity online is at worst harmless, often helpful, and at best amazing in the positive change it can effect in your life.

The Value of a Dollar

Now let's talk about what you have in your pocket. Let's discuss the value of a dollar. We call it the *value* of a dollar because we are here to champion its usefulness. A dollar is worth a good deal more than most people think.

Do you agree? Most people don't. Many throw them away all the time without thinking or caring. In itself, a dollar is not valuable: it's a slip of paper. If you're stranded in the Sahara desert (or on Gilligan's Island) with nothing but 4 million American dollars, they have no value to you at all . . . other than as handkerchiefs or toilet paper. (You can make a pretty good argument for turning them into one heck of a wide-brimmed paper boater, extending your life expectancy some five to ten hours, but statistics suggest that under a hot sun many of us would lack the patience and vision to construct one successfully. Cf. Hakov and Van Drivvel, pages 457–59, for more on this.)[1]

Fortunately, we have all *conferred* tremendous value on these particular slips of paper by agreeing to make them our medium of exchange. This has had the beneficial effect of moving us away from a barter economy, which had been a real pain in the butt—thousands of years ago—when you could only trade objects for other objects. Pack mules were no doubt worth more then than even the overpriced British Range Rover of today . . .

---

[1]This is an example of a completely fabricated and useless academic reference designed to impress people who don't take the time to read footnotes.

Anyway, dollar bills are worth much more than just an ongoing advertisement for George Washington, Inc. Before he achieved enduring fame as the face on the $100 bill, Ben Franklin wrote, "A penny saved is a penny earned." Well, it's been a few hundred years, so that quotation doesn't work terribly well anymore. As excited as we are about dollars, we do have a hard time firing ourselves up about pennies. Given the historical effects of inflation, we feel it now appropriate to update the maxim to . . .

A dollar saved is a dollar earned.

Not terribly original, that, but we weren't shooting for originality. We were shooting for effectiveness. You read it here first, dear Fool.

Do you have a dollar nearby? We're going to suggest you do something with it right now. Put this book down for a moment, go over and get the dollar, and park it, sequester it, quarantine it, tie it up, hide it. Save it. Regardless of who you are and what you're doing right now, make that your first dollar saved from this point forward.

Do something else for us—actually, for you. Tomorrow, make a point of pulling a dollar out of your purse or wallet at some point and put it right where you put your first one.

The day after, do the same. You might have some incidental change kicking around your pocket; you might find you don't *really* need potato chips with lunch; you might check a book out of the library rather than buy a paperback. Whatever. Squeeze that dollar out of the soaked sponge of your daily existence and bottle it.

And keep doing that, all year long. One dollar each day.

One year from the anniversary of your reading this page, you'll have $365 in savings. This goes for whether you are a student, a lawyer, an indigent, or Donald Trump (and, by the way, The Donald, King of Borrowers, would have been extremely well served by this strategy over the years).

OK, 365 bucks, right? Nice to have, but no big thing, right? Well, if you're saving $365 a year, you're actually *well* beyond the majority of the rest of *Homo sapiens.* In richer countries, many people suffer from a debilitating case of overspending that leads to chronic debt; in poorer countries, most own little, if anything, which is terribly sad.

Anyway, try doing the same thing the next year and the year after that, and so on. Maybe it's hard to remember to do this on a daily basis (although it's a great exercise if you can), so occasionally, you kick seven bucks into your kitty to account for the whole week ahead. Stay on schedule at the very worst; preferably, stay ahead of schedule.

Let's back off this for a sec, though, because we're not yet into our Foolish-savings-plan part of the book. Plus, practically speaking, you shouldn't do this if you have any credit card debt; we're attempting here only to demonstrate the value of a dollar. So, please, just take a few minutes more to step through this section with us. Here comes some fifth-grade math.

If you follow our simple dollar-a-day approach, fifty-five years from now you'll have $20,000 in savings alone ($20,000 divided by $365 is 54.79452, or 54 years and 290 days). *Or will you?* Actually, you won't . . . you'll have lots more. That's because the primary emphasis of this book is on finding simple steps you can take to get the money invested, making your savings earn its *own additional* savings.

Rather than sewing your saved money into your mattress, let's say you find a simple and safe investment like a government bond that returns a locked-in 5 percent annually. If at the end of every month you took your thirty saved dollars and plugged them into this savings vehicle, after fifty-five years you'd have $101,256.50. You were systematic, you didn't sweat market booms and busts, you took very little time to learn any of this—you just saved a Foolish dollar a day, socked it away in a conservative government bond, and you have $101,256.50.

That's over a hundred thousand in *savings* . . . above and beyond any money you're making at your job, or via any retirement plans, or through inheritance in any form. It was just a lousy buck a day! This also assumes you never began to add any additional bills to the money heap as you grew older and gained salary increases. You were just a fifteen-year-old kid, picked up a copy of our book, saved this way, and you're now seventy years old with a life expectancy of at least ten years more, if not twenty. And you have cash to blow.

Are we beginning to communicate the point?

Probably, but let's press it. Let's say you earn a higher return annually on that dollar. Call it 9 percent. How do the numbers work out then? Can you say "Four hundred eighty-one thousand seven hundred ninety-five dollars and ninety-five cents"? That $481,795.95 just goes to show how a higher annual percentage return dramatically increases your compounded savings over time.

OK, now let's go back to the first example for a moment. You, the fifteen-year-old putting a dollar a day into government bonds, end up expiring at seventy (sorry about that). You leave the money to your granddaughter, who coincidentally turns fifteen years old the *very day* of your death. She's a delightful young woman but a spendthrift, unable ever to save a penny of her own money. But she does manage to preserve the trust you left her. She just keeps it in the bank earning that same 5 percent annually. Fifty-five years later, when she turns seventy, it's $1.5 million. She never managed to save a buck, but she's a millionaire.

Now let's say that on the day of your death, your spendthrift but still savvy granddaughter instead made the simple decision to move the money from a government bond earning 5 percent to a more aggressive investment, with higher historical returns of 9 percent (keep in mind, that's still 2 percentage points below the stock market's annualized 11 percent historical return). If it's the only financial decision that she ever makes her whole life, that's fine, because she's brilliant. The $101,256.50 you left her will grow, in her fifty-five years, invested at 9 percent, to $11.6 million . . . 11 million pocorobas and then some.

Finally, let's just say (as we did earlier) that you had the dollar-a-day savings invested at a 9 percent return all along, then passed the money on to your granddaughter (using foresight to avoid the inheritance tax), and she keeps it invested at 9 percent, not adding a lick. One hundred ten years later, the next generation of your family will inherit $54.8 million. No joke. No cooked numbers here. Just a bloody dollar a day during your lifetime.

Is the point now obvious? You took the time to save—one dollar a day, from age fifteen to age seventy. You invested it at 5 percent or 9 percent, then passed it on to your granddaughter. She didn't even add to it—just kept your trust going, invested at the different returns that we went through hypothetically. You certainly have to acknowledge, of course, that inflation will make the money do less than it sounds. But even given that by the year 2108, inflation will make $55 million look more like $1.25 million (assuming a 3.5 percent inflation rate), that's a huge amount of money compared to where you started. And again, our examples are conservative in that they assume a very low savings rate (only a buck a day for you over your whole adult life, and nothing for your granddaughter) and returns below the stock market's historical average. (Our examples also do not include the inheritance tax, which is different for different people, always subject to change, and doesn't affect the overall point.)

The typical dollar is an afterthought, even for those people who don't think of themselves as having much money. Begin with that afterthought, take a few easy steps, and suddenly you're moving toward long-term financial independence—or, at worst, a family legacy that makes you the Most Beloved Ancestor. As well you should be!

Quickly to recap this section: The value of a dollar is huge when it's invested and compounding. And that's exactly where your dollar should be and what it should be doing.

And a Bunch
of People Want
What You Have

G IVEN THAT YOUR dollar bill may be worth far more than you'd originally thought, it should come as no surprise that some people who
have spent their professional lives studying its value want your dollar bill
in *their* alligator wallets. If this isn't already thoroughly evident to you,
pitch a dollar down onto the sidewalk in your local business district, duck
behind a poplar, and note how long it takes for that money to find a new
home.

Money doesn't actually drive our planet's orbit, but it has undeniable
gravitational effects on how our lives spin round upon it. Today, cold cash
helps you rent that beach house and pays for painkillers when you break
your collarbone surfing. The dollar bill paid for the Wright brothers to
build the first airplane. Money funded the collapse of apartheid after underwriting its dismal creation.

For most of us, money flows into our accounts twice monthly, in the
form of wages. After that, it seems to spend the rest of its time running
away in countless currents: $20 for gas, $52 for groceries, $37 on the
phone bill, $29.99 for that George Foreman Lean Mean Grilling Machine.
The corporations that provide us these goods and services—varying in degree of purpose—hunger for every incoming buck. What makes them
businesses, rather than clubs or charities, is their insatiable need for more
cash in order to fund more opportunity, hire more employees, and create

better products and services for you. When these corporations develop by servicing our needs and satisfying our desires—when they nourish and clothe us, or provide our family a memorable week of sailing around the Caribbean—they *should* be rewarded.

The trouble is that not all companies are intent upon building an enduring base of contented, healthy, loyal customers. In fact, too many businesses turn tricks and set traps designed to pull dollars out of your purse without providing *any* value in return. As we noted earlier, one dollar saved every day of the year and invested at 9 percent will grow into almost $500,000 over the course of a normal lifetime. You can just imagine how badly the hungry corporation would like to make your dollar bill theirs to save and invest, even if they have to be deceptive or dishonest to land it. Sadly, our nation's corporate landscape is littered with such entities, large and small, whose mission is nothing more than to confuse, to conceal, and to connive against their customers. And when these business models flourish, distrust and collective despair follow along as a natural consequence. We begin to think that a specific industry or—unfairly, by extension— business at large is injurious to the individual, a detriment to society. Hey, haven't you wondered why businessmen are the bad guys in all the movies lately?

Sorting out true service and chicanery in the financial services industry is perhaps more difficult than in any other business. The industry has its unfamiliar terms, its hidden conflicts of interest, and a vested stake in keeping as many of its cards concealed under the table as possible. But donning our motley garb, we can sift through the bewildering array of options together, driving out those designed to sweet-talk and swindle. The aim is nothing less than to defend your salary payments against corporate raiding—to save *your* money for *your* future.

Remember, as we expound our Foolish spending and saving strategies, that we are not going to ask you to barter with your gas-station attendant, choose unbranded soups and cereals, wear unclean clothes an extra week, or consider establishing residence in a small tent on the periphery of your hometown. We're concentrating on approaches that anyone can take, that are often in fact *more fun* than what you've been doing.

Speaking in particular about your basic needs—food, water, sleep, shelter, and human companionship—we don't think you actually stand to save much money cutting back on these. The free market system aggressively drives lower the price of stuff that everyone regularly demands. If the average human requires two bars of soap per month, you can expect that huge soap factories are constantly forced into furious price competition for your repeat business. Those battles inevitably set a cheap, fair price on suds. The same is true for food, clothes, and other necessities. As long as you're not purchasing your 895th pair of shoes alongside Imelda Marcos or spending $47,000 on a platinum four-poster platform bed, you're probably operating realistically when it comes to the basics.

That doesn't mean good money can't be saved in other aspects of your life. Quite the contrary. The easiest and most substantial savings come from your *larger* and *less frequent* outlays of cash—what we call big-ticket items, things on which you'll be spending hundreds or thousands of dollars each year. Examples include homes, cars, insurance plans, and investment portfolios, all of which we'll take closer looks at later in this book. So please forget nickels and dimes saved on necessities and perishables. If you can just crack some basic numerical codes, you can preserve thousands of dollars on big-ticket items over a lifetime. Actually, strike that. You stand to save *tens* of thousands of dollars if you can just get the numbers straight! And now that you understand the value of each one of those dollars, you know that this is a life-transforming chunk of change. Because every dollar you save is a dollar you can put to work for you.

Let's begin our Foolish survey by looking at how a lot of people spend what they call their *play money* or *funny money*—those dollars set aside for mere "entertainment." A huge industry has sprung up to capitalize on this instinct. And while it's not a typical big-ticket item, when you add up the amounts of money many people waste here over a lifetime, gambling is a very big ticket.

Gambling

First stop, the world of high-stakes betting—where a dollar can explode into thousands overnight and where lifelong savings plans can disintegrate in a matter of hours. You may wonder why we're giving over a short section of this book to an industry that most people consider completely peripheral to their lives. The answer lies in the numbers. First—even if they don't gamble—too many people actually think that the betting world is unpredictable, magical, and possibly filled with opportunity. And, second, the gambling industry today does more than $100 billion in sales a year in America—making it bigger than McDonald's, Coca-Cola, Nike, the Gap, Viacom, and Microsoft *combined*. Big money is being spent, and we think a brief analysis of these "investments" will tell us plenty about our own savings and our investments in common stock. Even if you'll never bet a single one of *your* dollars, read on.

In 1996, Americans made sports gambling and the lottery the entrees of choice, spending an estimated $80 billion and $34 billion on them, respectively. That this can occur on such a grand scale speaks to our nation's collective struggle with multiplication. Looking past the bouncing balls, the whirring sirens, the pumped-in oxygen, the petite drink waitress, and the gallant shuffler in tuxedo vest, mathematics and reason tell us that the house *always* holds the statistical advantage. Depending on the game, the mathematical advantage that the house enjoys ensures that the average casino bettor loses between 2 and 5 percent every time he puts a dollar on the table. Yes, Fortuna will visit a few favorites sporadically, but her sister Statistica will win the endurance test over everyone, eventually.

This means that the common repeat player will witness the gradual disintegration of her savings, as alternating streaks of losing and winning and losing dissolve her money at the overall rate of 3.5 percent per bet. She puts up $100; it eventually works its way down to $90. She puts up that $90; it steadily shrinks to $60; she wagers the $60; it falls to $30. In any of these cases, random variation may cause her money to quickly double. But long-term statistical realities sink the player.

The reverse is true for the house. Have you ever drunk a thick coffee milk shake real slow, slurping through a straw? You just played the role of a big-time casino owner, draining your customer's savings money and drawing back hard on the final few bucks. Can you hear that last, loud slurping sound? Go into a casino and take a few minutes to study the appearance of its regular patrons: drawn, stooped, and hollow. Ready to be drunk through a straw.

Now, before we scrutinize a few specific gambling vehicles—table games, sports betting, and the lottery—it behooves the merry Fool to disclose that we aren't moralists or government interventionists. We have no desire to see bureaucrats in plaid suits overseeing the shuttering of gambling-shop windows or the disassembly of lottery wheels in your district. In our open society, Donald Trump should be able to turn the entire eastern seaboard into a giant pair of fuzzy dice falling toward a neon emerald carpet if the region and its people truly demand it. Freedom places the chief burden of responsibility and choice not on the supplier but on the consumer. So our review of the gambling world is just to help us follow the flow of dollars, not to judge the supplier. Armed with our counting machines, let's go off to the slot machines for a starter.

CASINOS

If the giant fountains, pink flamingos, light shows, and (behind it all) roulette wheels haven't arrived at a strip near you, something like them may soon be headed to a puddle near you in the form of a riverboat. The casino industry has aggressively negotiated itself out of various regulations over the past decade, earning the right to set up its glittering palaces almost anywhere today. At the heart of it, what this means for all of us, is that we now have a new, highly convenient, and electrifying way to lose much of our money incrementally.

Given that the odds favor the house, the gambler who enters a casino aiming to profit would do better to stake it all on one bet rather than make a series of smaller bets, which would allow the unfavorable odds to stack up against him. Consider a player who

1. Places one thousand $1 bets, one at a time, at roulette (95 percent payback)
2. Takes his winnings and bets them all, $1 at a time
3. Continues this until he's completed thirty consecutive rounds

SAVINGS DISINTEGRATION FOR THE AVERAGE GAMBLER

Cash	After 10 Rounds	After 20 Rounds	After 30 Rounds
$1,000	$599	$358	$214

After thirty rounds of betting, the average player has lost over 78 percent of his money. Truth be told, the more you gamble, the more closely your returns will resemble the statistical realities—losses again and again and again. Addicted gamblers are, in essence, repeatedly walking up to a counter and exchanging $100 for $95. That's precisely why Gamblers Anonymous meetings aren't packed with dashing Omar Sharifs and darling Marilyn Monroes. Instead, they play host to frail, beaten men and women who have spent years methodically giving away their money—often all of it.

Time, you see, is actually the gambler's dreaded enemy, since it will with daunting dependability vaporize his savings. This is one of those classic zero-sum games: the success of the gambling house comes out of the direct failure of its customers. And the failure of its customers neatly correlates with the amount of time they spend on the floor. (That's where the free drinks come in. Indeed, casinos stand to make *such* good money on their betting tables that it's a sign of their greed that they don't give *everything* else away gratis.)

To hammer it home, consider the player with $150,000 in a suitcase. The figures below represent the returns if he took that $150,000, broke it down into $1 bills, and made 150,000 $1 bets on day one. On day two, the player takes what remains from his first day and again bets it all in $1 allotments. If the same strategy is repeated for three hundred consecutive days, here are the average returns:

SAVINGS DISINTEGRATION FOR THE ADDICTED GAMBLER

Cash	100 Days	200 Days	300 Days
$150,000	$888	$5.26	$0.03

Looked at from a strange angle in a different light, active gamblers are addicted to nothing more than bad mathematics. In less than a year, the bettor above would end up with a three-cent wad of Bazooka. A $25 calculator at the outset would have saved him $149,974.97. That's what house odds do to habitual bettors. That's why casinos want players down on the floor, right into the small of the night, placing repeated bets. That's why Las Vegas hates Texas Instruments and their pocket calculators.

If you're heading off to the casino for onetime amusement, willing to lose an inexpensive shirt or two, onward, Fool. We're not here to preach what is and isn't entertaining. But if you're hoping to make any real, consistent money using the casino, you're in for a dismal, southerly ride.

SPORTS BETTING

The estimated $80 billion gambled on sporting events in the United States in 1996 helped make it the fastest-growing segment of the gambling industry over the past decade. And that actually makes a heckuvalot of sense. Why?

Because it's fueled by games that people already love: baseball, horse racing, college hoops, boxing, golf. Unlike pushing coins into slot machines, which seems to entertain only the weariest retirees, betting on sports combines the glory days of our athletic past with the chance for big money. Hell, why not put $100 down on the New York Yankees in their race for the pennant? Be a part of the team! And what's the danger in betting a little bit of your savings on the horse with the crimson colors in gate four?

Nothing at all, from the standpoint of entertainment. The infrequent, small-money bettor is hardly putting herself at risk by centering a hat of iridescent flowers on her head, tipping back a mint julep, and risking an Andrew Jackson on the sixth race at Churchill Downs. But from the standpoint of speculative *investment,* sports betting makes no more sense than shaking bones over a craps table or betting red on the roulette wheel. No matter how well you think you know sports, all bets favor the house. This doesn't mean that the house will win on the next bet, or in the next day. It does mean that the house will *eventually* win.

As with casino betting, the average sports wager will lose the bettor a few percentage points per bet. That makes your hometown heroes as lousy an *investment* as sitting dumbly in front of a slot machine rattling your white bucket of quarters for good luck. In as many bets, your $1,000 or $10,000 or $500,000 will disintegrate into nothing but a pink blob of sugar in a candy wrapper. You may even find that by the end of it, you no longer enjoy sports.

THE LOTTERY

If you think casinos and sports wagering offer lousy opportunities, dear Fool, consider the state-sponsored lotteries currently running in three-quarters of the United States. Our lottery system slurps down in excess of $30 billion in revenues per year, as Americans venture out to corner convenience stores in record numbers to take a shot at multimillion-dollar jackpots. What the players probably didn't know is that the average bet brought back an expected return of negative *50 percent* . . . far worse than in Vegas. This is particularly stunning when you consider that some of these same bettors are adamantly opposed to casinos—places of ill repute that they are, run by scoundrels taking advantage of the public's numerical ignorance. Curse them. Drive them out past the city limits. Fiends! (Reread the last three sentences with appropriate sarcastic tone.)

But whoa there! At least your unfriendly neighborhood casino pays back 95 percent of its wagers! All of that with none of the hypocrisy. It's not like casino payrolls include state representatives sworn to serve the public good, dedicated to the education of your children, committed to strengthening weakened communities. (OK, maybe *some* state reps are on casino payrolls . . . but allow us to play the naïf.)

Bah! How good and instructive and empowering is this *lottery* that they promote?

Let's run some numbers here, as well. Consider the results of five thousand one-dollar bets on the lotto. On the second day, with his winnings, the player repeats the approach. He continues this for thirty consecutive days. Below are the average performance figures for ten-day periods, compared to the casino gambler's identical approach.

AVERAGE PERFORMANCE FOR $5,000 WAGERED

	Rate of Return	After 10 Days	After 20 Days	After 30 Days
Casino Bets	-5%	$2,993	$1,792	$1,072
Lottery Bets	-50%	$4.89	$0.01	$0.00

In just ten average days, $5,000 worth of lottery tickets is reduced to less than $5. Would you believe that $10 million in one-ticket allotments would dissolve into one penny over thirty days? And $500 million over the same period would shrivel into forty-seven cents?! What about Bill Gates's $30 billion fortune? It shrivels into $27.94 after a month of methodical lottery wagering.

In a world that offers so many good investments with *positive returns,* our friendly state governments provide us a way of torching our lifelong savings almost overnight. And, sadly, that is happening to people in America. The damage that lotteries are doing to the personal savings of repeat players is so insidious and ironic—coming from the government itself—that we ought to spend a couple of pages taking a deeper look. Don't worry—it'll be brief.

The three decades of success since lotteries were again legalized in the mid-sixties have created expert designers and promoters of the games. Agencies have developed multimillion-dollar rollover jackpots and have achieved ubiquity through successful positioning of the games in convenience stores. They've broken new ground on how to generate consumer enthusiasm via their witty, expensive, successful ad campaigns. From billboards to striking radio and TV spots to commission incentives for store cashiers who sell tickets to their customers, the lottery is the single loudest clarion call the state blasts to its citizenry each year, *by a long shot.* Did we elect our state representatives to preach good health, to champion learning, to talk up community projects—or to hype the lottery?

As a consequence, today's lottery tickets are less expensive, more accessible, better promoted, and more profitable for their promoters than at any other time in our nation's history. Close to $4 billion in tickets were purchased in New York State alone in 1999, and systematically, the state paid out nearly $2 billion in winnings. That simple public accounting reveals that, on average, in order to win $100 playing your local lottery, you'll need to pony up $200. To win $1,000, you'll have to spend $2,000 on tickets—an expensive way of feeling like a winner. Those returns make our *casinos* look like benevolent banks.

How the heck did the business of these games get so profitable? By capitalizing on monopoly status.

At present, no organization can compete with state-run lotteries, even though the industry turns thirty-eight cents of profit for every dollar in sales, a profitability rate well above that of one of America's greatest and most profitable companies, Microsoft. Ironically, the Justice Department continues to pursue that company for monopolistic practices, while our states operate their screw-the-customer lotteries sans competition. Is it legal for state treasuries to operate this multibillion-dollar megaprofitable industry *as a monopoly?* That's one of the questions we've put to the president in our open letter to the White House (see Appendix III). Though it's not even our strongest argument against lotteries, the operating structure of these games fundamentally violates the spirit of the Justice Department's crusades against anticompetitive practices in other fields. Since we are but Fools, we'll leave any court challenge up to some young hotshot lawyer looking to hang his hat on a Supreme Court case and a Hollywood deal!

Whether legal or not, there's no debate that state lotteries hugely benefit from their monopoly status. They have rather conveniently allowed themselves to earn the highest payout ratio in the history of American lotteries. They've exempted themselves from the promotional regulations that society enacts against casinos. And they've blocked access to reams of information about how they target markets and manage operations.

Is that what we want from our elected officials?

The answer to that question niftily transports us back to our concentration here on consumer finance. Criticizing states for dishonorable business practices ignores the driving force behind these games: *the demand from the people.* In nearly every vote on state lotteries since their rebirth in 1964, and in documented surveys dating back to 1938, Americans have voted overwhelmingly in favor of them. The votes, which typically show more than 60 percent of popular ballots supporting the adoption of lotteries, disclose the public's hunger for lower taxes and win-a-million games. But it's a short-term gain bringing long-term pain, because while lotteries mislead some into thinking it their only hope for prosperity, they also create and promote enduring poverty. The old saw about lotteries is that they're a tax on imbeciles, a tax on people who don't know the numbers.

To take it full circle, the state ends up promoting poverty, which it must later bail out with emergency taxes.

Are we calling for the end to lotteries here? Have the Fools lost their sense of humor as they clamber up on orange crates and moralize in the town square? Nay, dear reader. Our belief in open society demands that even such a waste of personal savings as the lottery be allowed. If the nation wants the game, it should get it. But let's welcome a little competition onto the scene. America is not about monopoly; we're a nation that prides itself on enterprising competition. The states should be forced to allow competitive games with higher reward ratios. (And you can make a pretty sure bet about which emerging media conglomerate based in Alexandria, Virginia, is ready to sponsor its own free Internet lottery!)

As we closed our section on gaming, so we close our section on the lottery. If you find it entertaining to pick up two $1 tickets when your state jackpot balloons to $50 million, go for it! If you derive pleasure from infrequently watching numbered balls fly around a compressed-air machine with your fortune riding on them, plunge in. You're helping to grow your government, if that puffs you up with patriotic pride. However, if you're methodically buying lottery tickets in the hopes of getting ahead, stand on your head, walk backward for a day, wear your clothes inside out, and eat breakfast at 7 P.M. Invert and you'll find the truth; the lottery will ruin your savings account.

To boil this entire "Gambling" section down to a few lines: gamble for frivolous fun. Bask in the neon, fill your lungs with more oxygen than nature ever intended them to hold, and take a chance at winning or losing a small amount of your money—if you must! But to gamble repeatedly and consistently under the delusive hope you'll make money is the height of folly, stamped with the *smallest* of *f*'s. To boil this down one step further, now you understand both the value of a dollar and the power that comes from knowing the numbers. But there are simpler numbers ahead, and they'll startle you.

Credit Card Debt

On the face of it, there's nothing more injurious to consumer finances than gambling. It exacts a charge on every wager. When courted lovingly, gambling (you'll notice we never allow the industry its euphemism, "gaming," to sneak in here) can smash nest eggs under toe in the time it takes to say "I wonder if I'll get to meet Donald Trump while I'm here." But while the pace of destruction can be ghastly, the gambling industry harms only a fairly marginal group. Far more people either don't bet or play for sporadic, small-time amusement. Many more people are harmed more significantly by an industry that pleads every day with Americans to spend more of their money: credit cards!

As we already noted in our introduction, consumer debt is at record levels. As of this writing, Americans owe $240 billion to their plastic creditors, with over $65 billion due in interest payments over the last year. The average American adult who doesn't pay off his bill each month is plodding along with $7,000 of credit card debt. If that startles you, get ready for another shock. On average, that debt is financed at a lending rate of over 18 percent per year. The average in-debt customer will make annual interest payments of over $1,000, money that will not buy her *anything,* money that she will not be investing for her future. What's more, much of that debt is created needlessly, the result of "discretionary spending" (that is, stuff you didn't *have* to have). To best understand what this is doing to consumer finances, we must investigate whence the credit card came.

Credit cards weren't part of the American heritage until 1949, when the Diners Club card debuted. Designed for business travelers, the card was purchased by corporations and overseen by chief financial officers (CFOs). The lending rate was tied to the federal funds rate—the rate set by the Federal Open Market Committee at which banks lend money to one another. That meant that back then, revolving debt on the Diners Club card amounted to average annual interest payments of 7 percent. If you had

$1,000 in debt on your Diners card, you would pay $70 in interest payments for the year. Simple math.

With time, other card companies sprang up to lend money not just to businesses but to individuals as well. Credit cards presented customers with convenience and a greater (and often misleading) sense of financial independence. ("Honey, apparently we can afford this Dolby system!") *Buying* suddenly became a whole lot easier. And credit card companies noted that consumers, operating without a CFO looking over their shoulder, were a lot less careful with their money. Lenders also rightly evaluated consumers as a higher risk, which caused them to inch their fees up above the fed funds rate. The slight initial hike was justified.

But the separation of credit card interest rates and the federal funds rate changed dramatically in the 1980s. Lenders got Wise. They began to realize that many Americans didn't know the first thing about interest rates or that their grade-school mathematical training could actually be helpful in the money world. Lenders' market research produced one overriding revelation: *These people haven't a damned clue about their money.*

So what did they do? Did they aim to educate their customers? Ha . . . right! That's a good one. No, they jacked up their lending rates. Between 1980 and 1999, while the rate at which banks loaned to businesses *fell* from 13.4 percent to 9.5 percent, good God, the credit card companies drove their rates *higher* for the consumer, up to an average of 18.0 percent. The difference of a few percentage points between the two in 1980 had grown to a gap of 8.5 percentage points per year by 1999.

And you know what? They were right, and their strategy worked. People didn't breathe a peep of complaint. For the most part, they didn't even know what happened.

The effects of the separation of rates are now very clear. In both gross and relative terms, more American households are declaring bankruptcy today than ever before. On the other hand, the divorcing of the two rates has dramatically swelled credit card–company coffers. These guys now sponsor weekend company trips to St. Croix and the Seychelles.

Just to clarify the numbers above, consider that if credit card companies had maintained the four-percentage-point spread between the fed funds rate and their own rate, they'd be on course to take in about $20 billion *less* in 2000. That $20 billion is being plucked away from Americans only because we can't seem to work the multiplication button on our counting machines. The calculator *should be* the lender's greatest foe.

Any surprise that many of our creditors today encourage impulse buying? They offer to extend lines of credit coincident with reducing minimum payment requirements and raising interest rates. If you didn't catch that last sentence, read it again. It's important. That's how the credit companies are making loads of money. They give you access to more money, reduce the amount you have to pay each month on outstanding debt, and raise the interest rates on you. Think about the consequences of those three simultaneous acts on a mathematically challenged college freshman.

Just as the young beer drinker has nudged up against his borrowing limit of $1,000, his lender calls to inform him that his credit line has been extended to $3,000. *Congratulations!* In addition, his flat annual fee on the card will be forgiven. All *right!* Henceforth, he'll be required to make minimum monthly payments on only 1 percent, instead of 2 percent, of outstanding debts. *Hoo-ha!* And finally, his interest rates will be moved up from 18 percent to 22 percent. Well, OK. Whatever.

Our freshman is thrilled by the news. Just look at it: No annual fees now, for a starter. More important, he has gained access to more money. Even better, he'll pay *less* per month to borrow that money. Gosh, he muses. What a stupid business that would let him get away with that.

But as we can plainly see, he has been enticed to delay repayment of ever-larger sums in order to maximize the creditor's profits. As the credit card company extracts its full pound of flesh, the customer inches ever so slightly closer toward bankruptcy. Take a look at what happens to his existing $1,000 in debt under the proposed conditions above (we'll pretend he doesn't even extend his borrowing to $3,000).

$1,000 DEBT TURNS INTO . . .

	Interest Rate	5 Years	10 Years
Federal Funds	6%	$1,338	$1,790
Prime Rate	9.5%	$1,574	$2,478
Average Credit Card	18%	$2,288	$5,234
Proposed Deal	22%	$2,703	$7,305

Ten years later, our college freshman will owe nearly three times as much as a corporation would for borrowing the exact same amount of money. This isn't *just* because the corporation is more creditworthy. No, no. It's because the company has a chief financial officer, an experienced money manager who would *never* borrow at the rates proposed to the individual above unless he was in the most desperate of straits. Conversely, the average citizen, the college freshman, the common fool, doesn't realize what interest rates *are* and has long since abandoned his electronic counting machine. It will always be more difficult to mislead the chief financial officer than the layman. That is, until our layman gets his hands on this book.

On a side note, please observe the self-fulfilling prophecy here. In lending at these usurious rates, creditors are in fact *fashioning* consumers into higher-risk, less creditworthy debtors. Anytime I suddenly double your interest rate, you are instantly ipso facto a higher risk. Call it *manufacturing* high-risk profiles. Eventually, it has dismal results for everyone.

But a return to strength in consumer finances is attainable. What the providers of high-rate, revolving-credit debt may not like very much is the development of the Internet. Because of the global network, people are piling into editorial sites in search of objective guidance. We developed our own credit area at Fool.com expressly for the purpose of walking everyone through the process of managing debt, from the college freshman to the divorcé to the retiree.

The two most significant steps you can take (in this order) are (1) to negotiate lower interest rates on your credit card debt and (2) to aggressively pay down all debt as soon as possible, no matter the rate. You'd be surprised how easy both of these can be, once you've concentrated on them. The first is literally the work of a single afternoon, or more accurately a few minutes sliced out of a single afternoon. In almost every case, with a simple phone call you can negotiate your interest rate down, demanding that your credit card company set its rate at no higher than 12 percent annually. Use our Foolish Rate Negotiation Dialogue™ below to bully your lender into lowering your interest rate.

YOU: I just got this incredibly great offer from FirstUnitedBancUSANation'sEdgeChoice card for a Titanium card with a fixed APR of just five-point-nine percent for the rest of my living days! I don't really want to switch cards, your service has been great. But I've just started noticing that the interest rate you're offering me has crept up to thirty-three-point-nine percent in the past year. Obviously, I'm going to have to transfer my balance unless you can lower the interest rate.

THEM: *(The sound of typewriter keys tapping and your credit and payment history being scrutinized.)*

YOU: Did I mention the free toaster?

THEM: *(The sound of fake typing as the operator tries to psych you out with silence.)*

YOU: *(The sound of you filling out the FirstUnitedBancUSANation'sEdgeChoice card application.)*

THEM: Uncle! We'd like to keep you as a customer, so I am prepared to lower your interest rate, and waive your annual fee if you choose to stay with us.

At this point they should offer you something around 12 percent. If you get a dud operator who isn't feeling generous, ask to speak to a supervisor. Granted, if you're perpetually late with your payment, yell at dogs, or litter, your lender may prefer to let you walk. So be prepared to follow through with FirstUnitedBancUSANation'sEdgeChoice. But if you have an even vaguely solid track record with your card you should have no problem whatsoever negotiating a lower lending rate.

As for the second just described step, in our experience it's always easier than one might think to pay down debt, once you make this your primary professional mission. More on this later. For now, let us close with a word about the very worst use of credit cards we've ever run across—an uncharacteristically pessimistic way for us to end a section. The worst use of a credit card that we have ever encountered was a fellow's buying lottery tickets with an 18 percent credit card. He managed to combine the 18 percent annual lending rate from his creditor with 50 percent average losses per ticket. If you have foes, real down-and-dirty enemies, the sort that just won't leave you alone, encourage them sweetly to buy lottery tickets on their Visa card. You'll have them sunk before the month is out!

So ends "And a Bunch of People Want What You Have." Now that you know this is so, know why it is, and know many ways to avoid it, let's put what we've learned into seven savings strategies. These are the components of "Surprise Them—Save It Instead," our next chapter, as we hurtle headlong into how to make money off of all this wealth you're preserving!

Surprise Them—Save It Instead

B^{oo!}

Sooo-prise!

It's time for all of us to shock our friends and family, to startle our communities and corporations, and to rock the world with a smart and simple plan designed to save money. Together we've survived, largely unscathed, the grim and gray considerations of gambling, the lottery, and credit cards. May these matters never again rustle loudly through your life. And Godspeed!

Not far down the road in this book, we'll be thinking about the best ways to buy some pretty expensive stuff and a bit about how to invest all of your money intelligently, but before we can airlift you out of the mire of personal finance and into the buzz and bump of the stock market, we need to briefly consider *savings*. How much money should you save? Do you need a budget? Where should you put money that you'll need in six months? Can the brotherly Fools actually make this chapter any fun to read? These are excellent questions you're asking. Permit us to make a few suggestions about your savings strategies.

Actually Try to Have Fun

A lot of savings tips are depressing. You follow the fashionable advice in the paperback bestsellers and find that you haven't bathed in a week, you aren't washing your clothes very often, and you've been alternating between ramen noodles and oatmeal all winter. We don't think you want to live that way.

You have necessities, like every other living, breathing creature on the earth. They must be provided for. To this list of standard daily requirements—food, water, shelter, sleep, human contact, and Nutter Butters—we'd like to add (look at the big letters a few lines above) one more necessity: *fun*. Yes, surprise the world and actually have fun saving money.

Not possible, right? When it comes to saving money, most suggestions add toil and drudgery to the process, stripping any remaining nobility from our days. It's no wonder so many Americans reject financial planning, with its spate of acronyms, with its accompanying commissioned salesperson, and, far worse than these, with the pettiness it forces into our lives. When you think of da Vinci, Einstein, or Mozart, does the idea of budgeted savings cross your minds? No, nay, never. Those guys thrilled the world by being brash, sublime, and spirited. Do you think they spent their free hours balancing checkbooks and rolling up pennies?

It is our honest opinion that if Foolishness doesn't make saving money uplifting, it ain't worth it. As much as Ebenezer Scrooge seemed a master of his money, he was defeated by it. That is, until the introduction of joy. Bring to your savings plans the good humor that pulled Scrooge out of hell. Your enjoyment isn't merely crucial to the process—it is the process. But how?

Take Friends Along with You

Kapow! Surprise everyone and involve your friends in your financial life. Pitch them ideas, catch some of their suggestions, and make fun of any really bad ideas that they have, like saving quarters by not washing clothes next week or earning $20 by spending your weekends with a metal detector, hunting for watches and coins at the park. Making fun of your friends is a core part of Foolishness.

But beyond trading tips and barbs, you'll actually want to have your friends physically travel with you during any important transaction. In the money world, you should never, ever haggle for expensive stuff without assistance. In fact, just the opposite. You need to bring as many people along for negotiation as you can coerce. Offer up a steak dinner to your ten closest friends who agree to cruise down to the local car house with you. Imagine the look on the managers' faces when they see your squad descending on them with notebooks and pens, calculators, a laptop, a measuring stick, automobile guides, a dictionary, and three giant bags of popcorn.

If you need one more push into bringing friends along, ask yourself, "Am I going to have more fun haggling alone with the salesman, or doing so with a bunch of my friends?" Case closed. Now when you're out there buying and selling like a madman or crazy Jane, try the following . . .

Focus the Use of Your Credit Cards on Growth

Some folks stuff them at the bottom of desk drawers, others jam them under their ice trays, but credit cards always seem to crawl back into the more prominent pockets of our wallet. But that's right where they should be. They weren't designed to fit tightly into an old shoe or slide neatly under a floorboard.

The Fool now formally proposes that even if you're carrying any kind of debt, you keep that credit card in your wallet at all times, view it as a weapon against inconvenience, and for the time being not toss and turn at night if your line of revolving credit has expanded, month over month. Nope. Even though the *average* American household carrying a credit card balance may carry as much $7,000 in plastic debt, we are not going to propose that you divorce your credit cards, accepting stiff alimony payments and relegating yourself to sleeping in a big lonely bed. Instead, we recommend that you begin with a shorthand classification of your borrowing habits, itemizing your credit card purchases in three groups: survival, growth, and luxury.

In the first category, include all items you've purchased on plastic to meet your *survival needs.* Chicken sandwiches, winter socks, and clean water count; leather pants, computer games, and beer do not.

In the second group, note all purchases that act as *growth investments.* For example, if you're a professional guitarist and just upgraded to a new guitar on your Visa, classify that as an investment in future growth. Buying a Jet Ski if you're an attorney, however, does not count.

In the final group, note the *luxury items* you've bought on plastic—from Scandinavian furs to Minnesota Twins season tickets to Nancy Sinatra's greatest hits on CD. That stuff is fun; that stuff is great; unfortunately, you won't be buying it on your credit card anymore.

You can guess what specific suggestion we're going to make now, right?

Until you've worked your way out of debt, eliminate all card buying for items in the third, or luxury, category. Unless you're consistently *reducing* the debt, also eliminate buying from the growth group too. Finally, never stop borrowing to buy stuff that meets your survival needs. If you can hold to these three categories and maintain this approach throughout your life, you'll greatly reduce the risk that you'll run into trouble with your creditors. And as you work off the debt, you'll move up into a world where you can make prudent investments in your future growth using credit cards: that ukelele for the professional crooner; that exercise machine for the young baseball player; paints, brushes, and canvas for the aspiring artist; books for the scholar. Used very carefully, credit cards can enhance your professional life.

Finally, never, ever, never, never, under any circumstances, ever, never, use your credit card to buy luxuries for which you cannot make payments in the month ahead. Revolving debt for personal luxury is wasteful. If you can afford to make the monthly payment, shop like mad. If not, don't dig yourself deeper into a hole for those Neil Young tickets, that trip to Zanzibar, or that brand-new leopard-skin pillbox hat.

From here, we have something of a strange twist, an underhanded knuckle curveball, some reverse-reverse-reverse-reverse-*reverse* psychology.

Buy Snowshoes in the Summertime

This suggestion would make Pythagoras proud. As we mentioned earlier, the Greek mathematician proposed that to see the truths around us, we must train ourselves to *invert*. He might champion acts like treating the endurance of failure as your greatest victory, regarding the Wise as mere fools, and eating ice cream in Antarctica.

Pythagorean inversion down at Shopper's World translates into the purchase of mittens in May and short-sleeved shirts in September. There's money to be saved in going shopping when the demand is at its low and supplies are still sitting on the shelves. Looking forward to telemark skiing in Switzerland next winter? Buy those skis in June. Planning to snorkel in the Bahamas this July? Pay for all your swimming gear in November.

You might want to purchase your car during the winter, too, and preferably just before the new models roll onto the lot. But how important is it that you save money when buying a new car? Well . . .

Surprise Everyone and . . . Spend Little on Your Car

It's a stunning statistic, but new cars lose up to 30 percent of their value the moment they depart the dealer's lot. Did you just spend $15,000 on a spanking-new convertible? As soon as you park it in your garage, its underlying value is closing in on $10,000. A few years later, it could be worth less than $5,000.

Youch!

From an investment standpoint, it doesn't make a lick of sense to spend big money on stylish wheels. We're not going to suggest that you pitch around the country in an unroadworthy buggy with a dreary interior that smells like four-month-old chicken soup mixed in a pair of veteran running shoes. Bleck! Let's not take the savings plan to an unhealthy extreme. But you should know that automobiles are one of the very worst places to park your savings money.

And, Fool, we saved the best idea for last.

Methodically Save 10 to 15 Percent of Your Salary

If you're making $28,000 per year, can you not squirrel away $3,000 of it? That amounts to putting away $115 out of your biweekly salary payments. And while that amount of savings might not seem important to you, it's just absolutely huge. If you are twenty-seven years old and able to put $3,000 away into the stock market each year until you're sixty years old, any idea how much money you'd have if the market maintains its historical rate of return?

Tick, tock, tick, tock, tick, tock, ti—brrrrrring!

Before taxes, $920,512. Wow. And all of that without a single pay raise, without a single opportunity in your entire life to add more than $3,000 per year.

Now, we have to make it clear that once you've saved that 10 to 15 percent for your future, we hope you'll take the remaining funds from your salary and enjoy them. By blindly putting away your money, you've saved yourself from having to track every dollar and cut back on brand-name potato chips. Woo-hoo! The philosophy behind this savings strategy is that you should have opportunities to enjoy every year of life. No one should sacrifice all of his or her youth for financial independence in middle age, particularly when that's unnecessary.

Yes, put 10 percent of your bucks away. Be smart with the remaining money.

Oh, but how do you do that, anyway?

You Can Get
and Keep More
Than You Think

THE FIRST STOP on the road to keeping more of what you have should be your bank, and we'd like to start with a few quick questions. What interest rates does your current bank pay? Are you leaving significantly more money in your checking account than you need to pay the monthly bills? Do you know where the best interest rates are for money market accounts? Have you checked out the possibilities of online banking? Do you know where to find the local ATMs that won't charge you any fees?

"Hey, hey, wait a second," you're saying. "I just innocently turned over the page to find how to get and keep more than I thought. I didn't expect the Spanish Inquisition." Well, as others more comedically talented than we have pointed out before, nobody *expects* the Spanish Inquisition. But perhaps it's time that you put *yourself* through the third degree. Goings-on in the banking industry today show that most consumers are not giving their banking behavior much, if any, inquiry, and the consequences are significant. Just as brokers, credit card companies, the mutual fund industry, and car dealers have been preying on consumers who don't know the rules of the game, banks are counting on their customers not doing even the least little bit of homework before opening an account.

Consider these facts:

- More than $1 trillion is currently in low- (or no-) interest checking and savings accounts
- ATMs currently charge fees as high as $5 for a single transaction. Banks make more than $2 billion annually on ATM fees alone
- There is virtually no use at all today for the inappropriately named "savings" account, yet it remains one of the most popular ways for Americans to store their money

When you stop and think about it, this all makes perfect sense. There are some good reasons why it isn't profitable to you, dear reader, to bank with the PhirstCitiBancs, which hold so much of our collective money in their vaults. After all, there's a *lot* of marble that has to be hewn out of Italy, flown over on the Concorde, and kept clean in those cavernous downtown branches where they shoot those lovely commercials. Those powerful CEOs of the biggest banks also need (*need*, we're telling you!) some very extravagant corporate jets. And don't forget the cost of having a football stadium or sports arena named after a bank. If you like seeing a stadium on ESPN's *SportsCenter* and being able to point at the screen and say, "Hey, my checking account fees helped name that place!"—by all means, keep banking there and skip the tedious chore of wading through the rest of this section.

Assuming for the moment that you haven't riffled a few pages ahead, let's begin by pointing out that the games and tactics used by banks to anesthetize their customers are the same ones that the Wise men of Wall Street use. Here are some signs that banks are deep in the Wisdom racket:

- The use of jargon to keep the customer confused
- Offering high introductory interest rates and then quietly lowering them
- Hiding the fees and costs in the small print
- Loudly proclaiming the value of expensive "personalized service"

Keep in mind always that your ultimate goal with banks should simply be to obtain the services and convenience you need, with the lowest costs and the highest interest rates available. If you're ready to bank online, you'll almost certainly find that the lowest costs and the highest interest rates are available there.

In any event, whether or not you're ready to give online banking a shot, let's take a few minutes to identify your banking behavior and set some easy goals for yourself.

How did you pick your current bank? Maybe it was the one that had the most ATMs in your immediate area. Or maybe it was the one that advertised the highest interest rates for a checking account when, several years ago, you were shopping around. Or maybe you just picked the one that had the coolest display of marble, red carpet, and polished brass in its lobby.

While there are many ways that banks have seduced people into placing their savings in one place rather than another, in all likelihood the top three reasons you're with a particular bank are location, location, and location. If you're like most people, your bank is pretty close to your home, your office, the train station, or some combination of those. You're banking where it was convenient to walk in, sit down, and start an account—even though there's a good chance that you seldom, if ever, actually walk into your bank to talk to a teller anymore.

But, if you're banking with an establishment that has a large number of locations that you can walk into, you are, most assuredly, paying quite a bit to maintain all those locations. That payment takes two forms: lower interest rates paid by the bank on the money that you keep there and ever-multiplying fees on almost all of your banking activity.

Ask yourself, really, how often do you need to go into a bank these days? With newfangled inventions like the telephone, direct deposit, the U.S. mail system, and even, dare we say, the Internet, you don't need to be particularly close to a bricks-and-mortar branch of any bank if you know how to find the account that fits your needs and keeps costs low. Right now, at this very moment, there are scores of banks that are no further away than your computer keyboard or your telephone. Keep in mind as you read on that virtually all of those banks will have rates and fee structures that are an improvement on the majority of bank accounts maintained today.

People out there haven't just been casual about where they bank. Many have also been extremely casual about leaving large sums in the wrong accounts—and passing up on hundreds, and occasionally thousands, of dollars of interest in the process. To get truly Foolish with your banking, you'll need to identify how much money you need to keep in typical banking accounts. The answer to this question, for Fools, should be, "Not much at all." Money that is left in typical banking accounts (that is, savings and checking accounts) is earning very, very little in the way of interest. The average interest paid on checking and savings accounts does not even rise to the level of the rate of inflation, yet Americans today have more than a trillion dollars in such accounts.

If you leave significantly more money in your checking account than you need to pay the monthly bills and avoid a service charge for maintaining a minimal balance, then you're leaving too much money in that account. Furthermore, though many national banks require you to maintain a balance of perhaps around $1,500 to get interest on your checking account without paying monthly fees, with a little research you can open an account with as little as $500 and be paid interest.

Are we advocating that you get all of the money beyond your immediate needs into the stock market? Hey, we're Fools, but we're not idiots. The stock market, though a wonderful vehicle for *long-term* savings, is in no way insured, and can be a great place to see money disappear over the short term. As we've stated before and will reiterate throughout this book, the only money we advocate putting into the market is money that you believe you're going to leave there for a minimum of five years. Five years—minimum. That's M-I-N . . . You get the picture.

Certainly, we all need to keep *some* money around and readily available. Not just to pay this month's bills, mind you, but dinero for a rainy day, for the occasional shopping binge, and as a security blanket to allow us to sleep at night. It's just that this money, if left in typical savings and checking accounts, will not return you even half the rate of interest obtainable through equally insured accounts. Your best choice may be an out-of-state bank, an Internet-based bank, or perhaps just a discount brokerage account (more on that anon).

Before explaining what these accounts are, though, the first step in every Foolish personal finance decision is to know thyself. And the only way you're going to truly get to know yourself in this instance is to start gathering up your old bank records and create a checklist of banking needs.

Forgive us this felonious accusation, but we think there's at least a decent chance that you're not looking very carefully at your detailed monthly bank statement. So as we figure out together how to improve your banking, let's cobble a few of those statements together. Records in hand, we'll discover what types of fees you're being charged, what your average account balance is, and what your typical low balance figure is. Since virtually all checking and savings accounts are going to inflict low balance fees on you, you need to know how much money you'll be able to keep in your account to find the deal that's right for you.

Try using this checklist to see just how much you've spent over the last three months and to see where the money is going:

Item	Month #1	Month #2	Month #3	TOTAL
ATM surcharges				
"Foreign" ATM fees				
Other ATM fees				
Overdraft fees				
Monthly maintenance fees				
Check printing				
Deposit/other slips				
Call-center charges				
Debit-card fees				
Low-balance penalty				
Per-check charges				
Return check/NSF fees				
Money-order fees				
Traveler's checks				
Other bank fees				
TOTALS				

Calculate those fees. This will give you a real idea of where your money has been going, and what you need to change in either yourself or your bank to keep your money in your own pocket.

With your calculation of fees firmly in hand, tap your ruby slippers together and repeat the following to yourself over and over again until you have it completely memorized: "There's no such thing as free checking. There's no such thing as free checking. There's no such thing as free checking."

If ever you should hear "free checking," immediately ask yourself, "What's the catch?" While many fine checking accounts charge no explicit fee, they also typically feature much lower interest rates than accounts that don't advertise themselves as (ruby slippers!) "free."

The opportunity cost of putting money into an account that does not have the highest interest rate makes these accounts not quite free. Even though the payment you make doesn't necessarily take the form of actual charges, by accruing less interest than you otherwise could get for your savings, there is a real cost for this "free" service. Put another way, the nation's banks (which are very profitable institutions) aren't exactly going broke by offering lots of free services. They're making piles of pretty pennies from all the services they claim are provided for free by paying very low interest on typical checking and savings accounts.

Furthermore, "free" checking accounts typically (though not always) come with strings attached in the form of numerous fees. Come to think of it, all checking accounts come with strings and hidden fees attached, and the number of strings has been growing at an explosive rate over the last few years as banks have been dreaming up even more fees to inflict on their customers.

At the same time, the largest national banks are offering interest rates on their checking accounts that are about one-quarter the rate that can be found at smaller regional banks or through Internet-based banks. According to a recent report published by bankrate.com, *none* of the fifty largest banks in the country make it onto the list of banks offering the best checking accounts. Between the nasty fees and the missed interest, the worst checking accounts in the country cost around $300 a year for someone who maintains a monthly balance of $1,500 a month.

Checking Accounts

Even though the Wise world of banking trots out dozens of different category names, there are really only about three different types of checking accounts:

- Accounts that pay no interest and charge relatively lower fees, which might be called something like "economy checking"
- "Basic checking" accounts for low-income earners, which also won't pay interest, but charge lower fees and require a lower monthly balance
- Accounts that pay very low interest (ironically, often called "High Interest," "Super Interest," "Mondo Interest," "Checking DoublePlus-Good," "Success Checking," or any number of other misnomers), charges higher fees for your mistakes, and requires a higher opening balance and higher monthly balances than other accounts

Any one of these might be called "free checking" (since the term "free checking," has no precise meaning), but here's something to keep in mind when deciding which account might be right for you: Depending on the account balance you maintain and the interest rate offered, you may be better off in a no-interest account. According to a recent survey, the average amount that an account holder needs to maintain to avoid minimum-balance fees on an interest-bearing checking account is greater than $2,000 a month, and the average monthly service charges (per-check charges, bill payment fees, etc.) assessed on an interest-bearing account are almost $10 per month. Keeping $2,000 a month in an account that pays about 1 percent interest a year (earning $20) while paying $10 per month in fees (losing $120) means a net loss of $100 a year. You can do a lot better than the average consumer out there is doing.

Customers who keep an average of $5,000 or so in their checking accounts get better deals from their banks, but they really shouldn't be maintaining that much money in a checking account in the first place. The opportunity cost of leaving thousands of dollars in an account that pays virtually no interest is really quite high. You should keep about as much in your checking account as you need to pay the monthly bills and avoid a minimum-balance charge—the rest should be kept in a higher-interest account such as a savings account, a CD, or a money market fund. You can then transfer money from the higher-interest accounts to your checking account as needed, keeping in mind the limits and fees that apply to making transfers.

Go out and find the best interest rates available for your checking-account dollars. A smaller local bank or credit union will likely have checking accounts with interest rates double those of the big national banks. Internet-based banks have rates that are closer to three or four times the rates offered by the national Goliaths. Here's a checklist of questions to keep in mind when you're either sitting down with a bank employee to discuss opening an account or surfing the Web to determine whether an ad you've clicked on has really brought you to a site where you might want to do business:

- What is the interest rate on the account? If the account does not pay any interest, what is the difference between the fees charged on an interest-bearing account and the non-interest choice?
- What is the minimum deposit necessary to open the account? What is the minimum balance necessary to avoid a fee once the account is open?
- What is the per-check charge? What is the charge for ordering new checks?

- What is the charge for a bounced check?
- Are canceled checks returned with the monthly statements? If not, what are the charges for having a canceled check returned?

Another Tricky Misnomer: The Savings Account

Earlier, we pointed out that you're best off keeping in your checking account only enough money to pay the monthly bills and avoid low-balance fees. Beyond that, you should aim to get the best rate of interest available for your intermediate-term savings, and that means putting some of your extra cash somewhere other than a checking account. But millions of Americans today are going about this the wrong way and settling for very low yields on their savings. As we speak, there is more money deposited in savings accounts yielding 2 percent interest than there is in certificates of deposit (CDs) yielding an average of closer to 5 percent. Nearly $1.5 trillion is tied up in accounts that aren't paying any more than 2 percent. That needs to change, and, as usual, the best way to beat the system is to learn more about it.

Let's take a quick look into some of the cages in this zoo:

Passbooks.

Do people still use these? Apparently, some do. If you're older than Generations X or Y, you might remember a type of account where the bank gave you a little book to record your transactions. By law, these accounts paid 5 percent interest—until 1986, when deregulation allowed banks to set the rates. Today interest rates have drifted all the way down to 2 percent, or even less if you're banking with First Goliath.

Statement Savings.

You can distinguish this account from a passbook account only by the fact that there's no passbook—there's a statement sent monthly in the mail. The interest rate for statement savings accounts is about 2 percent.

Money Market Accounts.

Money market accounts are savings accounts offered by banks and credit unions that pay out a slightly higher rate on your money; as of this writing, they average 2.5 percent. (By doing a little research, however, the Foolish shopper will likely be able to find some with roughly double that rate of return. Check around online at bankrate.com or our site for the most recent national rates as part of your research.) Money market accounts may require a higher minimum balance, but you can make as many deposits as you like for free and you can write up to three checks per month. Like passbooks and statement savings, these accounts are insured by the Federal Deposit Insurance Corporation (FDIC).

Money Market Funds.

Money market funds are a type of mutual fund. Though not government insured, they are very secure, as regulations require these funds be invested in high-quality, short-term investments like short-term loans to corporations or government agencies. Currently, money market funds can snare you over 5 percent interest. Again, shop around for the best rates.

Certificates of Deposit (CDs).

Going beyond the above accounts, if you have money that can stand to be tied up for anywhere from three months to six years, certificates of deposit will offer even higher rates—currently slightly higher than an annualized rate of 6 percent. Of course, if you're putting money into CDs, remember that the longer the term, the higher the interest rate you'll get—but you also can't touch that money for the length of the CD term. There is a penalty for early withdrawal of funds, so be careful about the CD you choose. If you're likely to be dipping into some of that money to fix the house, take a vacation, or buy holiday presents, don't put too much into a long-term CD. Like savings, checking, and money market accounts, CDs are FDIC-insured for up to $100,000.

It Ain't Just the Interest Rate . . .

If you wish to maintain a checking account at a local institution (either because you want to have a branch you can walk into, or you enjoy being able to use its large local distribution of ATMs), you should still consider moving your intermediate-term savings into an out-of-state bank if that's where you find the very best rates on CDs or money market accounts. If you're limiting your savings to what your big local bank is offering, you're almost surely passing up an extra 2 percent earnings on your money.

Why is it that a small bank you've never heard of halfway across the country can offer much better rates than the gigantic NationsUnion that just swallowed up half the banks on both seaboards? Simple. The tiny thrifts and savings banks don't have to maintain oodles of branches, pay thousands of employees, and produce the television commercials necessary to convince otherwise sane people to believe in "free checking." These smaller banks can better afford to make their customers' money actually work for their customers.

Still, keep your eyes on the fees—always. If you're setting up any accounts out of state, in state, or (the best logical answer) online, keep in mind that the highest interest rates may very well be accompanied by some extra fees. Make sure that when you're shopping around you get the fee disclosure forms from all the banks you're considering. Again, get your past bank statements and compare your behavior and needs to the fees that each bank charges for particular privileges and services.

You will of course want other questions answered before finally deciding which bank gives you the best bang for your buck, but the best account is very likely *not* at the bank that has the most commercials or the one that just swallowed up your old bank. Although these large regional, superregional, or national banks might have the most ATMs in the area—which might lead you to believe that that is what's most important—have you really been keeping an eye on what's going on with ATMs lately?

A Brief History of the Automated Teller Machine (ATM)

When ATMs first appeared about twenty years ago, not many people used them. Banks had to resort to promotional gimmicks to get anyone to try these newfangled and frightening machines. All transactions were free. Historians now refer to those early days as the golden age of ATMs.

(Sigh.)

With all the fees attached to them today, ATMs, although more plentiful, function as profit centers for banks at least as much as they do as a service to bank customers. One of the primary reasons why you probably have a banking account is so that you have something to take out of all those friendly ATMs that are now on every street corner. And banks are quite happy about that. Banks discourage their customers from making transactions with a live teller (sometimes by charging as much as $8 for a face-to-face encounter), because that involves paying somebody to smile at you while they're helping you out. It costs banks about 27 cents to have a deposit or withdrawal processed at an ATM machine versus about $1.07 to handle the same transaction by a live teller.

But there's another reason that banks love to have people go to ATMs: the fees that can be charged. American banks make a bundle off these fees, we think because people are not paying sufficient attention to what they're paying to use those machines. After all, it's just a dollar here, a dollar there, right? Wrong.

The Center for Responsive Law estimates that banks today make more than $2 billion on ATM transactions. That total is going up rapidly, as banks have seen fit to continually raise the amounts they charge customers for the privilege of using the ATMs. Furthermore, nowadays it isn't just your bank that's socking you with a fee—if you aren't using one of your own bank's actual ATMs, the other bank is usually hitting you up as well.

There isn't too much you need to know about ATMs except how to avoid incurring fees when you use them. (You also need to remember to wait for your card to come back out after you've been given the money. But we're sure you've *never* come near making *that* mistake.) To avoid fees, simply bank at an institution that doesn't charge you when you use your ATM card at its own machines or those of a different ("foreign") institution, and learn where the free foreign ATMs are.

Are we just dreaming or nostalgic? Are we fabricating this notion of free ATMs? Hmmmmm. Have you seriously investigated credit unions, smaller local banks, and Internet-based banks?

WHICH MACHINES ARE THE MEAN ONES?

Yes, some ATMs are your friends, and some are your enemies. ATMs come in basically three flavors:

- *Proprietary:* The ones your bank owns. It is a rare bank indeed that charges its own customers to use its ATMs, but it's far from unheard of. Approximately 10% of all banks now charge their own customers for using the ATM. The fee tends to be around $1.
- *Nonproprietary:* All the machines that belong to somebody other than your bank. These will charge you about $1.00 to $1.50 to make your transaction, and they'll inform you that they're imposing a fee via either the "welcome" screen or with a sticker on the machine itself. But wait, there's more! Your own bank is probably charging you a similar fee for not using its own network. Find out how much your bank charges for this, but generally expect to be out about $3 between the fee from the ATM you're using and your own bank's fee.
- *National:* The bank is hooked up to a regional or national network, such as Cirrus, Plus, NYCE, Interlink, or others. When you use these out-of-town networks, expect that the fee will be no less than $1.50 and possibly as high as $3. Then add the fee that your bank is charging you.

Hey, every ATM dispenses cash in the same way—they all provide the same service. What you really need to know, dear reader, is which machines won't charge you, and whether your bank charges you. If you often find yourself using nonproprietary or national ATMs, then you'd better figure out just how much your bank is charging you per year and decide whether you aren't better off banking with an establishment that doesn't hit you with charges.

And know where those free machines are. More and more, free ATMs are cropping up at convenience stores as a way to lure people in. But don't *assume* that the machine is free—make sure by reading the "welcome" screen and any stickers on the machine. It's your three bucks!

Credit Unions

As you may have already gathered, any Fool exploring all of the alternatives to traditional banks should certainly not pass Go without first finding out what her local credit union has to offer. For many of us, a credit union will provide better service with noticeably better rates and lower fees than any GoliathUnitedBanc or even our friendlier smaller-scale local banks.

According to the Credit Union National Association, a credit union is "a cooperative financial institution, owned and controlled by the people who use its services. These people are members. Credit unions serve groups that share something in common, such as where they work, live, or go to church. Credit unions are not-for-profit, and exist to provide a safe, convenient place for members to save money and to get loans at reasonable rates." Essentially, credit unions are collectives of people brought together to loan each other money at fair rates. Pretty simple, actually.

The purpose of any business is largely to serve its owners. In the case of a bank, owners are outside shareholders, and the purpose of a bank is ultimately to serve those owners by making profits from its customers. Thus, at banks, fees are high and interest rates on deposits are kept low.

With credit unions, the members, depositors, and owners are all one and the same! Credit unions are run not-for-profit and thus are able to deliver substantially higher interest rates than banks for the same deposits. According to the Web site bankrate.com, the average yield on a money-market account at a credit union is about 1.5 percent higher than the national bank average. Additionally, the end of the year sees some credit unions rewarding their members with cash bonuses if financial targets have been met.

Because credit unions exist to serve their members' best interests, the service at a credit union is often superior. Credit unions also generally provide better financial guidance and better financial education to their members than do banks. The employees of a credit union have their fellow members' interests at heart, and (from what we hear on our Fool.com discussion boards) most credit union members love the personalized service they receive.

How to Find a Credit Union That You Are Eligible to Join

Today there are more than 72 million credit union members, so it isn't that hard for most Americans to find some credit union or another that will welcome their membership. Traditionally, the way to find a credit union you are eligible to join (remember, some are set up for church groups or specific employers) is to start asking around. You can ask your boss to set one up (if your employer, union, or professional association doesn't already have one), or ask your family or neighbors if they know of a good one.

With all this talk of how wonderful credit unions are and how much more Foolish they are than the standard three or four banks that are taking over the world, surely, you are saying, there must be some drawbacks. And, indeed, you would be right to say just that. Some not-so-wonderful aspects of credit unions:

Few Proprietary ATMs.

The main drawback to a credit union is that they don't have the ubiquitous ATMs that make the big banks attractive. Credit unions typically have a pretty limited number of branches—oftentimes just one. Or even none. However, to get around this, in most states credit unions have formed no-surcharge ATM networks among themselves, thereby multiplying the number of free machines available to all members. On the Internet are plenty of lists of the free ATMs available in your area, so for many this shouldn't be a problem. (Check out www.Fool.com/money/banking/services/atm.htm for updated information.)

Insurance May Not Apply.

In most credit unions deposits up to $100,000 are insured by the National Credit Union Administration, an agency of the federal government. The $100,000 protection is essentially the same as that offered on bank deposits by the Federal Deposit Insurance Corporation. However, approximately 3 percent of credit unions are not insured. Obviously, you should make sure that any credit union you consider joining is insured.

Checks Don't Come Back.

Credit unions have special wacky names for otherwise familiar things. A savings account is called a "share account" and the term for a checking account is a "share draft account." Not really a big problem. What *might* be a problem for some folks, though, is that at most credit unions, canceled checks are not returned to members. This may not be too big a problem— you just need to keep a carbon copy of the checks you write—but it is something to keep in mind.

Range of Services.

Many credit unions have a comparatively limited number of financial services available. While share accounts and share draft accounts are pretty ubiquitous, not all credit unions will have a full range of loan services or offer some of the more unique banking products of traditional banks. This is a problem that is quickly disappearing, though, as credit unions are expanding their services. If you're thinking of joining a credit union, make sure that it offers the full range of services that you think you'll need.

The banking industry really, really hates credit unions on account of the threat credit unions present to the lower-service banks. Banks have mounted intensive lobbying efforts to get Congress to pass laws to make credit union operations taxable. Thankfully, these efforts have all failed. If you're unsatisfied with your current bank for whatever reason, check out the competition that your local credit unions (or the online ones) are presenting.

Big Ticket Items

We now move to a final stop along this grievous adventure into how money gets misspent, after which we'll start exploring how to invest the money we're recouping. We'll briefly consider the purchase of some expensive merchandise, stuff on which you spend more than $1,000. Fellow Fool, these are potentially dangerous acquisitions, for well-trained salesmen are often compensated on the basis of how favorable a deal they can cut for their boss (and *not* for you). Because that new car and house and insurance plan are so expensive and so infrequently bought, most of these transactions require the dreaded practice of bartering. If you're like most people, you're happy that a medium called money was invented, and you believe that the barter system all but died for a reason. You're probably also distraught that bartering is still alive in car buying and the purchase of other big-ticket items.

So, since we're currently stuck with it, we'd better find a way to master it. Knowing the numbers and taking your time are critically important. In bartering, the very worst thing you can do is to rush to closure without properly estimating value. This is, of course, exactly what we most often do. In an effort to just get the deal done and get home to familiar territory, we race headlong into that which we can't value. In car dealerships and on house tours, the average buyer flips and flops like a fish on the riverbank. The Fool's aim is to forever put you back in the role of fisherman, since you are in the position of power. You are the buyer; they are the sellers. You have the money to keep; they have inventory to move.

Now, as hard as it may be to believe, we'll try first off to make the process of buying a car as much like a lazy long day on the river with your fly-fishing stick as possible. That runs contrary to your experiences, we know. You're used to being rushed through valuations and confused by jargon, being presented contracts that are intentionally too long to read, and accustomed to the sudden, eleventh-hour appearance of additional costs— all of which makes for an unfamiliar, uncomfortable process that has many people longing for the simplicity of bygone days, playing softball, say, under a crescent moon with the smell of barbecue wafting past the pitcher's mound . . .

Boom!

Wake up!

Larry McCloskey is back with another offer from the manager, and yer gonna like this one. Rest assured, it's a sweetheart deal.

If, for some reason, you're wondering why Larry is so aggressive, think about what would happen if you spent an entire evening walking through New York City with $3,000 prominently hanging out the back pockets of your trousers. You'd expect someone to try to snatch those bills, right? Well, that city straggler with cash hanging from his pockets is exactly what many dealers see when you walk across the showroom floor. You would be a common fool (small *f*) not to presume that salesmen like Larry dream about taking away as much of that money as possible. The lone car buyer wandering the showroom floor is like a dollop of lime sherbet in an infant's palm.

So how is a Fool to face down this threat and negotiate for the right car at the best price? He doesn't. It can't be done. Even if you nail everything just right, they finally get you on the alarm system, the special paint protection, the needless warranty, that financing, or the service guarantee. The whole darned process is so confusing, so dreary, we suggest you pay the list price. Heck, we think it's a good idea to just give in to every proposal offered to you by the salesmen of big-ticket items. They know best. They've been doing this for years. They've made thousands of customers happy. Just sign on the dotted line, whatever they want, and get on home.
. . . Just kidding.

Stroll with us through four key big-ticket purchases—a car, a house, insurance, and a college education—as we toss up some Foolish stratagems for getting a good deal without heightened blood pressure. Let's start with the automobile.

BUYING A CAR

We'll take it for granted that any attempts you've made at purchasing a car on your own have left you feeling in some way cheated, isolated, or degraded. The next time you're in the market for one, you may have some new hope: dealerships claim that they're approaching business differently today. Nevertheless, call us disenchanted cynics beyond hope of reclamation, but we think it's more than likely that your next sales visit will still provide a usual mix of half-truths, shifting eyes, and the blinding gleam of Super Bowl–style rings. You'll probably still sit for hours in the drab interior of a dealership, staring at the plastic flowers in an attempt to divine whether a lockable gas cap is really worth $75. And you probably should expect to be told that seven other people are dying to buy exactly the car you just test-drove.

The reason for your distrust and resentment is as clear as a squeegeed windshield. Dealerships trot out inflated list prices, hoping to ensnare every happy-go-lucky buyer with an open checkbook. Because they can't collude on pricing with other dealers, and because the car manufacturers squeeze them—by withholding commissions until inventory has been moved—salesmen are an anxious lot. In certain months their take-home pay can be as little as $1,000.

Because of this flawed business structure, car dealers run salesmen at you like pawns in a Ruy Lopez chess opening—applying relentless pressure, maneuvering constantly for a psychological advantage, systematically attempting to mislead you. They're directed around the board by the king—the manager—to whom buyers are usually presented late in the bidding process. This man (he always does seem to be a man) will be introduced to you as a fascinating fellow and model citizen, a longtime local resident who has greater interests than simply moving inventory. He's bookish, or maybe a water-skiing fanatic, or a savvy options investor. The whole scenario is well rehearsed, carried out by automatons to the inaudible click of a metronome.

No wonder today's buyer is short on patience and long on frustration.

Sure, we could sit around whining, kicking dirt, and spitting about our collective misfortune, or we could force the issue a bit. Sounds much more Foolish to take destiny in our own hands. Given that, here is our suggested eight-step battle plan for landing new cars at the best bid.

1. Test-drive the car. Don't be test-driven. Start by narrowing down your list of desirables to five cars and then pick a day early in the month to test-drive each. Schedule these appointments by phone in advance, and make it very clear to the salesmen that you're interested only in taking their cars for a spin. During your test drives, don't talk about anything but the weather and how the car handles. Suggested one-liners:

"Can you believe the grouse are wearing their winter whites already? This is going to be a brutal winter."

"Is this the sport-suspension model? I'm not getting any roll on the turns."

"The sun sure is sitting high in the sky today. Tonight'll be a fine night to get some of my roofing work done."

"You mind if I test how loud the stereo goes in here?"

Do not, under any circumstances, discuss how soon you want a car or how you plan to finance it—or anything about your financial situation at all. Or anything about anything, really, except the weather and how the car is performing.

After the test, obtain from the salesman all the information you can on the cars that you like. Take brochures, fliers, posters, pictures, pennants, price sheets—whatever they'll give you—and head home. Again, speak nothing of your actual buying inclinations or how much money you have to spend. And don't leave them your phone number, home address, or e-mail address—you'll want to eliminate the noise pollution.

2. Build your dream vehicle at home.   At home, on the floor of your living room during, say, the last six holes of the AT&T/Home Depot Masters tournament (that is what they call it now, right?), begin building your dream automobile out of the packets of information you've collected. Goes without saying that the Internet can be tremendously helpful to you in this regard. Many manufacturers today let you "build" your virtual car right online, adding and subtracting the appropriate options, and allowing you to rotate your vehicle 360 degrees so you can see that souped-up roadster theater-in-the-round style.

Beyond your talking to friends and searching through *Consumer Reports,* we don't have suggestions for which car you should buy. That's a matter of personal preference. We will say that, from a financial standpoint, you're always best off buying the least expensive of your favorite cars. Your wheels are a depreciating asset. The moment you drive off the lot, your new car loses 15 to 30 percent of its value. Thus, the more money you spend up front, the more you'll instantly lose. So, if you can stand it, buy the whiz-bang XLT2000 instead of the whiz-bang XLT4000.

As you build your dream car, patch together the make, the color, and all the accessories online or from the brochures. Itemize them. Then close your eyes and picture yourself in that very car whooshing through the Olympic Mountains in Washington . . . gliding west of Frontera past the burning Bay of Campeche . . . circling lakes in Maine . . . sitting in bumper-to-bumper traffic on the Verrazano Narrows Bridge in New York City. Whatever strikes your fancy.

There's nothing wrong with dreaming about your car; if you're like most of us, you'll be spending way too many hours in the contraption. Now we just need to get it for you on the cheap.

3. Wait until the last week of the month.   As impatient as you may be to buy that car, to slide on the seat belt and blast out into the great beyond, there's one guy who's even more impatient: the one who wants to sell that car. Most dealers are on a month-to-month quota system, and for this reason, you should always wait until the last week of the month to begin negotiating for a car. Why? As the end of the month nears, the dealers begin to sweat their own sales performance. This induces a neurochemical reaction in them that causes each of the cars sitting as inventory on their lot to appear four times its actual size. It's like in *Alice in Wonderland.*

This neurochemical reaction is due in part to the dealer's need to make space on the lot for incoming shipments. The arriving cars, with their full suites of technogizmos, are much easier to move than those that've been sitting unsold for weeks. If you start negotiating early in the month, you'll be doing so smack in the middle of a seller's market. Be contrary and wait until the last few days of the month to bid.

It occurs to us that if enough people read this book, we could together cause a massive improvement in the auto industry. That's because auto dealerships would suddenly be vacant, empty places until, say, the twenty-sixth of every month. By that time, all but the most phlegmatic salesmen would be desperate, scared, and hungry people eager to take the first offer thrown out at them—yours. You should now feel more of a sense of urgency than ever before to share this book with your 114 closest friends.

To restate step 3: Buy at month's end.

4. Fax your bids to dealers within a two-hour radius.   Step four constitutes the foundation stone for our entire car-buying strategy.

Never, ever, ever venture down to a dealership planning to negotiate. We're constantly surprised at how many people do just this, the deal-cutting equivalent of giving away home-court advantage in the NBA Finals for nothing. In every sport, without exception, teams win more of their games at home. You will, too.

You're in much stronger position in your recliner in the den than in a cramped office ten yards from your dream car, eating Good & Plenty from a penny machine. Down at the dealership, the salesmen root one another on; they have a bench of substitute players waiting to get a crack at you should things go awry. And so far as we can tell, there are no referees. That's an enormous disadvantage for you, which means that you don't want to be anywhere near the dealership when you're talking money.

So what can you do? (Foolish hint: A bunch of people want what you have!)

When the fax machine was popularized in the 1980s, did its developers know that they held the ultimate bartering tool for big-ticket items? Your fax machine may well save you thousands of dollars. After all, it needs to serve *some* purpose these days.

Toward the end of the month (step 3), having typed up that one-page description of your dream car (step 2), it's time to create your cover letter. It should read something like this:

Dear ————:

I'm looking to buy a new car this week. On the second sheet, I've indicated the make, color, and various features of the car that I want.

Over the next three days, I'll be taking bids from any local dealers interested in my business. After selecting the most attractive bid, I will formally secure financing for purchase within the week.

If you bid, I ask that you include all costs, itemized by option; all dealer-preparation fees; and all tax liabilities. Please fax your bid to (555) 555-1234. I look forward to doing business with you.

End, of course, with your signature and name.

You are now ready to begin the fax campaign. Get the fax numbers of all dealerships within a 120-mile range that sell your car. Fax your two-sheet proposal to them, with only your return fax number on it (again, you don't want them calling you, right?). Then fix yourself a tall glass of lemonade and put on your catcher's mitt.

Incoming!

5. Select the two lowest bids and fax again.   Over the next seventy-two hours, you should expect to receive faxes back from every dealership you contacted. Some of them will respond by refusing to deal without you on the showroom floor. Congratulations, you avoided them! Others will jump right in. Among the bidders, you can expect to see a wide range of offers. If you're looking at cars in the $15,000 to $20,000 range, don't be alarmed to see deviation by as much as $2,000 or $3,000 from best to worst bid. The pricing in barter markets is naturally badly inefficient, since personality and emotion enter the fray. By removing those elements, by refusing to bargain in the showroom, you are now getting a taste of just how diffuse the pricing is.

With these faxed offers in hand, dear Fool, you've already saved a significant amount of money (not to mention time and self-respect). If you end up saving $1,000 in this process and drop that into the stock market, growing at 11 percent per year, you'll be staring at $180,000 in fifty years. Not bad for a casual trip through Fooldom!

But we're not through yet.

You should now pull out the two most attractive bids and go back to the fax lines. What you'll need to do now is obtain the fax numbers of perhaps another twenty dealerships by widening your search to car dealerships 120 miles further out than your first range. In other words, your new range is from 120 to 240 miles away. Send them the same cover letter, except for one key alteration: post the lowest bid you've received on the car in your cover letter. If you got the Acura Integra of your choice down to $18,800 in your first faxathon, put that right in the middle of your fax for the second round. Follow it with the query "Can you beat that price?"

Over half the time, you'll already have the lowest bid in your living room, but frequently enough you'll get a better bid from the newcomers a distance away. In our opinion, saving $500 to $1,000 on your purchase is worth the additional hour or two of travel. Those savings put into the stock market for a few decades would show tremendous returns.

6. Select the two lowest bids and negotiate.   OK, so you have a folder full of faxed offers. Take all of the bids but the top two, fill out a short, one-sheet thank-you, and fax that off to the losers. (This is optional, but it's a nice thing to do and should formally end their sales pitches.) You are now moments away from owning your dream car, Corinthian leather and all, and you haven't budged from the armchair. (We suggest fifteen push-ups and twenty sit-ups, now!) You should almost be feeling guilty.

Fit as a fiddle, you now work the final two bidders: You're one counteroffer away from signing. Call the second-place dealership up and propose a firm offer $250 lower than the best bid. If your best existing bid on the Integra is $18,400, call the other guys and offer $18,150. You're making a firm commitment to stick to it if they accept. If you don't get a nibble, just take the lead bid.

Before signing any documents, though, you'll need to do an hour or two more research.

7. Do some final research.   We cannot overstate the value of signing on to the Internet and posting questions and concerns as you head toward closure on this deal. If you're buying a $14,000 car, that merits seven times more attention than the purchase of a new computer, fourteen times more attention than you gave your new stereo, and twenty-eight times more attention than the purchase of a refrigerator. Thus, if you spent an hour researching that new stereo, you should be putting in at least seven hours toward this new car. You can save a few thousand here that, when invested in stocks, could turn into hundreds of thousands of dollars fifty years hence . . . or even a couple more stereos right now, if you must.

The research isn't painful. Start by reading *Don't Get Taken Every Time,* an excellent and entertaining book written by Remar Sutton on the car-buying process. If you find it at your local book nook, great. You can conveniently purchase it directly online, too.

For that matter, we devote a healthy amount of detailed coverage to car purchasing at Fool.com. Just click in to our main screen and use the search engine to find our car section. You can find hundreds of tips and experiences posted by other car buyers, sharing opinions on what to look out for in the final hour of negotiating (beware the dreaded extended warranty), which cars have proven clunky, which options are worthwhile and which aren't, and so forth—you get the idea. The breadth of ideas is startling.

Spending an hour of your time online with us will practically ensure that you are not surprised by anything that happens at the dealership. It should also give you some crucial insights into the financing process as it pertains to your own specific situation. (That's too detailed and digressive to spend time on here.) The debate over whether to lease or buy a new car, definitions of residual value and Red Carpet leases, suggested time frames for lease agreements, calculations of insurance rates—you can find it all in our car sections.

8. Stay on your guard as you trot out Team Fool for the signing.   After shoring up any final research and solidifying your financing, you're ready to head down to the dealership. Looking back through our eight steps, you'll note that you show up on the lot only to test-drive a car and to sign the closing papers. If you were persuaded to visit the showroom at any points in between, you weakened your position. Negotiate from afar!

Believe it or not, when you arrive, the salesmen will be happy to see you, even if you knocked good money off what they might normally get. Why will that be the case? Well, because they're people, too! They like clean, simple, and signed deals, many are good-natured at heart, and most prefer win-win negotiating to toe-to-toe, dollar-by-dollar pugilism. This was an easy contract for them. Think how much more of a hassle you might have been.

But even here, at the final signing, you'll need to be on your guard. You now find yourself in the unbelievable position of chatting up the opponent before the World Series has ended. You haven't signed anything yet, no deal has been finalized, and here you are in the enemy dugout, exchanging pleasantries! Be careful.

The very best way to protect yourself is to bring Team Fool along with you. Offer a good dinner or other enticement to several friends, and feel like a rock star with an entourage as you go to the dealership. Forget ever sitting alone again in the office. This time, have your favorite lawyer (again, a friend—this is not getting billed!), your favorite mathematician, your favorite linebacker, and your favorite sweet-talker by your side. Team Fool will ensure that the contracts are in order, that the numbers are properly aligned, and that you look meaner than a junkyard dog while sounding sweeter than honeydew. The car-buying Olympics are yours for the taking.

To close: We made a seemingly insupportable proposition to kick off this section: We suggested that buying a car, Foolishly, might be as calming as spending an evening out on the Yellowstone fly-fishing for speckled trout. Did we not at least get part of the way there, keeping you on your duff most of the time and putting you in the role of fisherman behind your fax machine? Don't forget that fly-fishing isn't painless. The waders are heavy, the weather can be nasty, and finding the best hole can take forever.

So, we hope that we came close to fulfilling our claims. And we hope that you end up with a nice car, on the cheap and without heartache, by pursuing our Foolish Fax 'n' Save™ (you owe us a nickel just for reading that trademark) approach to buying a car.

BUYING A HOUSE

Get ready for the most important transaction you'll ever make.

Sorry to rattle your nerves and shake your bones, but buying a house is critical on so many different levels. You'll spend a good chunk of your permanent savings on it, and in many ways, what home you wind up with will greatly affect how you live in the decade ahead. Home buying is tricky because you're looking for "fair value" in a scenario replete with values that cannot be quantified.

Unfortunately, most home buyers end up misjudging the worth of their property—it's so easy to do. Between figuring mortgage payments, juggling ideas on multiple properties, assessing neighborhoods, and sorting through home inspections, a number of things can go wrong.

While we won't try to give you the complete A-to-Z on home buying within a scant dozen or so pages here, we've got a couple of Foolish thoughts on how to start you thinking the right way about buying a home and there are even more details (equal to 125 book pages' worth) available at Fool.com.

1. The buyer broker.   Traditionally, the real estate agent has always represented the *seller* of the house. So whenever you walk into an agent's office and say something like, "I'm ready to offer one hundred fifty thousand dollars but would go as high as one-sixty if I had to," that agent is duty-bound to tell the seller about your conversation.

Even though a traditional agent may spend hours and hours with you, her allegiance isn't to you at all. It's to the *seller,* and in this regard her main motivation is to get as much money out of you as possible. There are two reasons for this. One, it makes the seller happy to get a lot of money. Two, as we've seen in the auto biz, the agent's commission is based on a percentage of the selling price. The more you pay, the more she makes.

There are many agents who will take exception to looking at their business so coldly. And there are many fine and ethical agents in the world. But the bottom line is that sellers' agents are salespeople who make their living off commissions. Never forget that, no matter how nice they are.

So how can a good Fool make sure that the guy who is helping him is *really* helping him? By hiring a buyer broker.

Thanks to legislation and the changes in the real estate business, the buyer-broker business has really taken off, and it's easy to see why. Simply put, a buyer broker works for you. The two of you will negotiate a fee based on several criteria, according to the state in which you're looking to buy. Usually the broker is compensated by commission based on the sale price of the house, unless you negotiate your commission with the buyer broker at a flat fee. So, know that the payment structure still generally favors a higher sales price—and that does not benefit you.

Assuming that the buyer broker's remuneration is commission-based, however, the amount the buyer broker makes in commission if you get the house for, say, $247,000 versus $249,000 isn't enough for her to jeopardize her relationship with you. A typical commission for a buyer broker is 3 percent of the sales price. Three percent of the $2,000 difference between

$247,000 and $249,000 is only $60, after all, and that isn't enough for a good buyer broker to underserve your interests.

2. Choosing a buyer broker.   Some people like the extra attention that a hands-on real estate agent can provide. Others just want to be left alone as much as possible so they can look at the houses. If you take the time to educate yourself some about the entire process (read a book; visit us online) you won't need as much hand-holding as some people. Be realistic about your time frame for buying a house and about the amount of time you'll be able to devote to the process. Let any prospective real estate agent know what you expect from her.

Remember that this person is going to have a huge effect on your life for a few months at least and perhaps even more. Make sure that you trust the agent, above all else. Ask about background and training. Ask about the area of town that you're interested in. Does the agent seem knowledge able? Does she ask *you* questions about what you want?

You want a strong agent. That is, you want someone who knows the market well enough to advise you on any given house; you want someone who's had experience in negotiating with sellers and with closing; you want someone who can steer you toward at least three excellent settlement attorneys or building inspectors if you so desire.

By all means, test-drive your prospective agent by getting her to show you one house. Has she listened to your requests? Did you want to see a single family detached home with two acres and are being shown condos instead? A good real estate agent will let you know if your desires are out of whack with reality, but should also try hard to find you what you want. Is she showing you what you like, or what she likes?

Negotiate a fee.

Though a buyer broker is typically paid one-half of the standard 6 percent sales commission, you can also negotiate a lower rate. Here's one way. Start with what you expect to pay for your house. If you're looking for a condo that costs $100,000, tell your buyer broker that you'll pay her a flat $2,500 commission and then another $100 for every $1,000 that she saves you under $100,000. This means that she will make money no matter what. Plus, she has the incentive to make it as cheap as possible for you.

Remember, though, you are going to be signing a contract. Make sure that the services and method of compensation you expect are spelled out in the agreement. Will you have to still pay the fee if after three months she hasn't found a house that meets your criteria? Probably not, but get it down on paper.

If you don't hit it off . . .

Interview another agent. These folks are professionals and are used to having prospective buyers shop around for their services. Thank her for her time and say that you have decided to use another agent. Don't waste her time (and yours!) if you'd rather work with someone else.

What if the agent does a bad job? You can call the local real estate board if you feel that you are being treated unfairly. Agents are held to standards by a state regulatory board, and if they violate any of the rules or regulations, they can lose their licenses.

3. Shop around.   Regarding the actual houses you'll be considering—comparison shop like mad. Get ready to build an enormous and enormously useful spreadsheet, dear Fool. Identifying the value items and comparing them house by house in the surrounding area will take no more than three hours of work (tops) and will reveal a fair-value range for your ideal home.

Before presenting some key ratios, it behooves us to state that we believe your home should be worth a lot more to you than the simple numbers dictate. We wouldn't suggest that you buy the very best deal in your county if it's a dreadful home in a neighborhood you can't stomach. You say you can't stand all those Spandex-clad joggers buzzing past (and looking in) your windows? Skip that one. Great deals are not about just money, and houses are the proof in the pudding.

But once you do find the right house, that's when you should go to the numbers to divine the underlying value. Buying the best product at any price is as bad an idea as buying the worst product on the cheap. Given that our spreadsheet takes but a few hours to compose, you have even less excuse for allowing this ever to happen. So here again, a rainy Saturday given over to this may save you thousands of dollars. Compound that saved money in stocks for a few decades and you might start rooting for rain every Saturday!

How do you get the information to build whatever this spreadsheet thingie is? Simple: call up your real estate broker and request comparables on every house that's been sold in your chosen neighborhood over the past two years. The number of listings you'll receive will depend on the size of your neighborhood, but an average metropolitan neighborhood will turn up something like fifty listings. Obviously, the houses most proximate to the one you're considering will provide the best comparison.

What will you receive in those sales listings? For each house sold, listings will include:

- The list price
- The sale price
- The age of the house
- Total square footage of the house and of the land
- Number of bedrooms and bathrooms
- Last year's property taxes

Take this info and list it out in spreadsheet form (one row per listing, with one column for each of our variables). Like so many things, it's easier and quicker to do this on computer, but you can do it by hand as well.

For starters, you should be concerned chiefly with the relationship between the last sale prices and the last list prices of houses that have sold in the area. If homes have consistently been listed at 8 to 10 percent higher than their sale prices (for example, a home listed at $143,000 sold for $130,000), you will tend to mark your prospect down by that percentage.

After that, you should compare the sale price against the total square footage of the house, against last year's property taxes, heck, even against the number of bedrooms. You can develop simple ratios for each (for example, sale price is $100,000 and square footage is 4,000, for a dollars-per-square-foot ratio of 25 to 1). Some of these ratios will be considerably more valuable than others. But when you have dozens of them spread out before you, a voice from above will begin whispering the fair price of your house to you.

No, these ratios will not give you a firm, fair price. Other variables are critical, including the age of the house (always a factor, but not easily figured into any ratio) and the always consequential variable of how much you really like the place! Still, that said, simple ratio analysis could save you some big bucks.

4. Don't consider your house the ideal investment. Right after we propose a simple and effective valuation technique, here we are warning you not to treat your house like the perfect investment. What gives? Well, many of our forebears believed they made wonderful investments in land

and property. Perhaps one of your great-grandparents bought a house in upstate New York for $1,500 eighty years ago. Today it's worth $195,000. On the surface, that looks great. But dig into the numbers and you'll find that the return on that initial investment has been 6 percent per year. Not bad, but—as you learned in the introduction to this book (you did read it, yes?)—over that same period the stock market has grown at a double-digit annual rate, which would've turned that same $1,500 into something closer to $10 million. We recommend that you not play smart aleck to your great-grandparents when they gloat about their longtime ownership of American soil. But you know the truth: Neither bonds nor gold coins nor commodities nor real estate have outperformed the stock market this century.

And not only does real estate underperform common stock, but it's a lot harder to trade into and out of, as well. You can call up your stockbroker tomorrow morning, announce your intention to sell two hundred shares of PepsiCo stock, and expect that within the next ten minutes your position will be sold. Try getting that response from the real estate market. Some houses take months, even years, to sell. On average, common stock is both more rewarding and more transferable ("liquid") than real estate.

We don't mean to suggest that houses are poor investments. Nay. Most do actually make you money, which shows you what a bummer buying a car is! But truly, if you're looking to maximize your returns, study the second half of this book carefully. The stock market is home to more potential value than your house.

5. *An oldie but goodie. It's always better to buy the worst house on the best block than the best house on the worst block.* Here's an extreme example. Say you live in a 2,500-square-foot colonial that's only two years old. You happen to look out your breakfast nook window one day and find that the lot next door is being cleared. "That's nice," you say—until you find out that your neighbor's new house is only as big as your living room. What does that mean to you? It means your property value is going to fall. Why? Because the value placed on your house also takes into account the homes surrounding your property.

What does this say about your new neighbor? She's one smart cookie. Her property value will increase because she's living next door to your beautiful abode. However, this doesn't mean that you can't despise her. Go ahead. We'll understand.

Once you've transcended your petty emotions, though, you should know that many communities have covenants to prevent such things from happening. But you can apply this rule to any neighborhood: The least-valuable home benefits from the more-expensive homes and the most-valuable home is harmed by the lower-valued homes. Keep this in mind while you are shopping.

6. Know the tricks to the trade.   There are some things that your agent might not want you to know, some things he or she just might not tell you. Here's a little sampler of things that you probably won't hear from your agent:

"You're the lone bidder on this house."

If your agent is not a buyer's agent, well, this one won't be a surprise to you. Why should this person, who's motivated to get as much money as possible for his client (the seller), tell you that you're the only one bidding on the house?

"I could be working a lot harder for you."

If you have children, or think you'll have children while living in your new home, you'll want to know about things like school districts and crime rates in your neighborhood. Sure, you can find that out for yourself, but a good agent knows the area and is familiar with these kinds of things. If the agent isn't offering all kinds of salient nuggets about this neighborhood and why it is or isn't a good place for you, find another agent.

"This house is stale."

Again, this is a problem for a seller broker. "Stale" means that the house has been sitting on the market, unsold, like an open bag of potato chips at the back of that corner cupboard in your old kitchen.

"My fee is negotiable."

You may be able to restructure the way your agent is compensated (by making it a flat fee, with added incentives for helping you to lower the price, for example). If that doesn't happen, though, you may still be able to knock off a percentage point from the agent's commission. They will tell you what's "normally" the commission, but that figure isn't exactly writ in stone. You can rewrite it.

"Both the seller's agent and I might kick in some money to make the deal happen."

Imagine that you're an agent. You stand to make a few thousand bucks if this $250,000 house gets sold. However, during the negotiating process, things have gotten a bit acrimonious for one reason or another. Your client (the buyer) just absolutely, positively will not fork over the $450 for a new washing machine, or maybe the $129 for a new garage door opener is the sticking point. Wouldn't you be willing to pay $225 (half of $450, with the seller's agent kicking in the other half) in order to make those few thousand bucks? Of course you would.

Legally, agents can't hand off checks to buyers or sellers. It happens, but it shouldn't. However, an agent *can* take a cut in his/her commission. So, at closing, the commission may be modified, with the broker getting the modified commission amount and then handing off the correct portion to the agent.

"You can use more than one agent."

Certainly before you sign an exclusive agreement with your agent, you can—as you're shopping for agents just as much as you're shopping for houses—have several people showing you around. You don't want to do anything sneaky, though: you need to make it clear to the agents involved that you're not interested (at present, anyhow) in having an exclusive broker. (It's very much like saying to that person you've just met, "I don't want to date only you—I'm still looking around." Sure, they may be crushed, but doggone it, "if you love something, let it go. If it comes back, it belongs to you; if not, you never really had it anyway"—and all that treacle that you can read on Hallmark cards.)

"This house hasn't sold for a good reason."

This is another reason to have a strong buyer's agent on your side. Brokers are required by law to tell you about any structural problems in the house, but they won't always tell you about anything else that might have happened there. Say that it's been renovated since that drug-running family of twenty trashed the place and that there was a shootout featuring AK-47-wielding thugs of the Transylvanian Liberation Army. A strong broker will find that kind of thing out for you. A seller's broker will do all he can to prevent the subject from coming up.

Certain states require disclosure of "stigmatized properties." In other states, what must be disclosed is not clearly defined, or not defined at all. For instance, some states may require disclosure if such information would make a material difference to the value of the home. This would presumably include the fact that there's a hole in the roof, but not necessarily the fact that a crime was recently committed in the house.

7. *Remember not to fall in love with the house.*   If you find yourself in a state of high anxiety, step back. This may seem like your dream house, but there are going to be others. Really. Your agent should help you with this—if she feels that the sellers are just asking too much and that they ought to be coming down, she's probably right. There are many houses in which you can be happy, so stand firm when you've decided that you've reached your upper limit.

A Brief Guide to Finding a Mortgage

Where can you get a mortgage? There are thousands of mortgage lenders across the country, each offering many different loan products. From lenders who will sell only to the most creditworthy borrowers (at the best rates) to those who will lend 50 percent of a property's value (at high rates), there's a mortgage product for just about everyone.

One place to check is your local bank. This can result in a reasonably good deal for the qualified customer. But in many other cases, the bank will not have a program that fits your needs, or you may fall outside the guidelines of its lending ability. So, once you have visited your bank, look in the real estate section of your local paper for the rates at other banks. It's a good idea to start the legwork on your own, before bringing in a mortgage broker, so that you'll (1) avoid the hard sell from the get-go and (2) have a better idea of what you could find on your own.

Of course, there's one research resource that tends to be a favorite of ours—the Internet. Be sure to check Web sites such as Bank Rate Monitor (www.bankrate.com), E-Loan (www.eloan.com), and iOwn.com (www.iown.com) for the best rates in your area. With such sites, shopping for mortgage rates, finding a home or an agent, prequalifying for a loan, and applying are right at your fingertips.

You may well find the cheapest rates in town (or in the country) via the Internet. If, however, you end up working with a real estate agent, you may feel more secure with a lender that has a relationship with your agent. The idea is this: The agent brings business to the lender, so the lender has some sense of responsibility toward honoring commitments with that agent's clients. There are, to be sure, legal protections for you no matter where you go, but a hassle is a hassle and this might be a way to avoid some. This is not a reason to settle for a lousy deal, but, as Mr. Freud said, psychology counts. (OK, maybe he didn't say that, but you can't prove he didn't.)

By the way, there is also no reason why you shouldn't take out a loan with a bank in California if you live in Virginia, or vice versa.

The key to saving money on your mortgage is to get the best possible mortgage *for yourself*. Sounds so obvious it's silly, right? But the point here is that you don't need to do it the way everyone else does. In fact, if you're willing to educate yourself in the ways of the mortgage world, you can save quite a bit of money by being a little different. In the following pages, we introduce you to some of the strategies that other Fools have used. But remember, the only person who knows if it's right for you is you.

THE 6 PERCENT SOLUTION

There is something called a seller concession, and it can save you money. It works like this: Suppose you agree on the price of the house at, say, $200,000. You then ask the seller for a 6 percent seller concession. What this means is that you add (up to) 6 percent to the price of the house. That's right, you're now going to pay $212,000 for that house—but the seller is going to give you that $12,000 back when the sale takes place. You're going to use that money to cover all of your closing costs. The seller has no reason to refuse this—after all, the agreed-upon price is still the same.

If we pretend for a moment that your closing costs add up to precisely $12,000, then what you've done is folded those costs into the mortgage. Points, title search, recordation fees, and the like have effectively been included in your mortgage. Since your mortgage interest is tax-deductible, these costs have effectively become tax write-offs.

In addition, you don't have to come up with all that extra cash at settlement. Your down payment will be somewhat higher (if you're putting down 20 percent, then in the current example your down payment would be $42,400 as opposed to $40,000) and, of course, your mortgage payments will be higher, but it ends up saving you money in the long run.

What's the catch? The catch is that the house has to appraise for the higher value. If the appraiser comes back and tells you that this house won't appraise for higher than $200,000, you can't do it.

But let's say you can do it. Let's look into this a little further. Say you buy the house for $200,000. Your $40,000 down payment leaves you needing a loan for $160,000. You get a thirty-year loan at 8 percent. Your monthly payments for principal and interest are $1,174.

Now, say you decide to use the 6 percent seller-concession strategy. You buy this house for the price of $212,000. You put down 20 percent, and this leaves you needing a loan of $169,600. Your monthly payments will be $1,244, or $70 more per month. Is it worth it?

To begin with, for most people paying the extra $70 per month isn't going to make an enormous difference—not nearly as much as would having to fork out an extra $12,000 all at once. But what about the fact that you have to now pay this extra money over the course of thirty years? Well, over the course of thirty years, you're paying $25,200 more for that extra $12,000 ($70 more per month × 12 months in a year × 30 years = $25,200).

However, remember that that's $12,000 less out of your pocket at the time of closing. If you take $12,000 and invest it at 10 percent (less than the market average has returned over the past thirty-five years), then your money will grow to over $200,000 (before taxes) at the end of thirty years. So, in this scenario, it's well worth it.

Naturally, you'll want to run the numbers for your particular loan to see whether it would be worth it for you.

Another option is to take over the existing mortgage on the house you are buying. This is beneficial if, for example, the existing mortgage has a lower interest rate. By doing this, you can also avoid some of the administrative costs of taking out a new loan. In order to assume a mortgage, it must be transferable, and you must be able to pay enough cash (or get a second mortgage) to cover the difference between the purchase price and the outstanding debt.

A third option is seller financing, in which you, the buyer, pay the seller directly over a period of time rather than borrow money from a lending institution and pay all at once. With a seller mortgage, you can often negotiate a better interest rate and avoid various administrative fees charged by lending institutions. The seller gets a steady stream of income and return without being subject to capital gains taxes. And he has collateral: the house. If the buyer defaults, then the seller can take the house back.

Seller financing can be attractive for a seller who has had difficulty selling the house. (If this is the case, you'll naturally want to know why.) It may also be a good option if for some reason you can't qualify for a loan. And perhaps more important, it enables you to avoid the dreaded mortgage insurance you might be required to purchase (more on this in a moment). No matter what, though, keep in mind that sellers are not in the lending business. They will tend to want short-term deals—usually not longer than three years. After that, you will have to get a mortgage from a traditional lender and settle with the seller in full.

Finally, always remember that mortgage lenders must compete for your business. That means that they will negotiate. Don't assume that their published interest rates are final. Collect information on available interest rates and mortgage features from lenders in your area. Decide which features best meet your needs. Be prepared to ask for better terms—a reduction of at least a quarter of a percentage point of the published interest rate is reasonable. You will be in a stronger negotiating position if your credit history is good.

For most first-time home buyers, saving enough money for a down payment is the biggest hurdle to owning a little piece of paradise. Traditionally, lenders have required a down payment of at least 20 percent of the home's purchase price. However, lenders will now accept less than that if the borrower takes out private mortgage insurance. (In the last few years, innovative programs have made it possible to put down anywhere from 0 percent to 3 percent of the value of a home and still qualify for a mortgage. We'll talk later about those special programs.)

Should you put down less than 20 percent? Well, if you've got the money, there are advantages to putting 20 percent down. For one thing, a 20 percent down payment immediately gives you substantial equity in your home. This may be important to you psychologically, and as Freud said. . . . In addition, you'll avoid the need to buy private mortgage insurance.

Your down-payment decision will be dictated by your financial condition, the loan you can get, and your preferences. If you're financially secure, you may want to go ahead and put down the 20 percent. On the other hand, you may figure that by putting down as little as possible, you'll have that much more to invest. Then, if you know what you're doing and have a sufficiently long time horizon, your money will be earning more for you than it would if you had tied it up in your home.

For further details on how to get the right mortgage, or how to do anything else in the home-purchasing process, simply visit Fool.com. We can't go into greater detail here about mortgage-rate calculations, tax write-offs, refinancing strategies, and the like, which are much more appropriately taught in books dedicated wholly to these subjects, or online. At Fool.com, we've made available for the clicking articles and comments from our national readership about valuation strategies, home inspection tips, when and when not to prepay your mortgage, and so on—just the tonic to imbibe before you make any mistakes at your signing! The flow of ideas is invaluable.

When you go through the process of buying a house, find a place you love that fits your budget. Don't look at your home as a moneymaking investment, though if it winds up that way, even better. Just shoot for the best price on the property by running ratios against the comparable properties sold over the past two years.

Oh, and get a good home inspector! And good luck out there. It's a nasty game, but somebody's got to win it.

Buying Insurance

You see the title of this section; we see the title of this section. This one could be a snoozer, eh? Big-time. We struggled with whether or not to include insurance—a critical personal finance decision—in *The Motley Fool You Have More Than You Think*. It's a dreadfully boring subject, grim and confusing . . . it's that very last aspect, "confusing," that convinced us to spend just a few paragraphs tackling the thing in this chapter.

Are we right when we guess that upon your graduation from school you knew little to nothing about insurance? "Premiums," "variable annuities," "term" and "whole-life" plans . . . what is this stuff?! Even if you have insurance today, you probably know little about your policy and just hope to heaven that if you die suddenly before retirement, your plan will take care of your loved ones. Almost everyone shares that same ignorance about insurance. Top that ignorance off with tediousness and you have a great opportunity for huge insurance companies with teams of salesmen to make gobs of money.

The primary reason why most people buy life insurance is the fear that they'll die before retirement. Life insurance promises the hope of leaving one's spouse and children flush with cash should the future, ahem, prove graver than one had envisioned. If the key breadwinner in any young family expires without appropriate insurance, the risk of impending financial doom increases dramatically. The widow or widower will have to go to work and work hard, juggle the children's schedules, and somewhere between midnight and sunrise find an hour or two of rest. We don't need to get any more descriptive here; suffice it to say that the circumstances could be dire.

When you start a family, you, the wealth creator, may need life insurance. In your youth, the annual payment will be lower, as the insurance company shoulders the early risk. As you approach retirement, your premiums will rise considerably, as the insurance company and the world prepare for your inevitable end—and consequently you begin to shoulder the risk. But in your senior years, presumably you will have been working for many years and will have intelligently saved and invested loads of money. Thus, your family won't so desperately need the safety net of insurance when you take up your journey to heaven or the next troubled planet that needs your help—whichever it is. A lifetime of saving early relieves you of the obligation to purchase expensive insurance late in life.

Our short section on this topic will only compare term insurance to whole-life insurance. Though even this subject is too complex for the brief treatment here, choosing between these two distinct plans is primarily what it's all about. (If you're desperate for more material on this subject, you'll find a host of undoubtedly stimulating books near the section where you obtained this one. Choose the one with the blue cover.)

Term insurance is a no-nonsense plan that has you paying low annual payments ("premiums"), which will rise as you age. Whole-life policies are in many ways the same, but considerably more confusing. Whole-life insurance includes an investment component, whereby you pay substantially more money, which your insurance provider will invest for you.

You can probably guess what's coming next.

The whole-life provider takes a pretty thick slab for investing your money (call it a porterhouse) and guarantees you annualized returns that are much too low. Unsurprisingly (we like to be shocking, but we just don't see how to be shocking here), our suggestion is that you buy term life insurance and use your remaining cash for investment directly into the stock market. Not only will you generate more growth from investing it in stocks, but also you will have access to some of that cash if it's needed. Plus, you'll learn more and have more fun, and all that other Foolish stuff.

No need for hypotheticals. Read how fellow Fool Seth Madell put it in our online insurance area:

> Excuse me for being a simpleton, but whenever I speak to an insurance agent, I find a few things to be true: (i) the agent will push me to buy Universal Whole Variable Annuitized Cash Accumulation Greatest Thing Since Sliced Bread Life Insurance rather than simple term insurance; (ii) I have

never met an insurance agent who could explain their product satisfactorily without using a phrase like "Trust me . . ."

To me, life insurance is about one thing and one thing only. If I die before I'm done saving for retirement, I have a wife who will need money in order to live out the rest of her life in relative comfort. Trying to make life insurance into an investment is too complicated for my feeble mind, and turning it into an estate planning tool gives me heartburn just thinking about it.

Furthermore, since my view of life insurance is to provide income for those I leave behind (if I leave before the party's over) I figure—silly me—that once I can afford to stop working (that is, once I no longer need to provide income other than investment returns) I no longer need life insurance.

My answer to this simplified dilemma (at age forty, currently) was to buy three concurrent policies—ten-year, fifteen-year, and twenty-year level-term life. The policies were constructed (i) to provide a decreasing death benefit as I got closer to retirement, since the first policy drops out after ten years and the second drops out after fifteen and since, the closer I am to retirement, the less death benefit I need; (ii) to provide predictable and guaranteed premiums, something that lets me sleep at night having done my budgeting with known numbers; and (iii) to keep my expenses to a minimum, allowing me to invest to a maximum.

This lets me fund my retirement so I can enjoy it and, if I am really really successful on this planet, leave something behind for my kids.

Quite frankly, I am bringing up my kids so they won't need my money when I die. And, if I leave them some money, the taxes paid on my estate will simply be the cost of having come into what stands to be a sizable inheritance. They'll just have to live with that.

No matter how hard the salesmen push you to buy the whole-life package (from which they will take a substantial cut), resist them as you would a car salesman. Obviously, all of our other suggestions for dealing with financial salesmen apply here as well:

- Ask them how they make their money—and how they make more money than that.
- Take Team Fool with you into any negotiation
- Use the giant Q&A format of the Internet for assistance
- Do not rush into any contract

And yes, we do have more detailed material online which will help you.

Paying for College

Ah, college. The all-nighters. The finals. The frat parties. The anxieties, the wild abandon, the intellectual gymnastics. The chilly autumn afternoons of football, the steaming raucous field houses jammed with sweating underclass bodies in the dead of winter. The soaring hopes of meeting Mr. Right—the crashing disappointment when he's found necking with that short-haired girl from Ohio in the bird sanctuary. Having enough money set aside to send the kids to college without a crushing student-loan load is something that every Fool should be thinking about.

Before we get into the nuts and bolts of paying for a college education, though, we have a hard truth for you: Education is big business.

Sure, we all think of the large research universities as the good guys in white hats finding a cure for cancer. After all, college professors don't make very much money. And it's our tax dollars that go to support State when they make the NCAA tournament.

Well, all of those things are true. But some other things are true as well, and these other things are not talked about nearly enough.

Did you know that Judy who lives on Oak Street will get a different financial-aid package than Jack who lives around the corner on Peachtree, even though they have identical grades? Or that if your child applies as a biology major to a school with a world-renowned specialty in biology she may get less financial aid than if she spplies to the same school as a less-in-demand art history major? Or that if a student pays cash (instead of depending on financial aid) his chances of getting kicked out of college for academic deficiencies is almost nil?

Consider that for years tuition costs have been rising faster than inflation. Why is that? Because the universities know the value of a college education, especially from one of the most prestigious schools. Studies have shown that a college education has the potential to more than double the amount of money a worker can make in his lifetime. The average household income of a couple who both have college degrees is almost $80,000. The combined salary of a similar couple holding only high school diplomas but no degrees is $41,000. And the average for a family in which both spouses work but neither finished high school is only $25,000 annually.

Schools know this and are not exactly above charging accordingly. The most delusional approach one can take, then, is to think of the university as somehow generous or above the business fray. Not true. The most cutthroat politics are the politics of academia. In many cases, universities exist to generate grants (you know the old saw—"publish or perish") and accumlate prestige, and educating students is somewhat of a sideline from the business perspective. Consequently, the care that universities give their undergraduates can be seen as a function of how important students are to the survival of the university. Where grants comprise 70 percent of the university income, how much does Sally Undergrad matter?

Another consideration is parent and alumni giving. You don't just pay the university now, you pay later. If the university is smart, it may even give discounts (or have lenient admission standards) to people who will give a lot of money later on.

Many of you are saying to yourself, "Well, that's real life, that's just how things work." True. But knowledge puts the consumer in a far stronger position to make the right decision on this investment. Which, by the way, is exactly how you should be thinking of any college education. It is an investment. What is your child getting for your money? What will the returns be? You should take a realistic look at which schools will give you the most bang for your buck.

Regarding your plan to save for a college education, if you fall into the "I have lots of time" category, our hat's off to you! If, however, you're thinking of slacking off and waiting a few more years to start saving for your education, just trust us: It's better to start now.

We're going to go out on a limb here: There is a strong chance that some significant events will occur over the next eighteen years that we can't predict. The tax laws are likely to change. The way that financial aid is figured may change.

Put on your thinking cap, because we're gonna talk dollar figures. Let's say that you've figured out that you'll need $50,000 for schooling. You decide to invest prudently and expect an annualized return of 7.75 percent, which you leave in an account to compound. If you start when your child is born, you'll only have to put in $110.38 per month. At the end you'll have $50,000, but you'll only have put in $23,843. The rest will have come from the power of your investments. On the other hand, if you wait until he is eight years old, you're going to have to save $282.79 each month to get to the magic $50,000 mark. And when all is said and done, you'll have contributed $33,935 to reach it.

Once you've developed a plan, stick to it! As you can see from the example just proffered, the success of a good investment plan depends on a regular inflow of new capital. Make it easy on yourself: Have it automatically deducted from your paycheck. Make a commitment to pay yourself before you pay any other bills. Don't close the account, no matter what happens. You'll thank yourself later.

OK, so what if you didn't start early enough? What then? Well, if it's any consolation, you're not alone. A recent study by the Student Loan Marketing Association—better known as Sallie Mae—the country's largest source of funds for higher education, found that parents of high-schoolers applying for college had saved less than half of what they needed to cover their expected expenses. What's more, *one in five* hadn't saved anything at all.

So what's a Foolish mom and dad to do? Well, it's never too late to get smart.

1. Make sure that Junior is really *ready to go to college.*   An astounding 38 percent of all college students quit school (at least for one semester) before the end of their sophomore year. After going to what many young people consider prison for the first eighteen years of life, school is the last thing some want to continue being subjected to. Before plunking down (or borrowing) $10,000, make sure that this is really something your child wants. A year off in the real world, waiting tables or delivering pizza, may be just the ticket to convince them that college might be worth it after all. Also, if they are expelled from school for academic reasons, it will be very difficult to get more financial aid—and you have to start paying those loans back right away.

2. Choose a cheaper school.   Weigh carefully the true benefits of a private school against the cost savings offered by a larger state school. A college degree is an investment. Will a psychology degree from Swarthmore (a fine school, in its own right) really be more valuable than a psychology degree from the University of Virginia? Will it be worth six more years of debt to pay for it? Only you and your child can answer that. But the burden of debt after school is a compelling reason to choose State U.

3. Have your child attend a school close to home.   As an in-state student at a public institution, your child will not only pay a reduced tuition but also will probably be eligible for financial aid earmarked for townies. Also, travel expenses and long-distance phone bills add up, especially during the first year, when homesickness may be more pronounced than later on (when, alas, your baby realizes that he or she doesn't really miss you that much after all).

4. Think creatively.   Why not send Junior to a community college for the first year to get the more generalized courses out of the way at cost savings of 50 percent? More than one hundred colleges and universities now offer classes over the Internet, and most charge in-state tuition whether you're a resident of that state or not.

5. Look for co-op/intern programs.   Many schools offer co-op programs through which Junior can go to school for one semester and then work in his field for a semester. It may take him a little longer to finish his degree, but when he gets out he'll have experience in what he studied. He'll also have some money in his pocket, and possibly a job offer from the company where he interned.

6. Don't sell any securities for a profit in the year before you are applying for aid.   Any profits you see from sales of securities will be counted toward your income, the first item that goes into determining need on the financial-aid forms.

7. Reduce your income as much as possible.   If you have losses from a business venture gone wrong, now is the time to take them. Reducing your income will help your eligibility for more financial aid.

8. Don't take any lump sum distributions in the year before you need aid. This is the same concept as the previous two. Don't do anything that will stick you in a higher "they can afford it" bracket on the needs-assessment form.

9. Have your child classified as "independent."   The good news in this play is that your child will be judged on his own savings and income when the school assesses need for financial aid. The bad news is that you won't be able to claim him as a dependent for tax purposes any more, and he'll have to fend for himself for a year before the benefits of this strategy kick in.

10. Look for unorthodox and unusual sources of scholarships.   Millions of dollars in scholarships are given away each year to deserving students.

The problem is that everyone is vying for the same scholarships. Look for the out-of-the-way treasures. A good friend of ours who helped us with this section, for instance, is proud to have received a $5,000 grant for graduate school from a Southern heritage organization. Not only was he the only one to win the grant but he was the only one who had even applied for it in four years. What did he have to do? He had to prove that he was a direct descendant of a Confederate soldier who fought in the War of Northern Aggression. (That's the way he refers to the Civil War following his having received the scholarship!) Find out if any fraternal societies or religious groups that you belong to offer scholarships.

FINANCIAL AID

There are many scholarships, grants, and loan programs to help Junior go to the school of his choice. Unfortunately, the process of securing that money is something of a labyrinth and is actually the first test of your child's intelligence and resourcefulness, long before he ever sets foot in his first college classroom.

The process begins with filling out the financial-aid forms that help determine the "need for assistance." Private colleges typically use what's called the Financial Aid Form (FAF). The Free Application for Federal Student Aid (FAFSA) is used by all universities. These forms are available from your child's guidance counselor or can be swiped from most public libraries, and are available over the Internet as well. Check with the schools to which you're applying for information on which form they prefer.

Once you finish filling out the FAFSA, you will send it to a needs-analysis department that will assess your potential contribution. The analysts will look at things like your assets, your income, and any savings that may have been put away in your child's name. Money that has gone into retirement plans, such as 401(k) plans, IRAs, and annuities, aren't counted toward your assets.

Each school that your child applies to will receive information on your ability to pay and then will offer you an aid package. Since different schools will have different costs and resources, each package will be different. Typically, the school will start with what you can contribute and then try to find other sources of money. These sources may range from federal grants (Pell or Federal Supplemental Educational Opportunity Grants), which don't have to be repaid, to loans guaranteed by the government, to offers of on-campus employment. Some state schools also offer grants and loans to students who are in-state residents.

The trick is to find as much money as possible that neither you nor your child will be required to pay back. (Come to think of it, that's a good trick to apply to pretty much any situation in life.) The more scholarship and grant money you can find (these are outright gifts), the better. Getting out of college with a $50,000 debt is not at all unheard of and can severely limit your child's options for many years to come. Many couples have had to wait until they are in their thirties to buy their first home because until then their school debt was so onerous that they were unable to qualify for a mortgage.

Suppose, then, that with these words of warning ringing in your ears, you go to a financial advisor or guidance counselor for advice. Here are a few "rules of thumb" that you just might hear:

- You will be able to send your child to any school that admits her. The financial aid office will put together a package that will make it possible.
- You should be able to depend on (1) contributing a third, (2) borrowing a third, and (3) getting scholarships to cover the other third of costs.
- Loans should be paid off five years after your child graduates.
- Count on the student using between 8 percent and 15 percent of his monthly net income after graduation to repay student loans.
- If your child is going to major in a high-demand, high-paying field, it's OK to borrow more.

Well, as always at the Fool, we take some exception to the conventional wisdom. If you look carefully at these pieces of advice, you'll see that they're potentially misleading.

For example, let's say that you're looking at two colleges: Dream U and Second Choice State (SCS). Dream U comes in at $20,000 a year for tuition, books, and room and board, while at SCS the same costs will run in the neighborhood of $9,000.

You've filled out all of their dreadful forms and Dream U has offered a package that consists of a family contribution of $4,000, a scholarship of $4,000, a work-study paying $1,000, and loans of $11,000. Meanwhile, lowly Second Choice State offers you a package that consists of family contribution of $4,000, a scholarship of $1,500, a work study job paying $1,000, and loans of $2,500.

A superficial look at the aid packages will show you that your upfront money is the same at both schools. They both promise to find an on-campus job paying minimum wage. Scholarships are even lower at the public college. But the real difference is *how much your child will be expected to borrow*.

This figure is the critical difference in any financial-aid package comparison.

IN PURSUIT OF FREE MONEY

Wouldn't it be great if there were a loan you never had to repay? There is, of course. It comes in several guises, the first of which is called a scholarship. To procure a scholarship, a college applicant does not have to be a certified genius, nor even be able to play basketball like Michael Jordan or golf like Tiger Woods.

Sometimes he or she doesn't even really need the stuff. "Free money," otherwise known as scholarships, could mean the difference between traipsing around Europe after college and being in debt until your mid-thirties. The good news is that as of this writing, private-sector funding for education has increased 55.1 percent in the past five years, according to the *Chronicle of Higher Education*.

There are *billions* of dollars of scholarship money out there for the taking. That's the good news. The bad news is that there are several million students all wanting a piece of the action. How do you find that pot of gold, and how do you increase the chances that your child is going to be the one that gets it? Hang on, fellow Fool, we've got you covered.

First of all, let's make sure we're all on the same page when it comes to vocabulary. A "scholarship" is an outright gift to a student. It usually comes from a college, a nonprofit foundation, or a government agency. It never has to be repaid, but it can be cut off if you don't adhere to the guidelines (such as maintaining a certain grade-point average). Usually, scholarships are awarded on an annual basis and can sometimes be reapplied for the yearly (others don't allow repeat recipients). In some cases you have to prove need, in others you don't.

We polled some Foolish ex–college students from our online community and came up with the following tidbits for student applicants:

- *Be true to yourself.* There will be a temptation to present yourself in the best possible (sometimes unrealistic) light. Instead of listing the fourteen clubs you belong to, talk about the one or two most important to you. In general, scholarship givers look for depth in a young person more than just a list of things they supposedly did. And if you did something off the wall, good for you! Be proud of the fact that you collected 3,200 butterflies. Not everyone can be the quarterback or the homecoming queen.
- *Kiss butt.* On the other hand, organizations tend to give money to students who they feel reflect the organization's values. If you are applying to the American Association of Butterfly Collectors for their scholarship in lepidopterology, shout your credentials from the mountaintop. You'll be chosen over that quarterback, hands down.
- *Look in unlikely places.* Look for scholarship money in your own backyard. Not only do local civic groups usually offer scholarships, but your parents' employers probably do, too. What about the clubs to which you belong in school? Do their parent organizations give to students? How about your interests outside of school? You don't have to collect butterflies. Civil War reenactors, model-airplane makers, and Lebanese immigrants all have organizations that offer scholarships. Think about what makes you different and then find people who will celebrate your difference!
- *Use a personal touch.* Think how many applications scholarship committees must get. Depending on the scholarship, it could be anywhere from a few to several thousand. You have to make yourself stand out. But remember to be judicious in your use of "notice me!" tactics. Applications to a bank and to an art gallery are going to look very different. The bank is probably going to expect you to be very businesslike. Use nice stationery. Make sure that all of your forms look neat and organized. The art gallery, on the other hand, might appreciate your being a little creative. Instead of sending your application in a plain manila envelope, make a beautiful drawing of your college campus. Tell them that this is where you'd like to go, with their help. Make yourself memorable—the worst thing they can do is say no.
- *Only give the info they want.* A common mistake many applicants

make is that they give too much of themselves, thinking that this will impress the committee. One foundation member told us that the foundation's applications asked for a five-hundred-word essay and any application with a longer essay was automatically rejected because "the student obviously couldn't follow simple instructions."

• *Don't depend on one scholarship.* Apply, apply, apply. Just because you think you've got a lock on one, don't give up on others. The more money you can find from free sources, the less you'll have to borrow.

• *Don't give up.* Just because you didn't get a scholarship one year doesn't mean that you won't get it the next. Try improving your skills. If you think you qualify for a scholarship from a fairly small institution (your local Jaycees or your mom's job), wait until the off-season and call or write a nice note to the person in charge of the scholarship committee. Explain that you're sorry you weren't chosen this year and that you want to better your chances for next year. Could she offer any advice? If nothing else, you'll get yourself noticed, and you'll maybe even get some good pointers.

MORE FREE MONEY: GRANTS AND FELLOWSHIPS

Grants are often given when the money is going for postgraduate studies (that is, for students who have already finished their bachelor's degree). The same is true for fellowships. Neither grants nor fellowships ever have to be paid back.

The largest source of grants is the federal government, which provides two basic types: the Pell Grant and the Federal Supplemental Educational Opportunity Grant (FSEOG—sorry about these acronyms, but we *are* talking about the federal government). There is, in addition, the federal work-study program (FWS), which isn't really a grant—the student is given a job to help finance education.

The Pell Grant is limited to a maximum of $2,700 and is meant primarily for lower-income families. This is supplemented by the FSEOG, which is also based on need. Its maximum is $4,000 per year. According to *Peterson's College Money Handbook*, a family with $35,000 annual income and $50,000 in assets is eligible for $400 in funds from the Pell Grant.

The student applies at the college's financial-aid office, using the Free Application for Federal Student Aid (FAFSA).

As stated, the Pell Grant and FSEOG are need-based. To determine how much aid is needed, the basic formula is:

Needs = education cost − expected family contribution (EFC)

EFC = student contribution + parent contribution.

If more than one member of the family is attending college at the same time, the EFC will be less for each student.

The EFC is determined by a rather complex formula that takes into account the family's assets, debts, and income, as well as the student's assets. The parents are expected to provide about 6 percent of their assets, excluding IRAs and other retirement plans. The student is expected to provide up to 50 percent of summer earnings toward education, while parents are expected to provide a much lower percentage of their earnings—22 percent to 47 percent above a minimum living allowance. Included in the earnings are capital gains incurred during the year.

Obviously, federal grant money won't pay all of the college tuition. There are state grants that can be used to supplement the initial federal grant. For example, Pennsylvania has the Paul Douglas Teacher Scholarship Program, the Pennsylvania State Grant, the Prisoner of War/Missing in Action Dependents Grant, and the Veterans Grant. Generally, state grants are applied for concurrently with federal grants, using the same form. There is also grant money available at the individual institutions from their own sources.

A lot of these funds are limited and are awarded on a first-come, first-served basis. Therefore, it is critical to get the application filled out and submitted as soon as possible (it can be submitted after January 1 for the upcoming school year) at whichever institution your child is attending. If you feel that your child may be able to qualify for aid, have her ask for an early decision from the college in order to get the application in on time. June 30 is the deadline for the application for aid for the upcoming year.

In addition to needs-based grants, there are also grants made on the basis of a student's meeting certain commitments after graduation. Reserve Officers' Training Corps (ROTC) scholarships require a period of service in the military. Many states give financial assistance to members of the National Guard to attend college, and medical school tuition can be paid based upon commitments to serve after graduation or during internships or residencies.

In contrast to grants, which almost any student is eligible for, fellowships almost always go to graduate students. The money doesn't have to be paid back, but the terms of the fellowship may require the production of something, like a paper or a work of art, or require teaching or being a professor's assistant. Fellowships can be prestigious, regardless of the money they bring in—a great thing to have on the resume.

For further information on educational assistance, you might want to pick up a copy of *Peterson's College Money Handbook*. While it's obvious that there isn't a pot of gold available in grants for college education, a few little nuggets may find their way into your education-funding package. And as with every other topic in the book, you know by now where we've got a greater depth of coverage on this whole subject.

A Word for the Wise

As we close up this section on big-ticket items, some of the ideas we've discussed beg us to ink a short piece considering the role of financial-product salesmen in the twenty-first century. Various car salesmen, insurance salesmen, real estate brokers, and stockbrokers occasionally drop us notes at Fool.com, firing out some version of this question: "Shouldn't people be allowed to make some money for selling stuff?"

To which we answer: Absolutely!

In an open and free society, we should be allowed to sell you a Bottle of Air™ for $29.99 if we actually want to make a business of that. In that same free and open society, you also have the right to appear on the evening news telling the wide world how badly overpriced and how absurd our Bottle of Air™ business is. Bad products and bad selling techniques are part and parcel of America. But consumer response—particularly in a computer-networked world—is also a critical component of an open-air nation.

Our recommendation is and has always been that transaction-based financial services companies should concentrate on educating their customers, on bringing prices down dramatically, and on building a volume-driven, consumer-demand business. They should, in a word, serve. Given the increasing use of the Internet, every big-ticket-item enterprise should expect increasing numbers of buyers to gather online to find the right products at the best prices. Price shopping is coming to Wall Street. It will haunt the credit card industry. It is already rewriting the way automobiles are sold. It will flip insurance providers on their heads. And in these fields and others, the businesses and salesmen that are working for their customers, evangelizing for new customers, and operating with light shed on all their activities will find the digital world their greatest boon. Just as it ought to be.

The Ten Most
Common Financial
Mistakes

W E HOPE THAT by now we've shown you how to start thinking about money in a way that many of us never learned in school. We believe that you can (and *should*) think and act rationally with your own lucre despite living in a world full of people who don't think about it rationally or even think about it much at all. This status quo has given rise to a bunch of large financial entities and institutions that have fed off their customers' lack of understanding for far too long. So, set yourself free! Or at least get your house in order so you can begin building yourself a bright and profitable future. To that end, let's run down the *must-not-do*'s, the most common financial mistakes the American flesh is heir to.

Most of them are going to sound pretty familiar by now, because this is a recap. If you already know them all, skip forward.

#1: Wasting More Than the Rare Dollar on Your State-Run Lottery

Almost everyone likes the idea of getting rich. Too many people, however, hold up the lottery as their only real shot at doing so. Rather than work hard and put their additional money to good use—invested and compounding over their lifetimes, leaving them something to pass on to their children and grandchildren—they blow their savings on this sorry prospect.

Sure, the "$40 Million Jackpot!!!" ads look alluring, but the odds of your ticket actually winning are more like one in 80 million. Assuming your goal in buying lottery tickets is to get suddenly and undeservedly rich, consider our Foolish suggestion: Take off all your clothes, run around on the field during a nationally televised sports event, and try to turn this lurid incident into a six- to seven-figure book deal. Repeat the process to increase your likelihood. While not great, your odds of getting rich at this are certainly better than one in 80 million—we'd say at least eighty times better, probably higher if you have a sense of humor or can string a few sentences together.

One in 80 million is no chance at all, dear reader. Here, as in every other part of your financial life, remember: If it sounds too good to be true, it is. Run!

#2: Failing to "Pay Yourself" First

It is by now one of the great clichés of contemporary personal finance books: "Pay yourself first." We've already mentioned the importance of automatically deducting a portion of your salary into a retirement plan or savings account. That's what's called "paying yourself first." It's a way of making saving painless, or at least significantly less painful.

But that's been said. With #2 here, we're putting a new spin on "paying yourself." You see, one of the greater budgeting mistakes you can make is actually not spending enough cash to be happy. Trying to save money by cheapening the experience of living is like stockpiling munitions while enemy tanks are rolling over your village. We frequently come across "money-saving" ideas that propose trading away life's little joys for pennies in a plastic pig. *Use your finger as a toothbrush. Eat hard candy for lunch. Before sending it to the wash, reuse your dirty shirt as a towel. Then use that "towel" as a bed. Then use that "bed" again as your shirt.*

Who's going to do this stuff?

Extreme saving brings its own penalty—chronic lunacy. The obsessive saver may end up in divorce court, having saved all that loot for no one but his legal team. Do not trade joy for savings, and don't delay all gratification until there is none left to be had or little energy to have it.

Just to tie a ribbon on this one: By "paying yourself first" (as today's cliché runs) it'll be easier to enjoy "paying yourself first" (the Foolish way). Extract savings money automatically from your salary and then use what's left to enjoy a good supper. Clean your teeth afterward with a (WARNING: product placement) Reach toothbrush, and sleep the night away on a (WARNING: product placement) Sealy Posturepedic mattress. (Hey, we have to make some money at this, too.)

Dedicate to your future at least $1 out of every $10 from each paycheck. Use the other nine bucks to *let it be.*

#3: Not Taking the Afternoon Off to Renegotiate Your Borrowing Rates

Most Americans are paying around 18 percent a year to borrow money with their credit card if they carry a balance. A rolling debt of $4,000 each month racks up charges of $720 a year. When you consider what that money could be doing for you instead . . . OK, we can't stand it, we have to run the numbers: $720 a year compounding for fifty years in a stock market index fund at 11 percent is $1.3 million—for *you,* not *them.*

This is precisely the reason why your card providers are eager to extend your lines of credit! This is why they hunger for you to carry debt from one month to the next. While this "extra" money has brought some short-lived smiles to some short-term–thinking heads, the card providers' aggressive marketing and business acumen has ultimately put plenty of people in a hole.

From rural road to city street, from the mother of all mansions to the most minute molehill, far too many people in America are paying interest on monthly debt at sky-high rates. Perhaps now you can understand why the insects crawling around Visa's offices all have second homes on Kauai (OK, maybe that's going too far, so substitute "summer interns" for "insects"). It's ludicrous. You need to slash those exorbitant lending rates. Only a very, very select group of high-risk borrowers should see anything approaching 20 percent. More appropriate is 10 percent to 12 percent—14 percent if you're in dire straits.

Get on the horn to your credit card provider and tell those guys on the other end of the line that you plan to transfer your account to another provider unless they agree to bring rates down to somewhere about 10 to 12 percent.

It takes one afternoon; it could gain you a few years' savings.

#4: **Not Paying Down Your Credit Card Debt Each Month**

Now that you know about #3, your next step is #4. First, let's dispense with the nostalgia: Oh for the days when credit card interest rates hovered at 7 percent, as they did in the beginning, not up at 18 percent! That additional 11 percent lick off your financial ice cream cone is a slurp that the Visas, MasterCards, and their compatriots weren't taking thirty years ago. It's largely an unearned lick. And believe it or not, *they know it*. Executives of these companies have fallen into the habit of pinching themselves every day ("Duhhhh . . . can we be *this* lucky?") as consumers have willingly borrowed more and more cash at ever-higher rates. It's time for you to join our "Stop the Pinching" campaign.

The $720 that a typical American might be paying creditors for nothing each year is equivalent to about fifty copies of this paperback book. Or a dinner for thirty. Or three pairs of (cheap) leather pants. Far more important is that $720 invested in stocks expands, after fifty years, into $1.3 million.

Now is the time to be contrary. Aggressively pay down your credit card debt. That $1.3 million should be in *your* retirement account a half century from now. Keep it away from the corporate underground because (and we won't mince words here) if you can't muster what it takes to pay down your revolving credit, then resign yourself to a life lived in debt, a life lived dancing when other people say "Dance," a continuous existence of fetching sticks.

And if getting out of debt seems too hard right now, at least stop using your existing cards and replace them with a single one that requires full monthly payments. That's a good first step.

#5: **Not Talking with Close Friends or Relatives About Your Finances**

Somehow we've spent a few hundred thousand years learning to stand upright, modifying our brain stem, only to believe that intimacy and illness and financial concerns are to be shushed away. Obviously, natural selection still has some work to do on us.

In the money world, the most prominent taboos hold that it is crass and dangerous to discuss our finances. Sure, both can be true. Picture an old man sharing the combination code to his safe with a stranger at the local minimart—that's risky. Imagine a young, mildly inebriated debutante bragging about her inheritance to a crowd of baffled onlookers—that's impolite. However, extremes aside, there are plenty of circumstances where a little chatter can relieve substantial heartache. That anyone would suffer through persistently bad money management in silence is absurd. It's all the more ludicrous today, in a networked world, with information and conversation available twenty-four/seven right there on your desktop.

The modern world presents all of us with fiscal complexities, yet too many people share too few of their financial conundrums with others. And by this we don't mean to suggest that incessant banter about money is a good thing. And we're *not* proposing that you start casually loaning money to acquaintances, or borrowing. Nay, Fool! But we do believe that there are numerous scenarios where two or a few people—close friends, parents, or siblings—can mutually benefit from a little talk of money. If possible, organize a personal finance and investment club among friends. Call it the Lady Fools of Knoxville, Tennessee. Or the Gentlemen of Grand Coulee, Washington. Working together online and offline will eliminate some of the more boneheaded, less tolerable mistakes that seem to happen to almost all beginning investors.

#6: Grinning Broadly As You Borrow to Buy a Pretty Car

America sure does love its wheels. In 1999, the Big Three auto companies—General Motors, DaimlerChrysler, and Ford—sold a whopping 348 billion dollars' worth of horseless carriages—that's 19.1 million new cars.

Much of that buying wasn't frivolous. We need our automobiles. You're not going to hear The Motley Fool advise against buckling up, blasting Mozart, and vrooooming out into the unpredictable beyond. What we will advise against, however, is ever borrowing to buy an expensive car. This isn't a qualitative but a quantitative bias on our part. When you purchase an automobile, on average it loses 30 percent of its value *one year after you signed the purchase agreement*—and sometimes does so at the moment that you roll it off the lot. Your brand-new $30,000 steel transport with (roll the *r*) Corinthian leather will soon retail at $21,000. In fact, next time you buy a new car, for humor's sake, inquire of your dealer how much he believes he'd pay for that very car in mint condition one year hence.

Welcome to the ongoing bear market in automobiles!

Now, we know you need a car. We do, too. But from an investment standpoint, it's never a good idea to covet expensive automobiles. The only thing more painful than overpaying for more car than you really need is overpaying for that same car *on credit*. By doing so, you'd be borrowing to purchase an asset with declining value. Do the numbers: On average, you'll pay about 10 percent in annual loan interest, and on average that sleek motorcar will lose 30 percent of its value within a year, and 10 percent per year subsequently. In the business world, they'd call that sort of leveraged transaction "dumb." We're gentler in Fooldom; we'll call it "a mistake." Buy transportation. Buy utility. You are *not* your car.

Again, we're not saying that you shouldn't *buy* a car, though we do think Big Wheels (remember those things?) are underrated. Our recommendation is simply that if you can swing it, you pick an automobile that you can buy with cash or, the next best thing to do, pay as much in cash as you can. Remember, you are not your car. Impress your friends with your heart, your mind, those natural good looks, and your sense of humor.

#7: Not Hounding Our Schools to Offer Any Useful—Let Alone Clever and Engaging— Personal Finance Education

Tick. The very group—*tock*—of Americans that holds the greatest promise for the country—*tick*—our teenagers—*tock*—is instead today threatening to become our greatest financial liability. No, we don't think they should be run out of America to the left or the right. No need. Converting them to a global asset from a national liability actually demands very little effort. It just takes simple education.

High school graduates today are provided strikingly little guidance on a variety of matters relating to personal health. We count personal finance under that heading. As small loans puff out into larger ones, credit card promotional teams chase our youth down the sidewalks of life. And everywhere, the dollar seems to have lost its relationship to value. For instance, does the average eighteen-year-old today know that she is the envious object of her elders? With forty-seven years ahead of her until retirement, she has more time to compound growth on her savings than does 74 percent of America. Did her high school alert her to this great good fortune? Is she aware that a hundred bucks invested in the stock market today should be worth more than $20,000 when she retires? Has she been taught that by adding just a hundred new dollars each year to that initial Ben Franklin invested in stocks, she'll be nesting on an egg worth over $135,000 by retirement? A hundred bucks a year.

Over on the grimmer side of the ledger, are our high school students prepared for these credit card bogeymen lurking like scoundrels, cramped in their college mailboxes? Are students aware that these and other wretches would love to see the future savings of America's youth carefully repositioned inside various *corporate* savings accounts? Are our teenagers being taught about this in a lively, dare we say *Foolish,* manner?

In a recent poll, 92 percent of all high-schoolers cited their parents as being the leading personal finance instructors in their lives. Ironically, a few questions later, 78 percent of the same group responded that they'd learned nothing about money from their parents. Kooky. But why should they have learned anything? Should their parents be considered financial experts simply by virtue of their being *parents*?

Clearly, *students* aren't responsible for this oversight. While our schools may teach high-level calculus, require the study of obscure characters in Tsarist Russia, and demand the careful analysis of the Beat poets (aaack!), they have yet to introduce a comprehensive, spirited plan dedicated to personal finance. The great comedic tragedy in this is that a $1 bill in the palm of a fifteen-year-old is worth considerably more than it is in older hands. Building wealth is created off that principle alone. The long-term compounding of growth off a growing base doesn't take complex brilliance to grasp. It demands patience and discipline—and no enormity of either. And more than these, it demands a week or a semester of financial guidance.

#8: Trusting Someone You Don't

Believe it or not, your instincts are probably pretty good when it comes to determining whom to trust with your moola and whom to distrust. Too many fail to act on those instincts, though. Why? *Because he was my old college roommate,* or some such explanation. What a shame, considering that our initial take is on target.

For instance, consider the bad car salesman with a tendency to hustle you into transactions. Even hellos seem moist with coercion. Come the final review of the contract, your questions meet gruff replies. You actually feel a wet hand on the back of your neck *(eeewwwwww)* as you page through a contract that seems thirty pages too long. All of a sudden the shine in his office loses its luster. The windows look dingy. Was that a scent of whiskey that just trailed by? Look, he's taken his shoes off! Oh, this is bleak. As you pause over the final pages of the document, two dealership "managers" crowd into the room. They have mutual funds to sell you. Can you believe that? They're selling emerging-market value funds out of a car dealership! Then one of 'em pulls out a folder of whole-life insurance options. And now dozens of salesmen are rallying around you as they burst into song:

> *Sign here, sign there!*
> *Sign here, beware,*
> *The years are creeping up on you,*
> *Your sheen is lost, what will you do?*
>
> *Sign here, sign there . . . !*
> *Sign here, it's fair*
> *For us to charge you twice the price;*
> *Our service is what should entice!*
>
> *Sign here, sign there,*
> *Sign here, sign there,*
> *Sign here, sign there, sign here, sign there,*
> *Sign here, that's where, sign here, sign there!*

Something amidst all that joy doesn't *feel* right to you, does it? With stacks of investment products to your left and right, with the new car contract spread out beneath your Uniball pen, with no one to talk to and a singing salesman at every angle, it's probably a good idea to cap the pen, thank everyone involved, step away from the unsigned contract, and slide out the side door. But too often you don't. Too often we don't.

Fool, don't ever feel obligated to entrust thy future to those whom thou trusteth not.

#9: Not Being Patient

This demands one line only: "In finances and investing, everything good comes to those who wait."

#10: Not Being Foolish About the Budgeting Process

We abhor the idea that gaining control of your financial situation could prove a laborious, agonizing process. Our experience talking financial turkey over the past few years is that initially most people dread this stuff. *Really, really* dread it. To put that dread in context, ask yourself if when you were a child, you dreamed of a big red kite backdropped with blue, of peanut-butter-and-jelly sandwiches and warm sand underfoot, of fleet-footed sandpipers and water-bound pelicans, and of orange Frisbees and reaching up to hold your father's hand. Did you dream similar dreams, or did you muse on calculating effective interest rates and refinancing mortgages, of something called universal life insurance, of billing policies, cash management, revolving credit, margin loans, hard-money lenders, and prime rates?

If you did the latter, then we may have a job for you at The Motley Fool, 'cause we cannot think of many things more wildly tedious than tinkering around under the budgeting hood. In a gathering of Fools in Alexandria, Virginia, to talk about money management, a mother flanked by her son confessed that even though she'd been saddled with the responsibilities of constructing and maintaining the family budget, "They've got to tie me down at the end of the month. I just hate it." Another Fool spoke of the very, very *grim* satisfaction that comes from seeing the numbers add up when she balances her checkbook.

Very few of these financial matters are intuitive. It all has to be learned. But any of you intimately familiar with the canon of personal finance literature probably have bedsores. Brimming with admonitions like "You probably spent too much money on movies last month" and packed with pages of spreadsheets, this stuff can be *deadly*. Particularly if you don't bow down daily before that six-by-two-and-a-half-inch pale green slice of paper we call *the dollar bill*.

Chances are, though, that elements of Foolishness live on in different corners of your household. If you get your kids or roommates, spouse, or best friends involved in participating and building a savings plan that races you into investment, yes, the process will strengthen the spirit. It sounds impossible. Entire personal finance–training courses are built around the tacit concession that this stuff is tedious. We don't think it has to be. We don't think it should be.

PART II

INTERLUDE

Make Your Dog
a Trick Dog

O K, YOU'VE FINISHED the first part of the book. It took you anywhere from one hour (Woody Allen: "Yeah, I took a speed reading course. I read *War and Peace* in an hour. It's about Russia.") to five and a half weeks of unremitting misery. And you're now prepared to shed any debt that you have and start saving. But at this point, you're definitely looking for a little fun. Heck, you probably did what we just did: slammed down a couple of dozen ounces of a caffeinated soda while listening to Boston's first album (good tunes, horrible album cover).

It must be time for an interlude.

In medieval times, the interlude was a short farcical entertainment performed between the acts of a morality play. Yeah, that about fits.

(If you're the sort who'd prefer that interludes and intermissions had never been invented, just skip right on to page 131. Our feelings won't be hurt.)

Maybe you're unhappy with your present job. Or you read the first part of our book and quickly lost *all* your money. Or maybe you'd just rather put your lunch hours to more productive—even profitable—use. Well, have we got *just the thing for you*! We now proudly present eight original and brilliant entrepreneurial ideas that we call "trick dogs." Every one of them can be done right now, requires minimal start-up cash or none at all, few additional materials, and no previous experience. All you have to do is finish reading, set down the book, exit the room, and begin. It's that easy. The future is now.

Make Your Dog a Trick Dog

It's amazing to us how few people actually *nurture* their dogs. We're not talking about the constant walking, feeding, and petting—those are all good. But they're all maintenance. Nothing's being created. Your dog isn't growing.

So, for this one, you'll obviously first need a dog. (Lacking one, just pick your happy new guy up at the local pound.) OK, now let's bring your dog into the room and stare hard at the creature for a few minutes. Stare long enough and you should begin seeing dollar signs; if not, you will by the end of this section. Because it's time to make your dog a trick dog.

How many weekends of merely average devotion does it *really* take for you to teach your dog a few tricks? We'd say two, maybe three at the most. And not only will you be bonding with your dog, but your dog will also finally be *doing* something, learning lessons, growing. And (otherwise it wouldn't appear in this section) there's money in this.

Do you have a farmers market anywhere within a one-hour drive of you? Sure you do—very few people don't. Do you know how much the average early-morning farmers market is *crying out* for *any* form of entertainment? Not only are a bunch of cantaloupes and cabbages unexciting on their own, but many of the customers wander from one generic fruit stand to the next half asleep. This scenario simply screams for a trick dog.

Show up at 5:30 A.M. with your donation hat and your dog ready to go. It doesn't take much when your audience is starved for entertainment. Sit. Roll over. Play dead. (Your dog can do this too.) And if your pup screws up from time to time, they'll probably love you the more. And make sure to keep your tip cup in a prominent place.

You'll enjoy this, your dog will feel a sense of belonging and significance he otherwise would never have dreamed of, and you'll both go woofing all the way to the bank.

Bottle Your Own Water

Is this the ultimate entrepreneurial opportunity of our time or what? Sure, dozens of other people (or companies, whatever) are doing it. But don't be dissuaded: that just means there's money in this business. Is that any surprise? *You're selling air*—with two parts hydrogen.

We first stumbled onto this idea when a friend pointed out that a gallon of gasoline costs less than a gallon of bottled water. Isn't that outrageous? It costs more to serve bottled water at a short cocktail party than it does to drive to the Great Lakes and back. Ah, but wherever there exist egregious inequities, dear reader, there *you,* the Foolish entrepreneur, will be. It's called capitalism.

OK, you need three things here. First, you need a sexy-looking glass bottle, preferably blue tinted. Second, you need a handsomely designed label displaying *a pseudo-European name.* We say "pseudo" because you really don't have to come up with an actual name. It doesn't have to be a genuine word at all. In fact, if you want to add a couple of umlauts or tildes over a vowel or two, even better. It just needs to *look* European. Here's an example, and you can even use this one if you like it: Phéãlooçia.

(NOTE: Yes, you will have to hire a professional to design the label and the bottle, but the cash spent will be well worth it—you're going to make a ton of money at this. If cash poor, you can get the designer to do it for free by making him a partner in your business.)

The third thing you'll need is, of course, any ol' tap, or a bathtub.

Do you have to tell anyone? Of course not! Nobody's forcing you. And it's not as if people are going to make a big point of checking your label to see where you got the stuff. These days, there are so many different brands on the shelves that the presumption is they're *all* from diamond-clear springs bubbling up out of some Alpine crevice. It'll be just the same for Phéãlooçia. *Trust us.* Indeed, trust us all the way to the bank!

Borrow Your Friends' Books and Sell Them

We've all done it: loaned a book to someone else and never gotten it back. Or borrowed a book and never given it back. Most likely both. It's just human nature. Who has the time anymore?

So let's try a phrase out on you: "secondhand bookshop." If you don't have one nearby, just start your own—and we have a suggestion or two about how to build up some inventory.

Hey, the title speaks for itself. Borrow your friends' books and sell them.

Please note that we're not actually advocating stealing here. Like every idea in this section, this one is perfectly legal. Now, it'd be bad if the books weren't *loaned* to you, of course—that would be stealing, you thief. And it'd also be bad if your suppliers weren't your friends. Borrowing from enemies or strangers generally counts as larceny as well.

But these *are* your friends. And how many of these kind people are actually going to notice? In our experience, fewer than one in five friends makes a real point of hunting down a book. That means four out of five people will never really miss the thing you hawked at your secondhand bookshop. And to that special person who *does,* you can just say, "Darn, I may have lost the thing. Let me buy you a brand new one," and do so. In so doing, you've just made the person most likely to terminate your friendship into an even better friend.

Granted, the gig could blow up. A particularly bookish type may find one of her *own* books—the one she lent you last October—while perusing the very secondhand store you transact with. You have two options: Cut her in on the deal or come clean and move to another town. We prefer the approach of cutting your friends in if they find out and get mad. If you lose all your friends, find new ones. How difficult is that?! Not difficult, all the way to the bank.

Command Your Own Squeegee Army

It's a fact one simply cannot ignore: The windshield-wiping industry is fragmented.

And if you've read our other trick dogs so far, you'll instinctively recognize that in every fragment sits a little vein of gold.

Some of today's easiest money awaits those who embark on squeegee-team acquisition sprees for the purpose of monopolizing their local or regional squeegee markets. Talk about your win-win-win situations! The average wiper benefits from consolidation—gaining a strong support network, basic health benefits, and standard equipment, from squirt bottles to soap to color-coordinated rags and uniforms. The customer—the stopped motorist—gets the half-cleaned windshield that so many of us have by now come to expect. And, most important, you, dear Fool, stand to make a small mint.

While this growth by acquisition is definitely not going to cost much, we'd be irresponsible if we didn't acknowledge the breadth of your early challenges. You'll need to write up contracts, establish bylaws, appoint a chief financial officer, fashion a site on the World Wide Web, possibly talk to some venture capitalists, and consider taking your "Internet play" public. That stuff ain't easy. But it probably pales in comparison to keeping your squeegee army well regulated and organized in your quest to establish the all-important *brand recognition.* This means your guys will need to be retrained, in many cases, about how to approach cars and how to demand money in a nonthreatening fashion.

When the business commuter sees a purple-and-gold sweatshirt, khaki trousers, and a white ball cap with an upside-down blue swoosh coming his way, you want him to expect superior service and happy-go-lucky coercion at the right prices.

Once you've established the monopoly, are you worried about new competition? Yeah, right. With your ace-in-the-hole Web page created, within eight months you'll be selling shares of SqueeGeeNet Inc. at exorbitant prices in the public markets. If you devote the slightest attention to this business at all, you should be able to use the new capital raised in your public offering to corner the domestic market region by region, then eventually nation by nation. Call us visionaries, but one day we see *your* weightless squeegeenauts stopping shuttles and space stations in their orbits with that distinctive surprise soap-bottle squirt. You'll need strict financial controls to avoid cash-*overflow* chaos, as your minions spray, mop, and boldly collect where *no one* has collected before . . . all the way to the bank.

Attend the Bathroom at Expensive Restaurants

One touch of elegance missing at even the most extravagantly outfitted restaurants today is a well-dressed, completely equipped bathroom attendant. Do you know how to spell "opportunity"? Before starting you'll need to bring with you the proper accoutrements. Most of these can either be found around your own bathroom or be purchased at your local pharmacy superstore (everything's a superstore these days, eh?). Fill a large shoe box with cotton balls, fragrance bottles, dental floss, hand lotion, nail clippers, Q-Tips, deodorant, and the always-essential mustache comb (for men) or mustache clippers (for women).

Now you just need to set up. Put on a good dark suit or dress and select the most expensive restaurant in town. (Do *not* make the mistake of going anything but first class.) Pass furtively and directly back to the bathroom of your gender. Open up your shoe box beside you. Lay a clean white towel over one forearm. And then just stand there inside the bathroom entrance, very much minding your own business.

Believe it or not, *most of your money has already been made.* Just by standing there beaming with professionalism, you'll land a steady flow of tips. Up your "salary" by pretending to clean the place, scurrying about as they stand over a urinal or enter the stalls or primp themselves before the reflecting glass.

For many, this will be enough. But aggressive entrepreneurs can bring in so much more money with just a bit more effort. Start ahead of time by removing the rolls of toilet paper from every stall. Once your patrons are seated, nature running its course, gently deliver your question: "Will you be needing any *tissue paper?*" To which they will respond, startled, that yes, of course they will. Tempted as you may be to charge them for it, restrain yourself. Instead, just drop them the roll, consider the service complete, and collect their inevitable (and often quite high) tip as they exit.

But before they're out the door, do spruce them up a bit. A quick roll down their back with the ol' adhesive lint remover may be appreciated. The key is to be deliberate, but not forceful. May take practice.

OK, at some point somebody will question you or complain to the manager. You'll find out just how good a restaurant this really is during the inevitable confrontation. If you get kicked out, good riddance. You didn't want to work in that place anyway, and there are a bunch of other joints where you can ply your trade. But any restaurant worth its chef should congratulate you and hire you on the spot. After all, they should be asking themselves, "Why weren't we providing this service to our patrons *already,* charging the prices we do?!" Yep. Plus, hey, you were even bringing your own stuff with you. *The restaurant had failed to provide its own dental floss and nail clippers,* and it took someone with energy and vision to correct this. All the way to the bank.

Make Your Car a Collector's Item

For people who truly love cars, our Foolish tip about not spending much money (or at least not much borrowed money) on a car may be extremely depressing. But one obvious way exists to turn automobile losses into profits. And that is by making your car a collector's item.

How? Easy. Four simple ways, in fact.

The first is a correctly themed paint job. Spend $500 to hire a local artisan of average or poorer caliber to soak your car from bumper to bumper with an artistic interpretation of a theme of your choosing. The key here is not the actual interpretation, the color selection, or the quality. The key is simply the theme that you pick. Pick a theme that some people out there—and it doesn't even have to be that many—*love*. And we *mean* LOVE. *The* classic choice has to be *Star Trek*. But really, anything that has inspired fan clubs—particularly ones that meet in large urban convention halls—is a good choice. (Other possibilities might include the seventies disco and funk band Earth, Wind and Fire, or Tony Danza, or Edvard Munch's *The Scream*—you may be even better than we at locating such possibilities.) Then, when it comes time to sell your car, just hang out with the crowd that loves your theme and will call your car "classic." Hey, given how easy and distinctive this is, *everyone* should be doing it. Can you believe that our highways are still populated by so many plain blues and reds and blacks?

Your second technique is to associate your soon-to-be collectible car with celebrity. America loves celebrities as much as it loves collectibles. So let's say you're trading in your old Volvo for $9,000—don't you think you could get at least $5,000 more if, say, its backseat could prove a *verifiable* brush with celebrity? If you manage to lure Hugh Grant into an amorous embrace in your passenger seat, get him to autograph the steering wheel. Or if you can get your car within one block of Zsa Zsa Gabor swinging her pocketbook, sheepishly ask her to initial the dash. Make your car a celebrity collectible.

Now, not everyone can get Grant or Gabor. That's where minor celebrities come in: an Olympic athlete from an inglorious sport, perhaps. Or if necessary, go even deeper. Nipsey Russell might be your ticket, or Charles Nelson Reilly—he hasn't had many hits since *Cannonball Run II*. Really, any of the *Match Game* cast will do. And if you can't even get one of those folks, geez, drive your car up to one of our book signings and we'll sign the darn thing for you in the lot afterward.

Your third option is to turn your vehicle into what we'll call a "quest car." Do you remember when Evel Knievel's 1974 stunt jump between the Roman fountains at Caesar's Palace ended in a 120-foot skid that left the poor fellow unconscious for twenty-nine days? The very motorcycle he used is now an expensive collectible. We'll safely assume that you're not about to duplicate that feat, but you *can* learn from the example. Make your car a collectible by embarking upon some epic journey of consequence—consequence to somebody. "Hey, this contraption has been to every single Pizza Hut in the United States—no joke," you might be able to brag, proving it with a glove compartment containing complete photographic evidence. You get the idea. *Somebody's* going to be impressed, and may pay a lot of money.

Which brings us to our fourth and final option: Simply combine all three of these. Here's how. Always begin with your run-in with a celebrity: Let's say you run into John Travolta at the Laundromat, and he's kind enough to autograph your passenger-side seat cushion. Beautiful. Now just find any painter even vaguely familiar with *The Monkees* and do the quick theme job. Two down, one to go. Take a couple of months off and drive your automobile across America without using a single road. Memorable! Salable. Valuable, all the way to the bank.

Be a Broker to the World

A mere two ideas to go. Shucks.

You've already read some about brokers in our book, and you're going to read some more. If it hasn't already, at some point it's probably going to occur to you that thar's gold in them thar hills! But, dear reader, why confine yourself to the dismal limitations of stockbroking when you can be a broker to the world?

Broker anything and everything that you can.

Picture yourself near the checkout aisle in your local supermarket, promoting Chiclets. You're offering to buy them for customers at the counter for fifty-two cents per pack. True, shoppers can just pick the candy-coated gum off the shelf themselves for forty-five cents, but you're providing a *service.* You're going through the trouble of finding the chewables, talking them up, standing in line at the counter, and paying the cashier. All *for someone else.* Given this, is it unreasonable for you to take a 13 percent commission, a mere seven cents? Never.

Carry out other people's transactions everywhere you go; scalp the planet. Pay the lady at the window for the gas while motorists pump it; facilitate concession-stand purchases at minor-league baseball games; buy tickets at Disneyland and sell them in the parking lot; never relent. You should consistently charge between 5 percent and 15 percent in commission for all of your dealings. Adjust your rates at your leisure, but always avoid explanation of the pricing of your needless services. You're a businessman, not an academic; let the MBAs sort out why you charge what you do.

From there, just keep wheeling and dealing like a Hollywood agent. Stir up bidding controversy, then follow it along with compromise. Be unpredictable. Take your licks off *every* lollipop, all the way to the bank.

Take a Few Pennies, Don't Leave a Penny

Our last opportunity involves sharing in the most apparently free money available today. We say "apparently free" because this particular idea is only now entering testing. Its inclusion in this chapter represents a sharing of unproven, sensitive, and potentially highly profitable information.

Take a few pennies, don't leave a penny. Pure profit, without the effort.

It's the sort of business that monopoly builder John D. Rockefeller would have cheered. You don't need to hire squeegee forces, you needn't spend hours training a bloodhound in performance art, and you can lay off chasing down celebrities in your automobile. It's so much easier. You just have to claim a portion of the free money from the foam cups beside the cash registers of our nation's convenience stores, and don't leave any of your own. It sits there, waiting for anyone sufficiently perceptive or shameless. Take a few pennies, but don't bother leaving a penny. No big deal.

Probably about now you're thinking that wealth isn't built one penny at a time. Phooey on you! Pennies a day equal dollars a month, hundreds of dollars a decade, and invested simply, tens of thousands of dollars in a lifetime. It's a positive philosophy; it's a way of life.

Conventional wisdom says that you never get something for nothing. Well, you already know what we think of conventional wisdom. *ALL THE WAY TO THE BANK.*

Like every chapter in this book, our interlude argues that obtaining and managing money is not only *not* very difficult, but actually quite enjoyable. For many people, this requires a pretty severe change in attitude. It is our hope that through the use of trick dogs, attitudinal changes become easier. This all comes down to imagination, resourcefulness, and a hellbent commitment not to take things too seriously.

Finally, make sure that you report back to us any good experiences you had with our trick dogs. Photos to send? Even better!

E-mail us at help@Fool.com, or write The Motley Fool, 123 N. Pitt Street, Alexandria, VA 22314. We'll publicize your efforts.

And now, out of the interlude, back to the play. We take you from saving to investing in the stock market. Read on.

PART III

AN INTRODUCTION TO INVESTING

But Profit Off
the Savings

DEBT FREE AND SAVING MONEY, you'll have far surpassed the plight of the average citizen, American or otherwise. Most people are living at breakeven or worse, trying to balance paying the bills with paying off debts. Once you're free of that grinding balancing act, your combination of no debt, not overpaying for big-ticket items, and regular savings makes for a tremendous one-two punch as you quest for a knockout in the financial bout of life. In fact, let's just be silent for a second and listen to your fans:

"Rock-eee, Rock-eee!"

(This is *Rocky II, III,* or *IV,* where you actually win.)

OK, you're sitting pretty with an ever-fattening bank account (or at least you're supposed to be—if you're *not,* please stop reading immediately and give this book to a considerate friend who's more willing to play along). Now, we learned in a previous chapter that bank accounts are conveniences insofar as they enable you to quickly and easily add any amount of money you like to your savings hoard. But we learned also that the small returns you can expect from bank accounts barely keep up with inflation. This means that as long as your savings are sitting there, they're just treading water. Or, to lapse back into our pugilistic metaphor, bank-account holders with big balances look less like Rocky and more like the journeyman fighter who covers up and sits back on the ropes all match long, venturing forth only for an occasional clinch. Movies aren't made about that sort of fighter, and we're here to make you the stuff of legend. So keep reading.

In order to really profit off the savings—the subject of this chapter—it's necessary to find out a little bit about each of your different options. You've no doubt heard phrases like "index funds" and "brokerage firms" before, but if you're like most people, regular mentions of them on TV or at cocktail parties leave you with little clue about what the heck they are exactly. So it's time to knuckle under and learn, because your destiny and your money's destiny will inevitably grow entangled with one of these options.

"Full-Service" Brokerage Firms

In our leadoff chapter, on having more of a brain than you think, we touched briefly on some of the conflicts of interest affecting one's traditional options for money management. In the case of brokerage firms, we mentioned that the way their sales force (their brokers) gets paid is directly at odds with the greatest good of you, their client. But before we get into that, we need to step back a bit and stare at the elephant.

As a mere etymological curio: The word "broker" is first found in Middle English in the year 1355, and "stockbroker" was first recorded in 1706. So, for starters, these birds have done a few hundred turns around the sun. That's not surprising, insofar as middleman occupations have been around much longer than that. If the oldest profession is harlotry, for example, you can bet that pimping wasn't far behind . . . probably number three or four, since you had to have the tax collector getting a piece of the harlot's profits, followed by the rise of accountants to help the harlots avoid the tax collectors. So let's make pimps the fourth-oldest profession. And then came brokers.

Brokers and their firms are engaged primarily in trading stocks and bonds for their clients. Before there were stock exchanges, you had two choices when you wanted to buy or sell stock: find your own buyers or sellers, or get a broker. Once there were exchanges, you still had only two choices: get a broker or spend your lunchtime buying your way into the exchange—then run around until you find the buyers or sellers you need. Much better to have a broker.

For a few decades now, many of us have gotten a lot of use out of our brokers. Our brokers were there to locate investment opportunities for us, do our trades, provide ongoing news updates and offer their professional opinions to help us track our investments, and send us some forms at tax time. But as technology has continued to improve, a computer now handles many of these functions at least as well. In fact, ongoing updates in news and opinion are *better* handled by a computer. And we execute our own trades these days at the press of a button, which makes the substitution of computers for brokers both quicker and *cheaper.* Plus, the explosion in financial publishing has provided an effective educational alternative to the broker—with none of the strings attached.

You probably have friends who have accounts with "full-service" brokers, and you may even have one yourself. While we make lots of jokes about "full-service" (cough, cough) firms, there *are* good brokers, and perhaps you know one. We'll have more to say on this subject later, in our chapter on opening an account. For now, it's enough to mention briefly that the big growth industry here is the "discount broker" field. These are newer, upstart companies that offer fewer services at cheaper rates, ideal for do-it-yourself investors of the sort you're going to become after you slam closed this outrageous book.

At a certain point in time that you'd be hard put to pin down, brokerage firms changed from being mere middlemen—executors of someone else's orders—to aggressive, sales-oriented companies. Traditionally, they've been paid each time their clients called and made a trade. But at that uncertain certain point, somebody decided it wasn't enough just to sit back and wait for *you,* the customer, to call. *They* began calling you, their customers, for the purpose of inducing you to trade, so they could make a little more. And that's what set off a most unhealthy and destructive cycle.

We're not saying that every full-service brokerage firm tries to excite its new and existing customers with "hot tips," trying to get them to trade, but enough do that we can make some pretty unflattering generalizations about the industry. Still, the news isn't all bad. There was another certain moment in May 1975. Up until April 30, 1975, the amount paid in commissions had been uniformly fixed by the exchanges themselves. But starting in May of that year, the Securities and Exchange Commission prohibited the exchanges from doing that, opening up a new era of competitive pricing. The result: Discount brokerage services were born. A host of new competitors came into the field, undercutting the higher commission rates of the Merrill Barneys and the Smith Lynches. Commission rates charged by discount brokers have dropped steadily and dramatically in the succeeding twenty-odd years, and you can now find a host of discounters who'll charge you under $10 per trade. A few have even knocked prices all the way down to *$0 per trade,* making money in other ways, such as by charging interest on borrowings and from kickbacks for their order volumes.

Meantime, "full-service" rates remain very "full"—still averaging about $150 per commission—which causes cynics like us to wonder whether the "service" offered is really more like serving a summons or subpoena, or serving something (or someone) for supper. Brokerage firms are reinventing their business, which they speak of in euphemistic, unintentionally humorous terms. Take Donald Marron, the chief executive officer (CEO) of PaineWebber, who in a *USA Today* interview not too long ago said: "Right now, we are talking to our brokers and saying, 'You grew up in this business being a transactor, in which you did trades for clients and charged a commission. Now, you have to switch from that to being an asset gatherer, which means trying to get someone's assets into the firm.'"

Does this CEO's language attract you? It's nothing personal on Mr. Marron, who appears to be a stand-up guy and also serves on the board of trustees at New York's Museum of Modern Art. But, dear reader, how fired up are you to be working with your friendly "asset gatherer" across the mahogany desk?

We could go on about this, but then we might get boring. . . . So, OK, we'll go on a bit more. The problem with working with a full-service brokerage firm is that you could easily wind up with a broker who's mainly just a salesman peddling investment ideas (often ones in which his firm holds a hefty stake), with no more expertise than you! (See our forthcoming example.) Again, we know some brokers who are wonderful at their jobs and have a host of lifetime customers whom they've served brilliantly. If that were true of all brokers, we'd be playing quite a different tune in this section. If it were true of *most* brokers, we'd still like these guys a lot. But in our experience, many brokers are ineffective, and a fair number are unprincipled. One of our employees at Fool HQ came to us from a brokerage firm whose local branch routinely whited out the commission amounts printed on its customers' monthly statements, just so their more ignorant clients wouldn't notice how expensively their accounts were being traded ("churned"). Another friend of ours worked for a firm when he was straight out of college, but was told to lie about his age if asked during his cold calls how old he was. Such practices are all too common to this industry.

Then there are the sales tactics. A woman named Jody Beecher sent us a note about her own recent experience, which was not atypical (though it did, we must point out, involve a lesser-known firm—which is usually a special danger sign):

> I had just finished reading your Web page when a broker called me. The broker was interested in selling me stock in a biotechnology firm. As a Ph.D. scientist at a similar biotech company [Gardner note: Ouch, buddy, look out!], I feel that I have some expertise in the area and that with some research into the prospective company's business and science, I would be able to make an educated decision about investing.
>
> At the suggestion that I would look into it myself and not simply rely on his advice, he became insistent that I invest now. I had never spoken with this broker before, nor had I ever invested any money through his firm. When I asked him to send me information about his firm, he declined. He also became more and more insulting to me. He told me that I must not have enough money to deal with his firm since his clients are able to invest money if there is a good deal around. He implied that I simply did not know a good deal. Further, he insinuated that my scientific training and active research in the biotech field would be of no help in evaluating if this is a good company in which to invest, yelling, "It doesn't matter who knows more about the field!"
>
> Frankly, I am both amazed and appalled at his behavior. Had I not just read your comments about the "full-service" investment industry and their "subtle [or not so subtle] tactics to keep customers undereducated and dependent on them," I would have been completely ill prepared for this phone call and his barrage. Thank you and all of the rest of the Motley Fools for empowering and educating us.

If you do decide to put your account with a full-service broker, make sure that you understand the way he or she gets paid. And you should also be sure you're getting your money's worth, in terms of both the advice and the performance you receive from your broker. Because you'll be paying a lot.

Mutual Funds

Many of our readers have come to us following a bad experience with one broker or another. That doesn't surprise us, given the inherent problems with that relationship and the spread of awareness about the problems. What many people—many, many, *many* people—have done is put their money in mutual funds instead. Let's talk about those.

As drab as the phrase "mutual fund" is, it actually does make sense. When you invest in one, you're effectively combining your money with the money of thousands of others into one "fund" in which you all have a "mutual" interest. Presiding over the fund is a manager (or managers) responsible for achieving the fund's stated objective. The typical objective will say, "This fund seeks capital appreciation; current income is incidental." Or it'll say, "This fund seeks income consistent with preservation of capital." There are thousands of funds with many similar-sounding objectives.

But we have yet to see a single fund whose stated objective is to BEAT THE MARKET!

And therein lies our big gripe with mutual funds. Year in and year out, the vast majority underperform the average return of the stock market— the figure you should use as an annual benchmark against which to measure the growth of your own savings. (We'll talk about what that is and how to track it later.) With well over $4 *trillion* in stock mutual funds today, invested in thousands of funds, that's no easy task. Upon further investigation, we find some interesting figures.

Over the five years ending December 31, 1999, only 17 percent of mutual funds invested in stocks outperformed the market's average. The overall market (as measured by the S&P 500, which we'll explain in a moment) rose an annualized 28.6 percent during that period, while the median average fund came in a full rock-'em-sock-'em 6.2-plus percentage points below that, on an annualized basis. Yo! Mr. Emperor? You ain't got no clothes!

Mutual funds come in two varieties, "load funds" and "no-load funds." The "load" is simply a percentage you have to pay up front to the salesman who sold you the fund. (This is another way brokers get their licks off your ice cream cone.) No-load funds have no active sales force hawking them, instead being offered for sale directly from the company that manages the fund. (You call the company up, get an application to fill out, send a check, and become invested in the fund. No additional commission.) Insofar as history shows us no distinction in performance between load and no-load funds, it makes little to no sense to us to invest in loaded funds. Which would you purchase in the supermarket: (1) a cabbage for $1 or (2) the same cabbage for $1.05, paying a nickel to the person who hands it to you? (Did you even want her touching your cabbage?)

Please note: Some funds have additional fees (12b-1 fees, "back-end" loads, and so on). *Make sure you understand the function and breadth of all fees you'd pay on any fund you're considering for investment,* before *you invest in it.* In other words, look at the fine print. We can help: Come on over to www.Fool.com/school/mutualfunds/mutualfunds.htm and we'll point you to exactly where you can find out all the fees to a mutual fund you're considering. Wherever there's a dollar sign, it's probably costing you.

The trillions of dollars now invested in mutual funds clearly demonstrates their popularity, and frankly, it's not hard to see why. Besides the endless amounts of dull financial journalism lavished on the subject, there is the endless number of fund-company advertisements supporting the endless amounts of journalism. These things are out front in the public eye, to say the least.

But further, when investing in a mutual fund you are handing over the care and responsibility for your money to someone else—really a very typical response people have when faced with something they don't understand. It feels safe and comforting to give our money over to others who wear expensive suits on television and tell us they're Wise and prudent and successful. But mutual funds make money by taking a percentage of assets, *your* assets; their top goal is to capture as many investors as possible (there are "asset gatherers" everywhere in this world, eh?), and they have the marketing budgets to prove it!

Those marketing budgets do come directly out of your money if you own some of the fund. And if the fund markets itself well, it'll attract huge amounts of new money. But as the fund gets bigger, it gets less nimble, less responsive, and ultimately less profitable. Forced to spread its additional monies further around, the fund ends up with so much money in so many different stocks that it ends up doing what the market does; heck, it is the market. But at the end of the day, each fund still has to pay its marketing budget and the salaries for all those suits. Where's that money coming from? You!

So it should not surprise you—now that you're becoming Foolish—to learn that an average of 80 percent of mutual funds underperform the market every year, a fact we often mention because so few others do. The fundamental problem of the mutual fund industry is that it just has too dang much money to manage!

To mask their mediocrity, some fund companies run silly advertisements on television. One not too long ago depicted a fellow trying to do dentistry work on himself. The idea was that investing your own money is as difficult as trying to execute your own root-canal operation. Yeah, right. And you need someone to brush your teeth for you, too.

Of course, we hasten to add that for every four bad funds, there is one decent one. Unfortunately, that's easy to see *in retrospect* but very difficult to predict ahead of time. Studies have suggested that picking last year's good fund is generally a decent way to find this year's bad one. So it can be somewhat overwhelming trying to figure out which few hundred of the several thousand candy bars contain Willy Wonka's golden ticket.

What sort of information can you actually use to do analysis? Funds don't report their complete holdings more than quarterly, so you're constantly driving down this freeway using your rearview mirror to navigate. You could study your manager, of course—read where he or she went to college, how well he or she has done with the fund. Funds change managers, though, so if you're going to invest this way, you might want to keep an eye out. That said, if you're going to bother paying that much attention, why not devote your time to learning about individual companies and their stocks? If you just spend the same time finding two or three great companies (of the sort written about in our chapter "Obviously Great Investments," for instance), you're going to do much better over the long haul. People who spend inordinate amounts of time researching funds scare us; it's like researching and spending money to fix up the body of a car whose engine will never run. It's just a waste. These fund products are designed to serve people who don't want to have to do their own thinking—any of it.

In the end, much as with brokers, *we have no inherent gripe with mutual funds.* The good ones are helpful to their customers. So's cold oatmeal, of course. However, also like brokerage firms and cold morning oatmeal, most of the funds you encounter are unfortunately below average. They tend to serve their managers better than they serve their customers. This is especially obvious once you learn about index funds.

The Index Fund

Voilà! The first savings option in this chapter that really makes some sense to us. You already know what a mutual fund is. An index fund is just one type of mutual fund. Most mutual funds are "managed" funds; that is, the fund's money is invested according to the tastes, intuitions, and analytical work of the manager. By contrast, index funds are generally computer driven, designed to mimic the performance of a given stock market index.

What are stock market indices? They're simply measures of overall performance, just as points per game measures (somewhat) how well a basketball player or team performs, or that 3.8 grade-point average measured (again, somewhat) how well you performed academically. A stock market index measures the average performance of the group of stocks that make up the index. Analysts then use the index to gauge of how the market did overall.

Obviously, the stocks one chooses to constitute an index determine exactly what gets measured. For example, if you were to choose an exclusive list of bankrupt companies, your stock market index would gauge the performance of bankrupt companies (and yes, even though companies go bankrupt, they often will continue to trade on the stock market, as investors speculate on a turnaround). Or, if you were to choose a random smattering of tiny companies, you'd have developed a "small-cap" index ("cap" is short for "capitalization," which is essentially the total value of a company). If, on the other hand, you're trying to do a decent job of measuring the average market overall, you'll probably do what Standard & Poor's does. Standard & Poor's (S&P) is the company behind the market's consensus benchmark these days, the S&P 500. The Standard & Poor's 500 Index simply comprises a selection of five hundred of the very largest companies in the market; its daily performance is the weighted average of their daily performance.

If the S&P 500 rises 15 percent in value for a given year, most market analysts and watchers would attribute that same figure to the market overall. The S&P 500 is *the* most commonly used broad benchmark of the stock market's performance.

As you read in the previous section, some 80 percent of mutual funds underperform that average market return year in and year out. So, hey, wouldn't it be a neat idea if someone created a mutual fund that just mimicked the market's performance, thereby equaling it? And further, since the management of such a fund would be mindless, what if you just assigned a computer to manage it, thereby keeping the management fees very low? Do you think this might be popular with investors?

You better believe it. The Vanguard 500 Index Fund is an example of just such a fund. As of May 2000, the fund had a scale-tipping $102.8 billion under management, and it was providing investors with returns well in excess of the great majority of "managed" offerings. Following in the tradition of the victory of chess computer (IBM's Deep Blue) over man (Gary Kasparov), here's another computer success story, of a similar magnitude: mindless computers merely replicating the averages are kicking down the doors of mutual fund companies across America. It's a big-money blowout.

When you combine lower fees (the Vanguard fund, like most index funds, is a no-load) with higher performance, you have a killer competitive product. To an industry already overpopulated with dollars that is unable to offer many of its *existing* customers market-beating returns, the index fund makes for a menacing prospect—or, if you're an investor, a very welcome one.

Because the index fund makes for a brainless *and* respectable choice, it's really our first-stop recommendation to investors of all kinds, novice and experienced. Factor in convenience, performance, low expense, and simplicity, and these things beat the pants off the two traditional options, brokers and mutual fund managers. Of course, you will need a minimum of $3,000 ($1,000 in an IRA account) to invest in the Vanguard fund (phone number: 1-800-860-8394, Web site: www.vanguard.com). Many other mutual fund families offer S&P 500 Index funds with slightly lower entry requirements going down to a $1,000 minimum opening balance, but these other companies in most cases charge higher annual fees than does Vanguard.

While the Vanguard 500 Index Fund is better known, a potentially superior alternative to explore is the Vanguard Total Market Index Fund, which invests in all 7,000-plus companies publicly traded on the major exchanges. The Total Market Index Fund has the advantage of giving you even more diversity than is provided by the five hundred companies in the S&P 500.

Now that you know what an index fund is, shop around and ask some questions—perhaps online. Remember that an index fund is appropriate only for long-term savings that you won't need for any reason for at least five years, since over shorter periods the market could decline in value.

In fact, Foolish investing is *always* long-term investing. The no-load index fund makes a great place to start.

Stocks

If you have peeked ahead in our book or taken a look at the contents page, you'll notice that we don't actually talk about funds, index or otherwise, much more beyond this point. That's because we believe that once you've learned a few things sufficiently well, if you're comfortable taking some additional risk, you should begin investing directly in individual stocks. Done right, stock investing will take you where no other investment choice dependably can: to long-term, double-digit, fund-beating returns. By investing in stocks, you'll also learn a lot more about business and the world at large, and have lots of fun doing so. That's why the rest of our book focuses on stocks.

Before we dig deeper, however, let us make one point quite clear, one that we're echoing from the end of the previous section on index funds. That is, investing in stocks entails short-term risks; over some three- to five-year periods, the market can (and most certainly will) decline, deflating your savings. In some cases, your investments could lose a large portion of their value (more than 20 percent) in a matter of hours! This is exceptionally rare, but over any full lifetime of investing you can expect to see your share of dives.

Given these statements of the obvious, you have two main considerations. The first is, are you prepared for this? Can you accept declines, sometimes sudden and unexpected ones? Are you good at taking risks? If the answer is no, you should probably not invest in the stock market at all, and certainly not on your own. At your most aggressive, you should take a hard look at index funds and stop there, and getting a full-service broker or financial planner to create a safety-oriented portfolio for you may be money even better spent for you. (This portfolio would include bonds or bond funds, money market funds, and broad diversification encompassing everything from foreign investments to individual domestic stocks.) While this portfolio will underperform the market over the long term, it could be much better suited to your own psychology. Free of worry, you'll be able to focus on the many other things that life has in store.

If you decide instead that you do want to invest in stocks, you have one more consideration. Namely, you must make sure you invest only what we call your "hard-core savings," or money you won't need for at least five years, money you could ultimately afford to lose because you don't need it to live on. To reiterate, the stock market is inherently risky. If you're going to float some ducks on this pond, you have to be patient with them. They may go quacking off in directions you hadn't expected, and some may never return. Don't spend your money purchasing these ducks if you even *think* you might need the cash at some other point to pay someone or pay for something. Let's say it again for good measure: Invest *only* your hard-core savings in the stock market.

Now that you're prepared to invest Foolishly, let's take a momentary breather and consider what you've already learned in this chapter. Assuming that you're a complete novice, in just a few brief pages you've already learned what brokerage firms are and how they make their money, what a "load" is, what a "load" most mutual funds are, how you measure the stock market's performance, and how beautiful a thing is an index fund. Many of these may be ideas you never thought you'd ever think about in your entire life, as recently as half an hour ago. Is this stuff difficult?! WE DON'T THINK SO.

It's time to learn a bit about the stock market. We'll start with a brief taste, and dine on this further with the introduction of some new dishes later on (our "Stock Primer" chapter being one obvious example).

First off, what's a stock, exactly? Well, a share of stock represents a tiny piece of ownership in the company whose name is printed on the certificate. Every company decides whether it wants to be "public" or "private," which refers to its ownership. If it's private, you can't buy stock in it unless you have an in somehow, like your buddy Louie wants to let you in on his ostrich farm. If it's a public company, a portion of it may be held by anyone in the public at large, which means that Louie's letting some anonymous others in on the action as well. The way it got public in the first place is that Louie decided he wanted to raise some money. So he hired an investment banker (played tonight by the understudy, Eunice), and Louie decided what percentage of his business he wanted to sell, while Eunice estimated roughly how much she would obtain.

Shareholders in public companies demand "liquidity" from their investments. "Liquidity" refers to the ease with which an investment can be bought and sold. The creation of stock markets greatly increases liquidity, making people like Eunice (whose livelihood depended on it) very happy. The presence of a market enables middlemen to match buyers and sellers at an equitable price. And those shares, which represent "equitable claims" (or rights to ownership in a business), are known also as "equities."

Shares of public companies fluctuate in value every day, with values determined by the day's stock market trading. Thus, when you buy a stock, you're purchasing a piece of ownership in the business it represents, but you're doing so at a price that reflects whatever everyone else thinks a share in that business is worth at the particular moment you buy. Due to the constant growth of business and value over the course of our nation's history, the American stock markets have offered great investment. That's because the long-term growth of American business has outpaced virtually every other non–stock market investment. As an American investor, you have a front-row ticket to watch and *participate* in the growing value of some of the world's great companies.

But hey, how does the market put a real value on a business, one that constantly fluctuates in value? Sure, Louie's eggs cost $800 to $1,000 each, and the creatures that grow out of them can live eighty years and are capable of forty to sixty offspring per year. But those are only benchmarks—not necessarily actualities. So you've asked a great question, to which no single definitive answer exists. There are probably as many different ways to evaluate stocks as there are stocks on the exchange (and there are thousands of those). The three most important factors are a company's existing assets (its property, plants, and equipment), its level of sales and profits, and its expected growth rate and future prospects (often highly speculative, and more responsible than any other factor for constantly changing prices). Beyond those there are dozens of other factors, some of the most important of which include level of profitability, brand name, quality of management, and product diversity and distribution.

What else is there to say about stocks? Tons, and what we write in this book and wrote in *The Motley Fool Investment Guide* only scratches the surface. For now it's enough just to understand the function that the market serves, what a stock is, and why you should think very seriously about parking your money in this garage—without the valet.

To that end, let's close out by giving you a general sense of just how much the stock market has outperformed competing investment vehicles. In our chapter "You Have More Than You Think," we demonstrated how much money you can make over time with investments compounded at 9 percent annual gains. We're pleased to emphasize again to you now that the market's average annualized return is even better than that! For the seventy years ending 1999, our overall market return is approximately 11 percent. And as you'll find out later in the book, our interest is in eventually teaching you how you might beat that figure. Indeed, Fools that we are, we think you should!

We won't bore you with running the numbers here, as we've already done so earlier and will continue to do so in other places in the book. But you've already seen the power of compounding in our "Value of a Dollar" section, anyway. Suffice it to say for now that compounding is a very tempting prospect.

Other investment options don't hold a candle to stocks. Mutual funds will sit a couple of percentage points behind stocks due to management fees alone, not to mention subpar performance, while bonds over that same seventy-year period have scored annualized gains of 4.92 percent. CDs and T-bills and money market funds are well behind, at 3.62 percent. And while those differences may not sound *that* great right now, over time they wind up being HUGE.

401(k) and Other Retirement Plans

We'd be remiss if we didn't include discussion of company 401(k) and other such plans in this section. These savings vehicles are what will fund the retirements of many Americans into the next century and beyond. Given their tax advantages and the possibility of corporate matching (read: *FREE MONEY*), they are well worth using.

More than a dozen sorts of retirement plans exist today, and it'd just bog down this slim tome to include referencelike material on each one. Blah blah blah. (Yawn.) For our purposes here, we're going to focus on the very popular 401(k) plan, named after the Internal Revenue Code section in which it appears. The vast majority of American companies have these today. If you work for a nonprofit, you can do the almost identical 403(b) plan; if you work for local or state government, there's the somewhat similar 457 plan. Then there are SIMPLEs, Keoghs, SEPs (all for the self-employed), and the list goes on. The point is that most such plans encourage you to put away some of your normally taxable income into your own retirement fund, on which you won't pay taxes till your latter days.

(A full list and explanation of the various plans is included on the Motley Fool Web site.)

Here's the way the 401(k) works: You commit to contributing a specified portion of your salary to the plan, which is automatically deducted from your paycheck. The amount contributed and the earnings coming from it accumulate tax-free until withdrawn. And that's the sweet thing about retirement plans; the tax-deferred nature of this investment is highly attractive. Here's why: By your not having to pay taxes on interest, dividends, and capital gains year in and year out, your money grows to far larger amounts over your employment life. Then, when it's eventually time to withdraw the money and pay the taxes, you'll have a lot more left over at the end.

When do you withdraw? In general, a 401(k) plan limits withdrawals to five occasions: reaching the age of fifty-nine and a half, retirement, termination of employment, disability, and death. (Our favorite one there has to be "reaching the age of fifty-nine and a half.") Additionally, the plan may include optional provisions for loans and hardship withdrawals. You may still make early withdrawals, but those come at a steep penalty that you *don't* want to pay. (Consult your plan for more specifics).

You can see the reasons for these limitations quite clearly. If there were no such limits, many people would yank money out all the time, abusing the government's intent to make these plans serve as savings and retirement vehicles.

Indeed, not only do those withdrawal limitations exist, but a separate limit on the annual amount you can contribute tax-free exists as well. Without that, some people—those lucky enough to be able to afford to put lots away—might try to sock away *most of what they earn* into their tax-free 401(k). So the Internal Revenue Code currently prohibits contributing more than $10,500 or a certain percentage of pay, whichever is less. The percentage there varies from employer to employer, depending upon a number of factors, but typically falls into the 12 percent to 20 percent range; the dollar amount, on the other hand, is set by the government and increased periodically on the basis of inflation.

OK, now the $64 million question. *Should* you do this—should you enroll in your company's retirement plan? Yup. But a qualified yup.

The single best reason to use a 401(k) or retirement plan is your employer matching your contribution. For every buck you toss in, some employers toss in a little bit too. (Say it again: *FREE MONEY!*) You'd be a fool (small *f*) not to take advantage of that. A typical matching policy involves your employer adding an additional 50 percent of whatever you contribute, but your employer's share cuts off when your contribution reaches a specified percentage—say, 6 percent—of your compensation.

Thus, if you make $30,000 a year and have a plan allowing you to contribute up to 10 percent of that to your 401(k), it'd work like this. If you can afford to, you should contribute at least the full amount that your employer will match. Let's say that's 6 percent. Six percent of your salary, the maximum your employer will match, is $1,800, and your employer contributes another 50 percent of that—$900. So you just got a free nine hundred petunias to plant alongside the other eighteen hundred—or more, if you contribute a larger percentage of your own salary. Looked at in another way, that's an immediate gain of at least 30 percent on your untaxed investment! We all should be so lucky. And beyond the amount the employer is matching, you still will receive all of the benefits of tax deferment on your investment. While there's no additional FREE MONEY being contributed by the employer once you've contributed the first $1,800, you could well desire to max out on the amount you can defer, and go the whole $3,000 because of the tax advantages of doing so.

Some employers may, alternatively, share a portion of the firm's annual profits in the form of independent contributions to the company's 401(k). That's called profit sharing. Another good deal.

So, to close up this crucial point, *if your employer matches your investment, earn the maximum match by MAXING OUT the amount you're contributing, as necessary.*

Now, what can you put the funds into? Well, here's where the "qualified" part of our "qualified yup" comes in. You want to invest in stocks? Sorry! Or at least, you can't invest in stocks directly. The standard 401(k) plan has limited options, mainly mutual funds and more conservative income vehicles (things like "guaranteed fixed-rate income funds"—yuck!). The typical selection of mutual funds will include something like a "risky fund," an index fund, and a "safe fund."

You already know our feelings about mutual funds. Given those feelings, we strongly encourage you just to stick with the index fund, if it's one of your plan's options. If it's *not* one of your plan's options, it's time to take your plan manager to task *or* out to lunch and schmooze the afternoon away (whichever works). Alternatively, or in addition, you could present him or her a free copy of this very book (makes a *delightful* gift), perhaps with this page circled. You'll be doing yourself and your coworkers a great service, and making the world just a little bit more Foolish.

We've heard financial advisors emphasize the need for people to diversify their retirement savings plans by owning stocks, bonds, and perhaps even real estate. For the most part, we disagree. Unless you're very near retirement, you're investing hard-core savings that'll be salted away for decades. (If you are near retirement, more conservative options may work better for you, especially if you need this money to live on.) Given the long-term nature of this investment, you should be working to maximize your expected annualized return over that long period. The way to do so in these plans is through stocks, which mostly just means "100 percent allocated to the index fund." It's probably worth reiterating here what we have said elsewhere: If over the course of time we turn out to be wrong about the steady upward performance of stocks, take the Fools by the arm forty years from now on Spacestation *Harold* and demand from us a free Tang spritzer.

The index fund need not be *the* choice for everyone. If you feel there's a strong growth fund in your company's plan that will outperform the index fund, go for it. If instead you feel that the stock market is going to spiral downward out of control for the next few decades, be un-Foolish and select a conservative option like a money-market fund. (We don't believe *anyone* can predict the stock market.) Anyway, your company's plan manager can guide you toward an understanding of the relative risks and returns of each of your investment options. As always, stay informed and make a decision you can live with. For a long time.

One final note: In this increasingly do-it-yourself world we live in, many people today invest through an individual retirement account (IRA). This happens even more frequently given the rapidity with which people change jobs and wind up "rolling over" their old retirement-plan assets into a self-managed IRA. Fortunately for them, IRA account holders *do* have the ability to invest this money however they like. As Lewis Carroll wrote, "Oh frabjous day! Callooh! Callay!" For them, we recommend stocks. The second half of the book provides a host of good ideas about how to get started investing profitably in the stock market.

For now, we've reached the end of our simple little stanza (iambic pentameter enthusiasts, run for the exits):

> *You have more than you think,*
> *And a bunch of people want what you have.*
> *Surprise them—save it instead.*
> *You can get and keep more than you think.*

Your First
Investments

The Dow Graph

NO WORDS SPEAK as eloquently and convincingly of the reason to invest in stocks as the performance of the Dow Jones industrial average over the course of its history, from 1896 to the present.

And it is that image—that little line that zigs more than it zags, soars more than it sags, proceeds almost unfailingly up the Mountain of Eternal Growth—that you should hold on to as you meditate on your first investments. Having completed the first part of the book, you're already well on your way to having put your house in order. Now it's time to step outside and begin cultivating your garden. Because it's not your house but your garden—here, the stock market—in which stuff will actually *grow*. And grow and grow.

Look again, if you will, at the Dow graph. Notice three things.

1. Notice the direction it goes.
2. Notice that it doesn't proceed in a straight line of perfectly algebraic slope.
3. Notice *once again* the direction it goes.

You know, if our financial media and commentators just took that basic 1-2-3 approach to thinking about the stock market, the world would be a much better place. Some of the most experienced financial journalists do their readers a constant, ongoing disservice by causing them to focus on the short term. Talk about losing the forest for the trees. This is what we refer to as the "journalistic approach to the financial markets." *Gotta generate headlines. Gotta get people focused on the here and NOW.*

Yes, it's possible for us all to get caught up in short-term thinking from time to time. We may indeed find ourselves worrying about how our investments are doing *right now, this week, lately.* It's human nature to think that perhaps the market is terribly overvalued, or that we're entering a period of perceived economic decline, or to worry because one of our investments has been halved. Great journalism, though, should make us to question our nature, to think bigger than we otherwise might, and should remind us of history and truth. And when it comes to the stock market, history and truth are perfectly revealed in our just-described 1-2-3 approach.

It's not hard to figure out the reasons behind our disheartening status quo. Just as the general news media want to focus you minute by minute on the latest explosion, the latest environmental crisis, or the latest sensational murder trial, our financial media want you to think hard and worry constantly about where the market's headed NEXT ("next" being here defined as any time period up to six weeks). Why is this? Well, it's their business, folks—they need to get your attention for their advertisers. That's the whole game. Unfortunately, this prevailing practice induces huge numbers of adult human beings to think that the stock market is too risky for them, that it's something they couldn't ever keep up with because it's just so volatile and treacherous. They forget that the stock market simply reflects the long-term growth of American and international business and that when you buy into it, you're purchasing a piece of that future growth.

Obviously, if you focus in on any given two- to three-year period on that Dow graph, you might see the line zag more than it zigs—you might see a "bear market." And those who invested only during that time, selling out at the bottom and swearing off the market forever ("It's rigged!"), in most cases deserve what they get. If they're going to take that sort of approach, they're fools, not Fools. Anyone who invests in the stock market over a short-term period is doing the investment equivalent of spinning a Vegas roulette wheel. Which brings us to a point we want to be extremely clear about: *We have no idea where the market is headed over the next three years. Neither does anyone else. DO NOT LISTEN TO ANYONE ON TV, ON RADIO, OR IN THE PAPERS WHO IS PRESUMING TO CALL THE SHORT-TERM MARKET DIRECTION. THIS PERSON IS MOST LIKELY*

DOW JONES INDUSTRIAL AVERAGE HISTORY

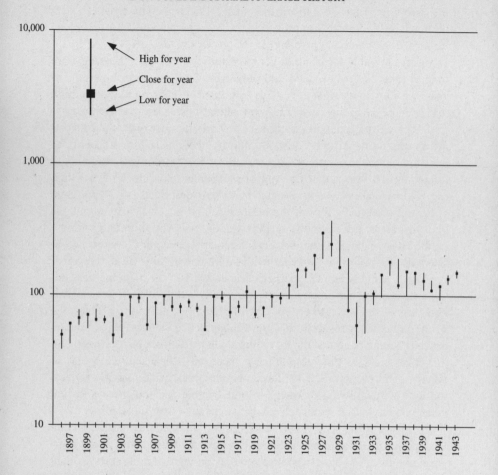

A CHARLATAN OR AN IMBECILE. If you're convinced otherwise, re-search all his or her previous market calls. Compare those to the actual *moves in the market. If you do this, you'll discover we're right. If you discover we're wrong, immediately e-mail us at help@Fool.com. We'll probably try to hire or marry this paragon.*

Interestingly, even if the person were fairly consistently right about the market's short-term direction, it wouldn't be smart for you to follow along. To play the short-term game requires jumping in and out of a lot of stocks.

DOW JONES INDUSTRIAL AVERAGE HISTORY (CONTINUED)

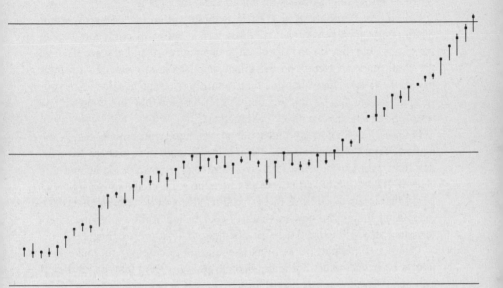

The amount you'd pay in commissions and capital gains taxes as you leaped hither, thither, and yon would likely leave you with fewer profits (and more headaches) than just buying and holding good companies.

Just a moment ago, we used the phrase "bear market." Even if heretofore you haven't been an investor, you probably know that this phrase characterizes a period of falling stock prices. Likewise, a period of rising stock prices is called a "bull market." While you may be familiar with these phrases, if you're like most people you may not know where they came from. So let us tell you. But before we do, you have to promise to quiz your financial professional friends on this to see if they get it!

OK, if you think about how each of these two animals attacks, you'll picture very quickly why we use these terms. Bulls, of course, butt with their horns, but they do so by projecting them outward and *upward.* Hence, the "bull market." Bears, on the other hand, strike *downward* with their paws. (Well, yeah, they also sink their teeth about ten inches deep into your ribs and savage you beyond the point of recognition, but that comes afterward.) So that's why we have "bear markets."

In an earlier section, on index funds, we taught you how to secure the market's return without anyone else's help. Through the purchase of an index fund, you can buy into that very line to which we've dedicated this chapter. It couldn't be easier, especially in the context of a larger financial world that tends to confuse things with its size and its complexities. The index fund shows you how to simplify your financial life and enjoy a performance that will exceed the vain attempts of most professionals.

The rest of this part of the book is dedicated to helping you make your first stock investments. For many people, an index fund may be all they'll ever need. Perhaps you're one of these. The very act of staying free of debt, saving, and investing is ultimately far more important than whether you merely earn market returns or, on the other hand, consistently beat the market. Thus, if you do become an index fund investor, you've *won,* and already made back far more than the cost of this frivolous and nonsensical book.

Some of you, though, want to beat the indices, beat the index funds, beat that ever-zigging line. We think we know some ways to do just that, so you'll be reading our thoughts on this subject as well. In fact, we take it as a personal challenge to beat the market indices, because we believe that it can be done by ordinary people like you and us who *don't* get to sit down with the CEOs of the companies we invest in.

But let's close with a question. At the beginning of the chapter, we somewhat facetiously used the phrase "Mountain of Eternal Growth" in describing the Dow graph line's ascent. Do we believe that growth is "eternal"? Will the market continue its rise on and on and on, until the ultimate cessation of the human race?

Good question. If you have a definitive answer, please let us know. From our point of view, we have a few thoughts on the subject that ultimately lead to no firm conclusion but do keep us coming back and putting our dollars in the market.

Over the long term, the market reflects the growth of business. (Over shorter periods, the market can move for a hundred different, ultimately less consequential reasons.) So the first question is, will business always grow? Now, obviously business doesn't *always* grow, because we have bad quarters and bad years. What we actually mean by this is, will there be a prolonged period—say, as long as a human lifetime—in which business (and the stock market) either does not grow or actually shrinks?!

Well, what grows business? A huge number of factors, primarily things like population growth, environmental conditions, and governmental stability (combined with lack of substantial interference). Increasingly, advances in science and technology also drive the growth of business. Thus the question becomes, do you at present perceive conditions that would lead to seventy years of stagnation or decline?

It's very easy to *create* scenarios in which that would happen, but most of those scenarios involve catastrophic events (nuclear war, lethal airborne viruses, alien invasion, an evil tyrannical force capable of mass brainwash—or all four at the same time). In each of those situations, may we suggest to you that you'll have a *lot* more to worry about than the returns of your investment portfolio? Each of these could bring about the effective end of our civilization. And the interesting point there is that whereas "civilization" has previously referred to one or another culture limited to a given geographical area, it may increasingly be the case that the whole world is its own single civilization. Swapping e-mails lickety-split with friends in Senegal, passing by a McDonald's in Paris, and hosting a Web site with tens of thousands of international readers every day just makes us feel that way.

Thus, our own best guess is that so long as our civilization is still around, you'll continue to see long-term growth in business and in the American—and the world's—stock market.

When Not to Invest

A S REWARDING AS the market continues to be over the long haul, cir-cumstances do exist that should dissuade certain individuals from buying. We must pause briefly now to consider those, before we plow onward into making your first investments. For some people, knowing when and why they *shouldn't* be investing in stocks is the essential first step toward success.

When You Owe Money

What a terrifying sight is the wild-eyed, contorted face of the debtor who crosses his fingers and rolls the dice on the short-term performance of stocks. Buying stocks when he owes other people money isn't prudent. Same goes for you.

Now, if this guy drops his dice onto the stock market in a year like 1995, when stocks rose some 35 percent, it's big-money time. All bets pay off, and it's time to tip the croupier. After market close, our man takes to strut-ting down Main Street in his golden shoes. He's all loud suits, loud ties, and free drinks if you half know him. He's in the money *now*.

But if—as is *always a possibility*—the dice crap out, they may produce a year like 1973. Daddy just lost his new pair of golden shoes. In 1973, stocks fell 17 percent, turning $100,000 into $83,000 in twelve months. Worse yet, the bloodletting wasn't complete. The following year, 1974, brought an even sharper decline—this time, 27 percent. So the $100,000 that became $83,000, then shrank to $60,600. And Big Daddy, who was buying stocks even though all along he had outstanding debts, is in big trouble. He already lost his golden shoes in '73, and in '74 a couple of Scorsese thugs push him down into trash cans in a back alley, and he wears a knee brace for a year.

Not a nice sensation, losing money on the stock market and *owing* money right through it.

Plus, it doesn't make mathematical sense. Does the stock market's average annual gain of 11 percent rival the 18 percent interest rate on your debt? Nope. Let's run the numbers (you're probably used to this by now) just to make that clear.

Below sits an investor with $2,500 in credit card debt who goes on to put $2,500 of her new savings into stocks.

What Happens with $2,500 Concomitantly in Stocks and Debt

	Stocks (11%)	Debt (18%)	Difference
At Launch	$2,500	$2,500	$0
Year 1	$2,775	$2,950	−$175
Year 5	$4,213	$5,719	−$1,506
Year 10	$7,099	$13,085	−$5,986

And you get the idea which way the trend is going.

A decade later, though she started the experiment with enough money to eliminate the debt, she's now in the hole by almost $6,000. But that's not the full extent of her troubles. When she sells those stocks trying to scramble out of her debt, she's going to have to pay back 20 percent of her profits, or about $900, to the government in capital gains taxes. So this approach has actually set her back nearly $7,000. That's a lot of bagels. That's nearly five hundred copies of this book. That's one front-row seat to a bad heavyweight boxing championship fight. That's a mistake all around.

Now, had she capped herself in bells and donned motley, she would have paid down the debt first and only after that begun a savings and investing plan. Nobody in America should let debt pile up on her credit cards. We've said that at least two dozen times now, but it's worth repeating, given how big a problem debt is in this country. Anyway (flourish of trumpets, Fool heraldic banner displayed) . . .

We now promise largely to lay off that point for the remainder of this book.

Before moving on to the next situation that would cause you *not* to put new money in the market, let's digress briefly and ask, "What sort of debt can you be carrying as a stock market investor?" So many forms of debt exist, it's a waste of space to consider each (pro or con) here. But here's a decent rule of thumb: *Any debt requiring interest payments above 7 percent per year and* not *providing tax write-offs—such as a mortgage does— will prove enduringly unbeatable.* And you must also consider stock market fluctuation, which is going to bite you in down years. If you're very aggressive, or in a higher income bracket, you may be able to get away with simultaneously maintaining an investment account alongside debt at or below a 7 percent interest rate. If you're neither aggressive nor well moneyed, we don't think you should be investing in stocks with any nondeductible debt carrying interest rates above 5 percent. The message, in the end, is the same: Pay it down. Prepay it if you can. You'll sleep better. Your acquaintances may stop facetiously calling you "The Donald" when you're not around. Sure, your *creditors* will dislike you because your interest payments to them will decline—but you want those guys to dislike you for exactly this reason.

You'll be a giant step closer to building broad and enduring wealth.

The first time you shouldn't be investing is when you owe money. The second?

When You'll Need to Spend Those Savings

Now that you've bid adieu to the misery of liability and have squirreled away, say, $1,000 or $2,000 to invest, are you now ready to get right into stocks? A brokerage office sits behind smoked-glass windows just a block and a half down from your office. Our nation's long-term business and stock market growth is begging to start rewarding you. Your future starts now!

But wait. Whoa there.

Not every nickel of your savings is created equal. That's especially true if you're going to need a handful of those nickels for lunch tomorrow, a bag of them for new clothes, a few thousand more for car and health insurance, tens of thousands more for travel and entertainment, and half a million nickels for the down payment on your dream house. In fact, much of your savings money could be eaten up by immediate concerns. A little preparation and planning—really, no more than a few hours of thought— will go a long, long way here.

You should never invest what money you'll need shortly, because over the short term, the market can get creamed! What would happen if you quickly lost half of the money you needed to *live on* in the year ahead?

Anne Scheiber tucked away $5,000 that she didn't need for five decades, giving it room to grow.

Bar none, the most important feature to sound investing is a recognition that you must give your money—your true savings—time to grow, compounding over the long term. Warren Buffett, the greatest investor of the twentieth century, has made more over the last five years than he did in the previous thirty. Think about what that means for just a second: the thirty years from 1963 to 1992 earned him less than the five-year tail end, from 1993 to 1997. So how much *time* can *you* give to your latest lump of savings? Answer that question and it'll help you determine where to put them.

We don't think you should invest in stocks *any* savings that you'll need over the next five years. That money should be parked extremely safely—in money market funds, for instance. Your aim with your shorter-term money is to make use of it as you or your family will need, whether for education, for braces, or to pay the rent. *Those things* are what your short-term cash is for; you need to spend it, so don't gamble with it.

When else shouldn't you invest?

When You Don't Yet Know Enough

You've wended your way out of debt. You've sectioned off monies that you won't need for sixty months. Hi-ho! Let's get that money into stocks.

Brrrrrrrrrrring!

It's Jordy Callahan on the phone, calling over from the brokerage firm of Sagacious, Crasher & Burns. Jordy's thrilled to hear you're ready to invest. He's giddy. And apparently the forces of *perfect timing* are working for you, because Jordy's got just the company for your first investment. It's a Georgia business franchising restaurants throughout the Southeast called Macon's Bacon. Management is ready to duplicate the all-day breakfast-lounge concept across the nation. Next stop, the globe. And if they ever find life on Mars or Jupiter, Macon's Bacon aims to serve corn fritters, bacon strips, and fried eggs to anything with a mouth.

It's gonna be *big*.

The company's shares trade around $5 each, so your $2,500 in savings could buy five hundred shares and help finance the expansion of (Jordy's words here) "a really great concept." With Sagacious, Crasher & Burns financially backing the undertaking, it's essentially a shoo-in. Who—Jordy wants to know—*who* is going to compete successfully with a twenty-four-hour breakfast house this *HOT*? Success is just a spoon swipe away.

"So, can I mark you down for five hundred shares?"

If your answer is anything other than, "Well no, Jordy. You can't," then you should not yet be investing that money directly into stocks. Our third reason not to invest is your not yet knowing enough. You will soon, though. Once you've wound yourself through to the end of this book, we think you're going to agree that researching smart investments doesn't need to take more than ten hours each year. But it is going to demand more work than just saying yes to salesmen.

Why risk *your savings* (it'd be OK if you were Jordy, risking someone else's) on something like Macon's Bacon when you've only just heard of it, when you can see no compelling reason for the company to dominate its industry, and when you could put *your savings* in an S&P 500 index fund instead that will give you a piece of Intel and Microsoft and Disney?

When you buy what you don't understand, you're going to lose money nine times out of ten. Which is easier to understand—the index fund or Macon's Bacon?

Oh, by the way, "Macon's Bacon" came from a story told us at a watering hole a couple of blocks from Fool HQ, in Alexandria, Virginia. It came from an out-of-towner, a six-foot-three leader of a visiting motorcycle gang who had been persuaded by a stockbroker to drop down $5,000 on a small restaurant company in 1988. The stock was trading at $5¼ per share. After the stock fell by 50 percent, the cold-calling broker phoned again to pitch him on buying more. He refused. That's a good thing, because today the stock is trading at 10 *cents* a stub; the motorcyclist's $5,000 investment is worth $95. He had never bought another stock again, having sworn off the market on the basis of his experience. We Foolishly pleaded with him to reconsider his view of investing. We eventually succeeded by asking him why he hadn't put the money instead into a company that he held dear and actually knew something about. Harley-Davidson was our example. His $5,000 invested into Harley in January 1988 would have grown into $165,000 as of this writing, thirty-three times his initial investment in just ten years.

"Makes a helluvalot of sense," he said.

Damn straight.

Had he done so, he could have treated *us* to a drink.

When You Are Dead

The fourth and final reason not to invest is that the blood has stopped moving through your veins and your lungs are no longer drawing in oxygen. When the background sopranos strike up, and you see that flash of bright light through a tunnel of clouds, and the Giant Hand reaches down to pull you into the next life, that's about as good a time as any to forget about your discount-brokerage account.

Let's count on the spiritual world offering more than just eighth and quarter points.

Once you've adjusted to life outside the corporeal, we hope at some point you'll pause briefly, just once, and consider what went before. Celebrate the fact that before departing, you paid down all your debts, set aside some inheritance for those who would invest after you, perhaps even conferred some useful investment principles for your descendants to mimic. The riches that you have extended down your family tree—mere earthly riches though they be—will go on to support the scholarship, creativity, and daring of your offspring. Sure, it'll also allow a few ne'er-do-well relations to drink Long Island iced tea through a straw and live recklessly among the sands and flowers of the Côte d'Azur. But the sum total of your monetary gifts will be a big, fat positive in the lives of many others. We give *thanks* for you. And we hope you'll say a few brief otherworldly words in support of us as well, and all the Fools still toiling down here— we would all appreciate it.

OK, you actually *are* still breathing for now, and you've paid down your debts and set aside money that you can afford to do without for at least five years. And you know enough to feel comfortable doing so, whatever the different sorts of pitches the stock market will be tossing at you in the coming decades. A 25 percent decline next year? Eight years during which the total value of your investments fails to grow? A market crash *tomorrow morning?* Yes?

You're ready to invest. And the rest of this book stands ready to teach you how.

A Stock Primer

Overview: The Stock Market and You

THE STOCK MARKET began as little more than a large farmers market long ago, in 1792. The market supposedly originated beneath a large buttonwood tree in New York, investors gathering beneath the heavy branches at noontime. As the number of traders and public companies grew, the whole process became more formal, and an ever-increasing number of trades took place at the new New York Stock Exchange office, a single room located at 40 Wall Street in Manhattan, first rented in 1817.

Now, many of us are intimidated by Wall Street. But really, it's only *bigger* than it once was—not different in its intent. Wall Street is little more than a giant shopping mall, the mall of American companies, offering "shoppers" partial ownership in thousands of different businesses. Instead of buying jeans from Gap stores, you can buy a piece of the Gap company. And when you become a part owner in the Gap, you'll start rooting for the success of their business, hoping that over the coming years they sell a bazillion more V-neck sweaters, T-shirts, and jeans. You're praying that teenagers think the brand name is cool, that the entire cast of *Friends* starts wearing Gap khakis, that companies extend dress-down day from only Friday to a second and then third weekday, that Gap successfully expands across Europe and then Asia, and that the managers of the business aren't wasteful with company funds.

By buying Gap stock, you've become an owner of the business, much as Bill Gates owns Microsoft, Steven Spielberg owns his own movie studio, George Steinbrenner (gasp!) partially owns the New York Yankees, and your uncle Garvin owns three floundering record shops in San Francisco's Haight District. Each of these business owners wants his or her "stuff" to gain in popularity. Whether they're selling software, movie tickets, ball caps, or Counting Crows discs, the owners want Americans to line up with their checkbooks each month, week, or day, and *buy*. The same, dear Fool, is true of you when you purchase stock in the Gap. As an owner now, you're hoping that only good things come to those who sell blue jeans.

To restate: Wall Street is nothing more than an enormous shopping area, like a farmers market complete with red potatoes, carrots, zucchini, green beans, green apples, peppers, squash, and the requisite gal in a Fool ball cap with her trick dog. Most of the food on the market is good and pure—but some of it's rotten. Your challenge as an investor is to scoot from one booth to the next, sorting through the options, kicking out the bruised apple swarming with aphids and plucking a ripe, clean one. Of course, Wall Street, our stock market, is distinct from this farmers market in one essential way: rather than providing a forum for the sale of edibles, it offers you a wide selection of businesses, some good and pure, others rotten.

Thankfully for us, our stock markets are the best in the world. The markets are regulated by the government's Securities and Exchange Commission (SEC) and they make sure that there's a system to the swirl of activity, that investors all have access to the same information, and that bad dealers are restricted from selling rotten goods to the public. The mix of sophisticated regulatory standards and the love of enterprise in America has created the healthiest market for stock selling on the planet.

The Stock Exchanges

Where is all that buying and selling of the shares of public companies happening? Mostly in two major markets in the United States, the New York Stock Exchange and the Nasdaq (which recently merged with the American Stock Exchange).

THE NEW YORK STOCK EXCHANGE

The largest stock market in the world is the New York Stock Exchange, often abbreviated as NYSE. When you add up the total value (market capitalization) of all companies on the NYSE the sum equals 69 percent of the total capitalization of all American stocks, with the stocks of many of our largest and oldest companies among its listings. For example, the NYSE holds most of the thirty stocks that constitute the Dow Jones industrial average, the figure that evening news anchors somewhat mindlessly quote each night toward the close of the program.

These thirty stocks—the most closely watched group of businesses in the world—are meant to represent the overall economy of America. A variety of industry leaders—from McDonald's to ExxonMobil to Disney—are tracked and averaged together by stock price, which results in that oft-quoted figure, the Dow Jones industrial average. The very best examples of which companies sit on the New York Stock Exchange are these Dow behemoths, each with billions of dollars in sales each year, each with business operations in all parts of the globe, each with products that neither you nor we can avoid for more than a few days. These blue-blooded blue chips are what the NYSE is all about.

THE NASDAQ STOCK MARKET

While the NYSE is home to the stocks of many of the oldest and most established companies in the country, the stocks of many smaller companies (called "small-caps" or "mid-caps") are traded on the Nasdaq stock market. Founded in 1971, the National Association of Securities Dealers Automated Quotation—or Nasdaq—system had grown such that by the mid-1990s its trading volume began to regularly surpass the volume of stocks traded on the New York Stock Exchange.

Many of the small companies on the Naz (our Foolish affectionate nickname) are growing or failing at an extremely rapid pace, and their stocks reflect these minirevolutions. Nasdaq issues are more volatile in price than the stocks of the giant companies listed on the NYSE, by a good margin.

The Nasdaq stock market is known for listing a large portion of the technology companies in the country, both young and old, from Microsoft to Intel to Dell Computer. The Internet boom, for instance, has largely been a Nasdaq-driven phenomenon, with Yahoo!, Amazon.com, eBay, and, heck, Cisco Systems residing on the Naz.

Whereas the New York Stock Exchange is comparatively conservative, proud, and secure, the Nasdaq is daring, aggressive, and volatile. This ain't to imply that the Nasdaq market is shaky, or that all New York Stock Exchange–listed companies will be around forever. With Microsoft and Intel, Nasdaq lists two of the greatest businesses in the recent history of man. Their enterprise, their tight fiscal management, their lead in technology, and their spectacular marketing strategies have all been partly enabled by the Nasdaq.

Does the Market Matter?

As with so many things in our capitalistic society, stock markets were created as businesses that provide a service, or a "product." Just as a mall offers a large area in which to shop for a variety of items, the stock markets offer an efficient and safe place in which investors can follow and invest in stocks. These markets are regulated and all of the companies listed must meet initial listing requirements, as well as periodic reviews, in order to remain listed.

As to which market you might employ, you really don't have a choice, so it needn't be a consideration. Each stock is listed on one of the two markets, so depending upon which company you want to buy, you'll buy stock listed on its particular stock market. If you wanted to buy stock in Coca-Cola, for example, you would place your order and your discount broker would buy the stock on the New York Stock Exchange. If you were to buy stock in Microsoft, you'd be buying it from the Nasdaq Stock Market.

The exchange doesn't matter. The merits of the business do, and the money you'll pay out in transaction fees matters, as well. Transaction fees? Ah, a nice segue into the subject of brokering.

The Brokers

If the stock market is a giant mall of American business, then stockbrokers are the clerks working inside that mall. They walk the aisles prepared to sell you home appliances, hoopskirts, and digital cameras. But if you've ever visited the New York Stock Exchange, you recognize that it isn't entirely like your favorite haberdashery. You can't just walk down onto the floor of the exchange, wave your hand in the air, and start buying. You'd probably get creamed by a guy with sixteen slips of paper in his fist and a half-eaten hot dog hanging from his mouth.

So, the only way to buy stocks is to pay a broker to place the orders for you. What type of broker you use is critical, though. In an earlier chapter we discussed some of the differences between full-service and discount brokers. Let's consider them again briefly here.

FULL-SERVICE BROKERS

If you were to shop for a big-screen television at an electronics store, a full-service broker would walk you through the showroom, pointing out individual TVs and their various features. After helping you decide which one to buy, he would then go into a song and dance about adjacent products—from lifetime warranties to cleaning kits to supersized antennae. Why? Because on top of his normal salary, he is paid a portion of every sale that he makes, in the form of a commission. If he sells you a $500 TV set, $10 goes into his pocket. If he then tags on a $55 lifetime warranty, another $10 flies his way. If he can make a compelling case for the cleaning kit, then $5 of that $25 sale goes to him as well.

This well-dressed salesman is being encouraged to sell you even that which you don't need. So too with the full-service broker on Wall Street, who pitches you on semiconductor stocks, telecommunications stocks, municipal bonds, corporate bonds, growth funds, international funds, limited partnerships, Treasury bills, and CDs. And he does so because for each sale, he gains a commission. The system is encouraging him to move you into as many different investments as many different times as he can; and just as with the television salesman above, the best interests of the customer don't always fit into that business model.

More recently, some brokerage firms are moving toward charging a flat percentage fee of assets, instead of the churn-inducing commissions model. Regardless of which way you pay your full-service broker, you should be focused on how much you're paying, and what you're receiving for those payments. Is "full service" worth it to you, or are you a self-directed investor who's ready for . . .

DISCOUNT BROKERS

We need say little more here about discount brokers than that they play the part of cashier, not salesman, at your favorite shop. The discount broker doesn't pitch ideas at you while you move from shelf to shelf, scoping

Bermuda shorts and then sandals and then sunglasses. Instead, he stands behind the register, takes your order, scans your credit card, bags your merchandise, staples your bill together, then with a wink and half-genuine smile wishes you a good day and sends you on your way.

The discount broker is growing in popularity in America because investors are improving their returns by designing their own investment strategies in clubs and through online forums. It's not surprising. If you are sold needless things by a full-service broker but don't know any better—well then, if you can get into a community of other investors, chances are you'll cut out the nonsense products and improve your returns. These groups are researching the subject together and now taking their money directly to the discount broker, who isn't commissioned by his employer to sell particular products. He is not conflicted. He doesn't have to choose between representing your interests or those of the firm—an awfully difficult decision for any employee. The discount broker, as cashier, just provides service and a smile.

Whether you use a full-service broker or a discount broker, you can expect to get regular statements on your account that look much like the reports your bank mails you each month. There are some unique features that you'll want to know about, though.

THE BROKERAGE ACCOUNT

What is a brokerage account?

Let's narrow our analogy a bit here and, for a second, imagine that your stocks are packets of seedlings that you purchased at Ernst. You've taken those seeds back home and planted them in a bed fifteen yards west of your sons' Wiffle ball field and ten yards south of your daughters' miniature log cabin. Nice-looking place you got there.

Fellow Fool, that garden bed is your brokerage account, holding the collection of companies whose stock you've purchased. Instead of chickpeas, Idaho potatoes, thyme, and azaleas, though, your garden bed may hold stock in Nike, Campbell Soup, and Pepsi. And just as you want your Idaho potatoes to take to the soil, you'd like your companies to shoot roots three hundred feet into the ground of your brokerage account. You'd like their yield to multiply with each year and your whole garden to burst like a summer-day parade.

Your brokerage account is simply your garden, a holding place for your investments. It isn't materially different from your savings account at the local bank, the only difference being that, in an average year, stock investments will grow three times faster than the cash in your savings account. Sounds like you'll want that money in stocks, then. Yes, you will. But, even though we mentioned it before, *what exactly is stock,* you ask?

What Are Stocks?

When you buy stock, you pay for a partial ownership in a company. That stock gives you the right to vote on major company decisions. Your stock also makes you eligible for quarterly dividend payments, puts you on the business's mailing list, earns you a fold-out chair at the next shareholders' meeting, and depending on the company, might win you some discounts or free products in the year ahead.

But most investors don't buy stock to gain a shareholder's vote or to land a couple of freebies; they buy the stock to make money. Investors have made the decision to move that money out of its sleepy perch at First Federal Global Banking and into ownership positions in public companies.

The businesses a Fool can invest in range from water purification to the milking of cows to asthma medication to hiking boots to Slurpees. And the aim of the investor is to find businesses that each year sell more stuff, make more money selling that stuff, and see the value of their enterprise expand. If the world succumbs to an addiction for cherry Slurpees in the years ahead, with the average adult female drinking more than six per day, then 7-Eleven will see its sales and profits soar; the overall business will grow in value; more investment dollars will come rushing in; and the investment returns for shareholders in 7-Eleven, Inc. will rise.

That sounds pretty easy, eh? Well, it's both commonsensical and yet increasingly complex; as with all great subjects, the more one learns, the more (one feels) is yet to be learned. But genuine scholarship always takes the researcher away from jargon and into simple principles, repeated once and again. Let's pursue that simplicity and ask ourselves, can investors buy into any company?

Maybe. Read on.

THE PUBLIC COMPANY

Nope, not all businesses have stock for sale. Companies fall under two categories; they are either private or public. If a company is *private,* the founders and subsequent management have decided to keep ownership of the company to themselves, much like the corner market run by former minor-league ballplayer Buster Scheele. Oftentimes, guys like Buster are perfectly happy with the way things are; they don't want to pursue growth at breakneck speed; they don't want hundreds or thousands of shareholders demanding higher profits every three months; and they don't need the money that comes from going public.

Money?

Yep, companies go public to raise cash. When a company like the ever-enterprising SqueeGeeNet Inc. wants to expand business, it usually needs more money. There are three typical routes to new capital:

1. SqueeGeeNet can raise money by waddling down to the *local bank* and getting a loan, which demands regular interest payments.
2. As a private company, SqueeGeeNet can look for investments from *venture capitalists*—investors representing corporations, trusts, and wealthy individuals. Venture capitalists, or VCs among the initiated (or "vultures" among the disabused), make early investments in rapidly growing companies. They aim to strike it rich on start-up businesses with big stories but with not enough cash to do more than tell those stories.
3. Finally the company can sell *stock* to the public, raising millions of dollars by giving up some control of their enterprise. They will not have to return any of the money taken in from selling stock, but they'll be beholden to a crowd of often impatient shareholders.

Just about every public company out there has gone through all three financing stages. They started by borrowing money, then they brought in some venture-cap funds, then they worked with an investment firm like Morgan Stanley to bring their company to the market, in an initial public offering (IPO). Once public, the business must release its financial statements to the world—including its competitors—every three months. At that point people like you and us can run a simple calculation to see what the company is worth. It's called "capitalization," and look below, it's the very next subtitle.

CAPITALIZATION

Why do stocks rise and fall? What does the price of a stock represent? Excellent questions both. Stocks rise because each company has a limited amount of shares available for purchase. Breathe deeply, Fool, a few numbers are coming at you. But they're a piece of cake.

Imagine that a small airplane business called Jefe Airlines goes public by selling 10 percent of the company to the investment community. If Jefe (pronounced HEFF-ay) Airlines sells 1 million shares at $10 per share, tell us, what is the company worth? Let's work through this one. When the company sells that million shares at $10 a stub, they just raised $10 million for the business. Since they sold 10 percent of the company, the total value of the company is $100 million. The owners from the private company's early days still hold 90 percent of the shares in its public form, or $90 million in stock. And on Wall Street they will say that the capitalization, or the total value, of Jefe Airlines is $100 million.

Now, if the company stirs up popular demand for its flights from Manhattan to Newark, if it is selling more tickets and making more money, then more and more people are going to want to own that business. More, more, more, more, more. Just as a major-league franchise becomes a more valuable "property" when the team makes it to the World Series three years in a row, so also does a bank, restaurant, publisher, or pharmaceutical company—or an airline—when it starts winning in sales and attracting more customers. The shareholders follow the earnings growth, and all of a sudden the value of the business has gone through the roof.

SUMMARY

We hope that it's clear that when you buy stock, what you're buying is partial ownership of a business and your hope is that the business increases in value over time, so that your stock increases in value as well. You want one more visual example? Try this one.

McDonald's plans to open an average of six new restaurants on this planet every single day of the year 2001, growing its present count by about 10 percent. Today, there are more than 28,000 MickeyDees restaurants in the world. If you'd bought stock in McDonald's three decades ago, when the company operated only one thousand restaurants, you'd be extremely happy right now. Your initial stake of ownership would have grown in value significantly. When McDonald's adds a new eatery, it consistently turns a profit on that establishment. Thus, McDonald's is still in a growth phase, looking for new places and greater profits.

The Business of Stocks

Once you've invested in common stock, you'll notice that stock prices fluctuate daily, occasionally as much as 5 to 15 percent or more. Given that your bank pays you back 3 to 5 percent on your savings money per year, the volatility of the stock market is no small thing. You will certainly be tempted at some point in your investing career to trade your holdings more actively, trying to dive in and cut out at the right moments. Going back to the garden analogy, you'll be transplanting embryo investments from place to place, selling two-day-old sunflowers and planting cotton in their stead. You will hear us say on numerous occasions during the remainder of this book that we think daily transplanting, or short-term trading of stocks, is a singularly bad idea. But for now, let's just consider why stock prices change.

Stocks fluctuate because people, pension funds, investment firms, mutual funds, and investment clubs buy and sell shares every day. They do so while trying to estimate the value of a business that day. If they can find a great bargain over in the computer section, or in home appliances, or in the bookshop, they'll exploit that inefficiency in pricing and buy or sell shares. At any given point in time, numerous stocks are reasonably priced, but many more are either over- or undervalued relative to the company's long-term value.

But how do they price these stocks?

Over the long run, a stock price most often follows the earnings growth of the company. If Jefe Airlines sells one thousand plane tickets for $100 each next week, it's generated sales of $100,000. Investors will then want to know how much Jefe had to pay in advertising, staffing, plane leasing, fueling, information technology, and old sandwich meat to supply flights for one thousand people. Also, does this business make money? Are there opportunities for an additional growth in profits for the business going forward? If the answer to these questions is no, chances are that Jefe Airlines will be bankrupt and forgotten, all in good time. If the answer is yes, then who knows? We might all be flying Jefe Airlines from Boston to Worcester. Who knows how high the company will soar!

The answer to how high, how fast, and how long actually lies in free information, a phone call or mouse click away. For starters, let's take a look at how to follow the performance of a stock like Jefe Airlines.

How to Read the Stock Tables

With a giant lemonade on the kitchen table, a bowl of oatmeal, and your children still fast asleep, open up the stock tables in your newspaper, and let's consider what lies in there.

As confusing as all those numbers may look, they're quite easy to decipher once you know what to look for. At the beginning of the stock tables, a small box usually quotes the most actively traded stocks for the preceding day, as well as the stocks whose price moved most in percentage terms. Take a look at those and gasp a little. There were probably one or two companies acquired at a real premium, given their previous price. Maybe one or two companies announced great earnings and saw their stocks rise 15 percent. Still others might have announced the departure of a key business partner and suffered a mighty blow.

Traveling beyond the biggest percentage movers, run your eyes over the reams of company names and stock quotes listed alphabetically by company, one stock market at a time. To find Disney's stock, for example, look under the D on the New York Stock Exchange. There it is. Nope. There it is. Wait. Grab your glasses. OK. *There it is.* A typical newspaper lists a stock in the following fashion:

52-Week Low/High	Stock	Ticker Symbol	Div.	Yield	P/E	Vol. (000s)	Last Price	Day Change	Day High/Low
23/43	Disney	DIS	0.21	0.58%	78	2890	36	−0.88	37/36

From left to right, we start with the fifty-two-week high and low for Disney stock. Over the past twelve months, Disney has been as low as $23 per share and as high as $43 per share, a spread of over 80 percent. It's been a volatile year!

Next, the *company name* is listed. Simple enough.

Following that sits the company's *ticker symbol.* Each listed stock has a ticker symbol as an abbreviation. Disney's is DIS. If you're flipping past a financial television station or grabbing your quotes at Fool.com, DIS will be used in place of the company name.

Following that in the newspaper tables is the *dividend* amount that the company pays annually. What the heck is a dividend? you ask. Dividends are simply payments that a company makes directly to its shareholders. Companies like Disney pull some money out of their flow of earnings and use it to encourage shareholders to hold on to their stock for the long term. Because investors get regular dividend payments, they can budget off the cash payments and presumably preserve their investment in the stock. In Disney's case, each year the company pays shareholders twenty-one cents per share. The payments are made quarterly, so Disney sends shareholders five-and-one-quarter cents per share every three months. If you owned one thousand shares of Disney, what would your annual dividend payment be? Yep, $210. Nice, quick thinking there!

OK, take a second and let's look back at what we have so far. We have the annual high and low for the stock price, followed by the company name, followed by the ticker symbol, followed by the amount of dividends per share paid by the company. Whew. OK, onward!

Div.	Yield	P/E	Vol. (000s)	Last Price	Day Change	Day High/Low
0.21	0.58%	78	2890	36	−0.88	37/36

To the right of the twenty-one-cent dividend is a simple ratio called the yield (the dividend yield). That's nothing more than the annual dividend per share divided by the current stock price. In Disney's case, you have the twenty-one-cent dividend payment, and all the way to the right, you have the stock trading at $36 per share. Divide $0.21 by $36 for the dividend yield. Tap-tap-tap-tap-tap. Woo-hooo, we're going to win! The answer? Yep, 0.58 percent. Why calculate the dividend yield? Well, so you'll know what percentage growth you'd get from the stock if it did not rise or fall all year. In this case, you'd get 0.58 percent, which loses badly to inflation, loses badly to plinking your money into a savings account at Intergalactic United Banking, and loses badly to mutual funds. Clearly, no one should invest in Disney for the dividend alone. Investors here are hoping that the stock price rises, in addition to that dividend yield, and that over time the company will raise the dividend. Here comes a fast-pitched softball question. Which company do you think investors are expecting more earnings growth from?

DIVIDEND YIELD

Disney	0.58%
Jefe Airlines	7.20%

Yes, you're right. They're counting on more earnings growth from Disney. If both stocks didn't appreciate, Jefe Airlines shareholders would be much more satisfied than mouse holders. The market is counting on Disney to continue posting strong earnings and sales growth; investors certainly wouldn't be happy to just sit there gobbling that low yield.

Unfortunately now, in the wake of a column that demanded some basic calculation, we run into a slightly more complex beast to its right: the *P/E ratio*. The numerating P in the ratio represents the company's *stock price*. The denominating E stands for the company's *earnings per share*. Thus, this ratio compares the company's stock price to its trailing twelve months of earnings per share. Gasp. What's that? Good luck, kid, you're never going to grasp this. (Just kidding. Relax and watch.)

Let's say that Jefe Airlines earned $100 million last year, after removing all costs and paying taxes to the government. Nice year, Jefe. For shareholders, public companies present these earnings also on a per share basis. You can figure out how many dollars of earnings the company made for each share of stock that you own. *Capisce?* Good. So, let's say that Jefe Airlines has 200 million shares floating out publicly in the marketplace, being regularly traded by investors. The $100 million earnings spread among 200 million shares makes for fifty cents of earnings per share. Yes? Sweet.

But we're only halfway there on the P/E (price-to-earnings) ratio. We now know the denominator, the earnings per share. It's time to divide the stock price by the earnings per share, and we'll explain why one would do that in a second. Returning to Disney, where Jefe had earnings per share of fifty cents, Disney had earnings of 46 cents per share. Its stock is trading at $36 per share. We must divide that price by those earnings per share (36 / 0.46), and we get a P/E ratio of 78.3. Even though you may be thoroughly confused at this point, isn't it kind of cool that now you can walk around parties saying, "Yeah, Disney's P/E is seventy-eight. The company is trading at seventy-eight times earnings"? Cool, eh?

OK, what is the P/E ratio used for? Well, we go into the greatest detail on this matter in *The Motley Fool Investment Guide* (a mere fourteen bucks for the paperback). But to get you started, the P/E ratio is used to show at how high a multiple of earnings per share the stock is trading. You are lost now, yes? Good. Read that sentence over five times fast and see if you're still lost. Yes? Don't worry, you're making progress even if you don't know it yet.

We'll take another stab. In the case of Disney, the company has $0.46 of earnings per share, is priced at $36 per share, thus is said to be trading at seventy-eight times earnings. What if Jefe Airlines also had $0.46 of earnings per share but was trading at $20 per share, or trading at forty-three times earnings? Hey, wait a second. Why is Disney trading at a stock price higher than Jefe Airlines, even though Jefe is making proportionately more per share? Aha! Disney is trading at a higher multiple because the market expects that company to grow more rapidly and consistently than Jefe Airlines. For now, all you need to know is that the highness or lowness of the P/E ratio reflects what sort of growth the market expects for that company going forward. At the time of this writing, take a look at some P/E ratios for well-known companies:

Yahoo!	363
Microsoft	41
ExxonMobil	27
General Motors	7

This indicates that the investing community generally expects Yahoo! to grow the fastest, followed by Microsoft, trailed by ExxonMobil and General Motors. If you dug a little deeper, you'd notice that, combined, ExxonMobil and GM have nearly 14 times more sales than Microsoft and Yahoo! put together. Naturally, the market is going to expect good smaller companies to grow at a faster rate than good larger companies. That partially explains the discrepancy in the P/E ratios listed above. OK, we've done enough of that; you get the gist of it. Let's move on.

P/E	Vol. (000s)	Last Price	Day Change	Day High/Low
78	2890	36	−0.88	37/36

So, what remains? To the right of the price-to-earnings multiple is listed the *volume of shares* traded on the market for the previous day. On that day,

Disney's stock traded 2,890,000. If that seems like a lot of shares changing hands, you're right. It is. Disney is an enormous company with a very broad base of shareholders. Some stocks routinely trade as little as one thousand shares per day.

Out to the right of the daily volume, your newspaper lists some relevant prices for Disney stock in yesterday's trading. In this case, Disney's stock ended the day at a *closing price* of $36. Following that is the *change* for the entire day, meaning here that DIS rose by ⅞, or 87½ cents per share. After that is the price range for the day—the high and low prices touched during the six and a half hours of market trading ($37 to $36). The daily high and low isn't terribly important.

Whoa there! Check it out. Disney closed the day at $36 per share. The stock was trading as low as $23 over the past twelve months and as high as $43 per share. Some investors, having looked only at the present stock price and annual highs and lows, will casually say, "Wow, Disney isn't cheap now." To which you should feel free to respond: *"Hooey."* While many people are leery of buying stocks that are near their 52-week highs, you shouldn't make that your instinctive response. You will come to notice that the stocks of truly winning companies fairly consistently score new highs, from one decade to the next. Sure, they may have a bad three-week run or four-month run, or even three-year run, but if sales and earnings grow, more investors will pile in. Don't be scared off by a stock hitting new highs unless you find out some other worrisome things about the company.

There you have it. You're now an expert at reading the stock quotes in your local newspaper. The Motley Fool can think of a couple of other great statistics that could be added to newspaper stock columns, but there just isn't enough space. Naturally, this has investors looking to newspapers for the latest news but less for data, which is best presented in digital form online. Whether you're following your stocks in the newspaper or at Fool.com, we recommend that you not obsess over the one-week or one-month moves of any of your holdings. Prepare yourself to think in terms of years instead.

How to Track the Performance of Your Stocks

This little section is just slightly ahead of its time. As you read the next few chapters on buying your first stocks, though, keep in the back of your head that you're going to need to account periodically for the performance of your investments. As we discussed in the earlier chapters on mutual funds and index funds, when smart Fools invest in stocks, the aim—aside from securing a solid financial future—is to beat the market average. So how do you know if you're "beating the market"?

First, a broker will always send you a confirmation statement for every stock transaction that you make, within two or three days of that transaction. This slip of info provides at least the following:

- The company name
- The ticker symbol
- The cost per share
- The transaction fee
- The date of the trade

These confirmations are important to keep for your tax records, and they can also come in handy to help you track your performance.

In addition to your transaction slips, brokers will provide you with monthly statements showing you the total dollars in your account, the collection of stocks you own, the price you paid for each, the present price of each, and usually the dollar and percentage-point change since your purchase. What many monthly statements today will not do is show you how your overall portfolio has performed in percentage terms as well as how that return stacks up against the market's performance. They should.

Here is how we advise you keep track of your stocks, measuring your performance against the S&P 500 Index. If you are without computer, you can do this on a pad of paper. Just line up your stocks, then line up the *total dollars invested* in them and the *total current dollar value* of your holdings. Divide the latter by the former and compare that percentage return to the gain in the S&P 500 during the same period. If you do have a computer, set this up on a (look out, product placement coming!) Microsoft Excel spreadsheet.

Let's take a look at one sample purchase.

Date Purchased	No. of Shares	Company	Price Paid/ Share	Current Price	Fees	Total Cost	Dollar Value	$ Change	% Change
7/11/96	25	Gucci	53.00	97.00	$25	$1,350	$2,425	$1,075	80%

The investor in Gucci stock between July 1996 and July 2000 earned 80 percent growth on that investment. Given that the stock market grows at an average annual rate of 11 percent, Gucci appears to have been a fine investment. But there's more complexity here. The four-year period being considered did not post merely average returns, so it's important to track what the S&P 500 did relative to Gucci's performance.

7/11/96, S&P 500:	645.67
7/11/00, S&P 500:	1,470.88
Total Gain:	127.81%

Whoops! It turns out that investment in Gucci wasn't so winning after all. Though the investment rose 80 percent, that growth did not match the market's average of 127.81 percent, and thus, the S&P Index fund would have been a better investment. This is not, however, to suggest that Gucci won't end up beating the market or that an investor in Gucci during this period has made a colossal blunder. Nope. The point of this little exercise has simply been to champion the idea that every investor should compare his or her returns to the S&P 500. In stocks, it isn't surprising that most people make money; it is surprising how many celebrate profitable yet subpar returns—particularly in the mutual fund industry! If you can't beat the market over a three- to five-year period, join it with an index fund.

Now, our example above showed you only how to measure the performance of a single investment. Tracking an entire portfolio is only a bit more time consuming (and it takes up a good deal more space, which is a problem in this medium). What we've done is to set up a number of sample worksheets in *The Motley Fool Investment Workbook,* the sisterly companion to this book. The workbook allows you to get your pencils out, sharpen them, and go nuts. What we hope you take with you here is that you must always know, from one year to the next, how your investments have performed relative to the S&P 500. Over the long term, we think you should squash the market, and quite Foolishly.

Closing Words

We just covered the stock market, the various exchanges, the qualities of a public company, the total value of a public company, who the various brokers are, how to follow stocks, and how to track your portfolio. We hope you'll agree, after that whirlwind tour, that much of the jargon on Wall Street is unnecessarily, if not intentionally, confusing. Any long, complicated words that you may run across as you dart into the world of investing should be summarily dismissed. You don't need that "information." All it takes to create enduring wealth from the stock market is commonsense thinking, plain dealing, and patience. Certainly Anne Scheiber didn't spend her days immersed in Wall Street jargon. She just purchased great companies and held on for decades.

As we move forward into a discussion of particular companies and select investment approaches, please recognize that philosophically all you need to know about stocks is already planted in your head: to invest in the stocks of the very best companies that one can find, to own those stocks for as long as their business prospects look sound, to be practical enough to realize that no one should spend substantial amounts of time quoting his stocks by the hour and worrying about his performance on a daily or weekly basis.

If, at a cocktail party on a patio overlooking some magnificent view, you run across a fellow spouting off about his hectic day-trading of stocks, understand that what he's actually doing is spending a lot in time and commissions in search of short-term gains, gains that he must then turn around and pay out in short-term capital gains taxes. Quite contrarily, you'll want to *own* your present and future as much as possible, to free up time for your friends, family, community, for touch football, bridge, bird-watching, or traveling. When the future finally rolls into town, with compounding returns speeding the growth of your savings each year, won't it be nice not to be spending hours each day watching the prices of your stocks wiggle up, over, around, and down on a glowing computer monitor? By then, your savings will be working all out for you, not the reverse.

OK, OK, so how do you actually make that first stock purchase, and in what do you invest? The remainder of this book is dedicated to just that— starting on the very next page.

The First Federal
Bank of Coca-Cola

Y OU'VE ALREADY LEARNED that most bank savings accounts and CDs pay low annual interest that doesn't do much better than inflation. Treating your savings to such low returns will really hurt in the long term. But the reason so many people still do so is the safety and convenience that banks represent. Unfortunately, these people don't know what they're missing.

As we begin to scour the investment world to search out your first investment, we're ideally looking for companies that offer the same safety and convenience you get from a bank, but at a much better return. American business has matured today to the point that certain all-American companies have achieved such success and stability that they have almost become like banks. You can feel very good, that is, banking with them. They're dependable, almost never getting crushed in bad markets and rarely going down much in *any* market. And their returns are actually *well above the stock market average* (which is itself so much better than interest on bank accounts). And their shares can be purchased easily, through any brokerage account or even from the companies directly.

These are exactly the sort of companies in which you should make your first investment. If you choose well, you may never ever sell this first investment!

Our first stop is the sole subject of this chapter, America's single greatest consumer brand name. We think you've heard of it—Big Red down in Atlanta—the Coca-Cola Company. So much has this company done for investors that we've been inspired to name this chapter "The First Federal

Bank of Coca-Cola." Perhaps we should've made that the title of our entire book; Coca-Cola has been that stable, that strong, and that good.

The primary aim of this chapter is to understand why. We'll begin by looking at what you and we should care about most: da performance of da stock (the company's ticker symbol is KO, and it trades on the New York Stock Exchange). Having ogled KO stock for a while, we'll traipse through an easy-to-read examination of the company's business model, which should go some way toward explaining exactly *why* the stock has done so well. By the end of the chapter, we'll have in hand a few general principles we've learned from Coca-Cola that all of us can use in our investing. It's a generous teacher, and a superb candidate for your first investment.

Da Stock

Whence came this gallant champion, this world conqueror of the soft drink industry?

Coca-Cola first sold shares to the public in 1919, after twenty-six years of scrappy growth. Beset by public relations disasters, the company had almost gone bankrupt several times in its early years. Up until the turn of the century, Coca-Cola's drink was a frightful mix of sweet syrup, alcohol, caffeine, and a pinch of cocaine: Robitussin with a shotgun kick. Back then, though, cocaine's miserable effects weren't known. It was celebrated as a wonder drug in medical institutes across America and Europe. Health enthusiasts cheered the effects of the coca leaf, as kids tossed back midday jars of soda.

As the dangers of its concoction became apparent, Coca-Cola was besieged by outraged former drinkers and the press. As the tide was swelling, executive Frank Robinson made a critical decision. He all but terminated promotions that implied Coca-Cola was medicinal, and the company began marketing the potable as merely a refreshing, delightful soda pop. This sudden reinvention of its product was the company's defining moment. It worked brilliantly, and (as one might expect) the market for refreshment has turned out to be much, much larger than for liquid curatives. It was eight years later, in 1903, that the coca leaves used in Coca-Cola were quietly decocainized.

Then came 1919, when Coca-Cola announced it would go public. It issued common stock priced at $40 per share, valuing the company at $1 million. Had you purchased one hundred shares of Coke at its initial public offering, an investment of $4,000, just a year later you'd have been pretty upset: Coke traded down to $21 per share. In a single year, you lost $1,900, or 47.5 percent of your investment. Investing was better left to the professionals, right?!

That wasn't the only time you, the patient long-term buy-and-hold investor, would have been discouraged. At six other points in the company's seventy-nine years of trading on the stock market, the stock lost more than 20 percent. Those include the Depression-era loss of 36 percent in the early thirties. Then there was the sinking of the "Nifty Fifty" in 1973-1974; the Nifty Fifty were several dozen huge companies whose darling stocks had been bid sky high, to be subsequently crushed during a sharp rise in interest rates. Coca-Cola lost 63 percent of its value—no pocket change, that. The investor with $100,000 in Coke during that bear market lost $63,000, in just *thirty* months! It would take ten long years to make it back to even.

But let's retract our lens now and take into account the entire history of Coca-Cola stock. In so doing, you'll quickly discover that one can make anything look bad by focusing on just a short-term period. What matters is not the weekend series away at Wrigley Field—what matters is the whole darned season. Because while investors in Coke have occasionally watched their Atlanta team get completely blown out, in the end they've been treated to as many home runs and pennants as Atlanta's real baseball team has in recent years.

You see, $4,000 invested in the company in 1919 is today valued at . . . at . . . *cha-cha-ching!* $606 million.

Yep, $606 million, one of the single greatest twentieth-century investments in the United States. Imagine the investor who bailed in 1920, sickened by the 47 percent loss. That sickens *us.* Why be negative, though? Instead, let's imagine the investor who purchased $1,000 of Coca-Cola stock for a family trust just as KO bottomed at $21. (Hey, you gotta figure *somebody* did.) As of this writing, that $1,000 investment would be valued at over $250 million. That's enough money now to buy a minor-league baseball team, a houseboat on the Thames, a garden rivaling Versailles, full-time cooking and cleaning services, three Derby-winning horses, a twenty-two-year-old trophy spouse resembling Juliette Binoche or Brad Pitt, a trip around the world with two financial authors of your choice, political clout (supposing you'd actually *want* such a thing), and an opportunity to help rebuild broken neighborhoods across your state.

So did *your* Most Beloved Ancestor buy a little KO and pass it down through the family? Great! So when does our trip start?

Families that have bought and held Coca-Cola for decades *do* exist. Some of them attend the Coca-Cola shareholders' meeting each April in Wilmington, Delaware. Spend a few hours hobnobbing at the refreshments (er, Coke) table and you'll discover some broadly shared similarities from one to the next. We'll summarize a few: They didn't listen to any broker who told them, "It's looking a little overvalued right now, so let's move you into Macon's Bacon"; they were sufficiently unimpressed with the rise of mutual funds to trade their shares for a holding of Fidelity Overrated fund; few have ever bought any lottery tickets since the state lottery resurfaced in 1964. One also imagines them never impatiently buying insurance or a house or automobiles without a little consultation down the line, through the family. We don't mean to apotheosize the long-term shareholders of the Coca-Cola Company, but mayhap a Fool rightly imagines them not feeling rushed about financial decisions.

Ah, but amid all this wealth and patience, one piece of the equation is missing. *How could anyone have known ahead of time, or along the way, that Coca-Cola would one day earn Foolish Federal Bank status?* Who could have scried in 1927 that seventy-plus years later Germans in Traunstein, Greeks on Ios, Canadians in Port Cartier, New Mexicans in Wagon Mound, Tanzanians in Rungwe, and Fools in Alexandria, Virginia, would all be saying every day, almost without even thinking about it, "Um, yes, another Coke please"? What possible clues lay spread about the conservatory for amateur sleuths?

To be honest, at various points it would've been nearly impossible to foresee Coca-Cola cans shipping to every corner of the planet. The company suffered frontal assaults from competitors, struggled through fierce internal battles, endured periods of poor managerial guidance, and had its stock kicked like garbage around a junkyard. Who could *possibly* have known? After all, history has left hundreds of once-great companies in, or teetering on, bankruptcy: Macy's, Bloomingdale's, Montgomery Ward, Chrysler, Barings Bank, Texaco. Geez, one of the wealthiest counties in America, Orange County, California, announced its bankruptcy in 1994. Burt Reynolds went bankrupt. So did Willie Nelson. What if you bought the wrong guy or company, thinking it was the next big thing, and it wound up being no thing?

Did Coca-Cola investors this century get *lucky*?

That's the subject of the second half of this chapter, which follows shortly. We think not, of course. You see, we continue to believe that to understand business you need not have a master's in business administration from a costly ivy-overgrown university. And take the Ph.D. from the London School of Economics if you like, but you don't need that either. Neither, last we checked, did you need a writ from Caesar or from heaven. Verily, dear Fool, all you really need is some intellectual curiosity and the willingness to indulge it. (We're biased, of course, since all we took were undergraduate English degrees.) Online access helps.

To preview some of the next section, let's close with some insights from an old friend, Randy Befumo, who was once upon a time the senior writer (as well as a juggler of many other jobs) at Fool HQ. Here's Randy's take on Coca-Cola, to close:

> Coca-Cola controls a finely tuned, global system for distributing its drinks. Even better, as much as possible it gets other companies to do the labor-intensive stuff like bottling. Coke just creates the juices, teas, and sodas and then sends them to bottlers and distributors—businesses that it partially owns, but doesn't have to manage.
>
> Because its entire line of beverages shares the same distribution system—into restaurants, soda machines, sports stadiums, and supermarkets around the globe—*Coca-Cola can instantaneously launch new products into a mass market*. A fine example is the recent rapid growth of Surge, the drink brewed to compete with Pepsi's Mountain Dew. Within weeks, the company had its citrus-flavored green soda in the hands of customers across the world.
>
> You name the refreshing drink, and Coca-Cola will be offering it in the 21st century.

Da Business Model

Until we begin to develop our own hunches as to why great companies beat their opponents, outperform expectations, and repeat the act one decade after another—until then, we may never be truly confident of our stock market investments. It's true—if you can't explain why certain businesses have thrived, beyond crying, "Luck and magic!" you'll have a difficult time beating the market averages. You need to be able to locate great businesses in order to secure great investment returns. And the only way out is through, right through into the middle of their businesses, into an understanding of how they make money, how they plan to continue making more money each year for their shareholders, and whether those plans are realistic.

At this point you might be thinking, "What am I even *doing* reading this? I mean, I've never read a single book about finance or investing, and now these Fools are telling me that we're going to study *business*, how corporations make money for 'shareholders,' and that I need to assess whether such plans are realistic?! Come off it!"

Hey, hear us out. Because the good news is, it's really not at all difficult. The better news is, in the next few dozen pages we're going to present to you most of the attributes that we find in great stock market investments. And by now you're well familiar with our teaching tools: *the plain English language,* for one, and a certitude that the right answers lie squarely in the ring of common sense, and generally outside the span of conventional Wisdom. So let's take a look at Coca-Cola. What drove the phenomenal growth of a business that has turned investments of a few thousand dollars (that anyone could have made) into hundreds of millions of dollars, in one standard human lifetime?

Six things that we can see. (And six things that most of the best businesses will exhibit.)

REPEAT PURCHASES

Coke has a heck of a setup. Think about it. These guys don't sell you a "one-timer," something that will satisfy you for weeks, months, or years. When you buy a Ford Taurus, chances are you won't be motoring down to the dealership again for another few years, at least. Ditto for the new chandelier in the foyer, or the stuffed sofa in the den. And if you're like us Fools, you try to shop for clothes no more than a handful of times each year.

Little bit of a different business over in Cokeville. The average human being now drinks eleven Coca-Colas per day. In developed nations, kids under the age of thirteen are consuming these pops at the rate of ninety-six cans per week. And a controversial recent market study found that at the rate that infants (children under two years of age) are consuming Coke products today, by the year 2050 most toddlers will be weaned off the candy water, not their mothers' milk.

(OK, OK. So we made some numbers up for the fun of it. You can't blame us. Working to get all the numbers right in a book like this takes effort. Makin' stuff up doesn't, and it's a heck of a lot more fun. But now for something completely different . . . the Real Thing.)

What are the real numbers?

Of the sixty-four daily ounces of liquid consumed by the average human being, the Coca-Cola Company currently serves two. Another way of saying that is that Coca-Cola currently provides more than 3 percent of the liquid intake of the entire population of planet Earth. And because you return over and again to its stuff—whether it's Coke, Diet Coke, Sprite, Mello Yello, Minute Maid orange juice, Surge (heck, maybe you're even drinking some Fruitopia)—because you go back to it habitually, Coke essentially gets constantly repeating promotion at the points of sale and consumption. Those little red cans with cursive logos flash up in your eyes from every angle, whether at the local Giant or on your back porch! Habitual buying becomes its own best marketing plan.

The value of being in a business that creates repeat daily or weekly purchasing from consumers is nearly priceless. We offer this as our lead evidence in the search for great business. There's more. Allow us to pour another Coke before continuing. . . .

BUYERS IN THE BILLIONS

Coca-Cola is not involved in the repeat sale of drinks to an exclusive audience. It wasn't just trying to sell VW Beetles to spirited youths in the 1960s; it isn't targeting its video game machines at children and adolescents; the company likewise isn't engaged in the sale of "cancer sticks" to what will prove a dwindling number of smokers in the decades ahead. Coke isn't exclusive. It sells through to *everyone*, targeting *everyone* with its pricing and promotions.

And, also important, at seventy-five cents or so a can, the soda is affordable for billions of human beings. For this reason, it's an absolutely wonderful product group to dominate. Take a look at the handful of companies that reach the planet with everyday low-price products and you'll see that virtually all have made for consistently superior investments. Makes sense: The more buyers you have, the more defensible your business is. For instance, the loss of any one Coca-Cola customer is irrelevant—customers are just so much plankton to this whale.

Contrast that with the provider of jumbo laces to four major shoe companies. If at some point one of the shoemakers decides to develop its own bright, thick laces, JumboLace Inc. (Nasdaq: LACE) just lost a hunk of its business. And if its laces then go out of fashion with its select group of remaining buyers, roll out the lifeboats because the battleship is going down fast.

Coca-Cola is governed neither by a few business partners nor by a select and fickle audience of consumers. No single lost customer can mortally wound this company. Number a company's buyers in the billions and enable that business to sell through to them each week, each day, each hour (hiccup), and you are en route to a world-beating enterprise, a world-beating stock. Please allow us another swig as we proceed to . . .

A FEW MONSTER BRANDS

Coke has built its business on just a handful of great products, a few monster brands. Can you imagine generating $18.8 billion in sales in a single year, while mainly just selling Coke, Diet Coke, Sprite, Fanta, and Minute Maid? Shouldn't a company that wants a global business in the tens of billions of dollars have to design hundreds or even thousands of products each year, provide ongoing improvements to each, and dramatically lower prices month by month to force out its competitors? In order to win its battle, shouldn't the company nearly kill its management and employees trying?

Nope.

In fact, if you just Foolishly invert each of those notions, you'll have Coke's business pretty well pegged. It offers only a few big-name products, not thousands. Only in a few, notably unsuccessful ways has it ever tried to improve its products (excepting that fateful early decision to steer clear of the medicine business). And after working to ensure the wild success of just a few winners, Coca-Cola actually now possesses more flexibility than most businesses to *raise* its prices. Are you going to much care (or even notice) if the cost of your sixteen-ounce bottle of Coke or Diet Coke rises from seventy to seventy-five cents next week? Will the world battle Coke, with masses brandishing pitchforks and torches stampeding toward corporate headquarters in Atlanta, if the company inches prices up by a few pennies per can from time to time? Probably not; many of us are used to paying $1 or more for it in airports or at cinemas!

As trivial as that measly nickel price hike may be to most buyers, for Coke an extra nickel marks an extra 6.7 percentage points of net profitability. Speaking of which, during the decade between 1988 and 1998, the company improved its "profit margins"—the number of pennies of profit coming from each dollar of sales, expressed as a percentage—from 13 percent to 20 percent. Over the next two years, a frail Asian economy and a European health scare caused profitability to temporarily plummet. The world's strongest companies will all face bumps in the road sooner or later, but even during these tough times, Coke edged out 8 percent net margins. Now, as this is being written, Coke's profitability is beginning to return to its former glory. Most recently, Coke earned 16.5 cents of pure profit on each dollar of sales.

The Coca-Cola story is one of slow and steady refinement. Volume shipments of Coca-Cola beverages as of June 2000 had increased 7 percent over the previous year. That may not sound like much, but 7 to 8 percent volume growth rate has been Coke's average pace for the past seventy years. As Coke steadily expands around the globe, steadily increases its profitability, and steadily captures consumers' hearts through aggressive brand marketing, The Coca-Cola Company is well positioned to reward shareholders with returns far ahead of any savings account out there. Annual compounded growth of 11 percent seems quite achievable.

And that's 11 percent without any annual fees or taxes, as long as you just buy and hold, hold, hold. One thousand dollars invested today with compounded annual growth of 11 percent will become $8,000 in twenty years. If through diligent savings you supplement your initial $1,000 with another grand each year, your Coca-Cola investment would grow to $64,000 at the end of twenty years. That's how to get rich slowly, dear Fool. Swig.

AN IRREPRESSIBLE LOVE OF NUMBERS

The Coca-Cola Company has, more rigorously than perhaps any other company, collected and analyzed its industry data for nearly a hundred years. In its earliest days, the company toted up sales by region, as its syrup traveled from village to village. The marketing guys measured the performance of their advertisements and filed away the lessons they learned. Today, Coca-Cola has reinforced their promotional business with a strict adherence to mathematical reality. (When we say stuff like that—mathematical reality—wow, it's almost time to shut the book. Understood—that does sound kind of Wise. But please understand, dear reader, that by "mathematical reality" we mean nothing more than fifth-grade math—again, *we* use it, *Coke* uses it, and *you* can too.) Here's some of that math (here, addition) that the company presented in its award-winning 1996 annual report to shareholders:

> A billion hours ago . . .
> human life appeared on Earth
> A billion seconds ago . . .
> the Beatles changed music forever
> A billion Coca-Colas ago . . .
> was yesterday morning
> Our challenge:
> to make a billion Coca-Colas ago be this morning . . .

Perhaps in the year 2005 annual report the company's goal will be to make a billion Coca-Colas ago be this *afternoon.* Then, but one hour ago. Then, just the past minute. Then, somewhere in the middle of next century, a billion sold every second. Then . . .

Some say the world will end in fire, Robert Frost wrote, while some say in ice. Others have looked to Nostradamus for predictions about Armageddon; still others see Earth's demise bound up in a nuclear warhead misplaced in rural Russia. Some strange souls even thought, toward the end of last decade, that the Hale-Bopp comet held the key to our dismissal. But who'd'a thunk it was an overdemand of sweetened, caramelized, carbonated water?!

Thankfully, that scenario doesn't seem likely. We Americans have our Justice Department more than ready to step in anytime a company starts selling a billion items of anything per second. Innocent blather aside, Coca-Cola has made statistical work an internal trademark of its global domination. They've spent decades boning up on the numbers of their survival, enabling their systematic expansion of the franchise into new markets, no matter how distant.

Fellow Fool, you now have an extremely well marketed business that every day sells its few wares to billions around the globe and that has a corporate culture practically founded on tracking numerical performance. Yep, this just keeps looking better and better.

AT ALL COSTS, RUNNING AWAY FROM ALL COSTS

We come now to the fifth reason we can see for the phenomenal growth and emergence of the First Federal Bank of Coca-Cola.

For decades, the leader in sales of sugar water has made a practice of reducing expenses and getting itself out of any business that costs too much to manage. This doesn't mean that Coke hasn't blundered repeatedly. In fact, the only reason it would ever need to exit a business is that it had once decided to *enter* the thing in the first place.

In the 1980s, the soft drink giant decided that "synergy" existed between itself and Columbia Pictures. Interesting. The logic went that Coke wouldn't have to pay for expensive product placements in blockbuster films anymore. The two could cross-promote like crazy, with Rambo flicks on bottle caps, and bottle caps in Rambo flicks. The logic did not, however, take into account that running a movie studio takes a good deal of time, a good deal of money, and a good deal of unique creativity. It also may have failed to recognize that it's the *very unusual* film studio that rewards its owners with a steadily growing stream of profits. Before the decade was out, Coke was divesting itself of its cinematic operation at a loss and recommitting to the syruping of the planet, exclusively.

And just as important, the Atlanta management team has worked diligently to strip away as many operational costs as possible from its core business. Coca-Cola doesn't even bottle most of its own drinks! Long ago, the company opted to make a business primarily out of mixing the caramelized corn syrup and soda water and delivering it to outside bottlers. Of course, Coke could certainly have owned all of its bottling operations if it had wanted to, and doing so would have dramatically increased sales. But Coke's CEO, the late Roberto Goizueta, had pointed out again and again that the greatest curse to any business is a worship of sales growth, irrespective of earnings. Publicly owned businesses are not charged with getting larger and breaking even. Quite the contrary. They're expected to stay lean and earn money for their shareholders. By lightening its business, First Fed of Coke has concentrated attention on its earnings.

Before and since, the company has mostly steered clear of the temptations to buy unrelated businesses (no more Columbias) or expand the cost structure on its core business. It instead uses the surplus cash it's building up to repurchase shares of its own stock in the open market. In reducing its overall share amount, Coke inflates earnings per share (and earnings per share growth) even more. It's one of those things that's great to do, if you can possibly afford it. Coca-Cola can, as have so many of the companies into which Warren Buffett has bought.

With just one growth driver still left to trot out, let's now update what we're working with. At this point we have a company selling just a few well known products, to billions of customers each day around the globe, that loves to study the numbers of its operation, and that works furiously to eliminate its business expenses. Can you think of any other companies that meet these criteria? Aha, good.

A Rabbit Before the Dogs

Quietly, Roberto Goizueta, then Coke's CEO, convinced the company that though it's a century old and now valued more richly than almost any other U.S. corporation, Coke is still very much an upstart. By serving a *mere 3 percent* of mankind's daily liquid intake, theoretically the soda giant has a lot of growth opportunity left. Those numbers successfully make an unlikely underdog out of a true overdog.

Yet it isn't a ploy.

Coca-Cola faces the challenge of having to sell more liquids to more people every year until the end of time, or risk disappointing investors on the corner of Wall Street and Broad. Because of this, Coke will expand into more juices, into bottled water—heck, who knows? Maybe it has to get into the rainwater business someday—seeding clouds, collecting the water, and turning it over to global bottlers. Or what about caffeinated milk? More seriously, what the challenge will require is an even more aggressive global-marketing and expansion strategy, and the outright domination of Pepsi.

What Coke has done so well over the past quarter century is to give its employees numerical expectations and to put scorecards in the hands of its shareholders. By aligning the interests of both, by making them all partners in the business, Coke has freed its constituents to imagine opportunities limited only by the rate at which the universe is expanding. If the Coca-Cola Company continues to concentrate on profit margins and numerical success, can it possibly miss additional profitable opportunities that present themselves in time? Sure it could, but we wouldn't bet that way. Barring disaster, in our estimation Coke will continue to make for a world-beating investment in the decades ahead.

Chances are good that $1,000 of KO today will not turn into another

$150 million over the next seven decades. But the jury's out, of course. We'll see. Regardless, the value these shares deliver should stomp the market over decades. Why? To recap, that's because of (1) the company's repeat-purchase products that go out to (2) a huge number of loyal customers every day, despite involving only (3) a few company brand names that are greatly helped by (4) the company's love of numbers, which also helps Coca-Cola (5) eliminate costs in its business. And because management has effectively aligned the interests of employees and shareholders, (6) Coca-Cola feels like a rabbit running from dogs.

Other multibillion-dollar multinationals, eat your heart out.

Coca-Cola would truly today be the first common stock investment we'd make, with the intention of keeping that money in there for at least ten to fifteen years—if possible, for a lifetime. We are suggesting that you use Coca-Cola as your savings bank, which is made even easier by the advent of direct-purchase plans (see "Opening an Account" for more, where you'll discover that you can start with as little as $75 via direct-purchase plans). Through direct-purchase plans you can add small, two-digit sums on a monthly basis to your KO holdings. And even if the company does 5 percentage points worse than its seventy-eight-year annualized returns of almost 17 percent, you should beat the market. And perhaps most important, you would be way ahead of whatever you would have gotten from a certificate of deposit or money-market fund in a "real bank."

Consider banking with Coke.

Obviously Great
Investments

COCA-COLA MAY BE GREAT, but it certainly doesn't possess any monopoly on greatness. It's worth examining several additional companies that, if not equal to the syrup mixer, are at least in the same county. The U.S. markets are in fact swollen with public companies that, by filling a need profitably, have compounded extraordinary growth for their shareholders for decades running. Which companies? Our personal favorites are those that generate a slew of profits while serving the regular needs of the billions of men, women, and children across the globe. We're talking about companies like Microsoft, Gillette, Pfizer, the Gap, Cisco, General Electric, Wrigley, Johnson & Johnson, and Intel.

A nice introduction into this group of Obviously Great Investments is to ask ourselves what sorts of companies we *don't* like, which businesses are best avoided by the individual investor.

First, we don't typically cotton to corporations whose products or services aren't immediately visible to us as consumers. For example, the companies that manufacture parts and equipment for heavy industry, crankshafts for tractors or steel bits for oil rigs. They're never onstage in front of a large assemblage of buyers. Because of this, we have a tougher time studying their wares and assessing customer response.

Second, we aren't interested in businesses that demand very large investments to get started. Ever wonder why so many start-ups these days are of the software and Internet ilk? It's because those businesses take very little money to launch. Five guys with beards and computers that boot are about it. Conversely, restaurants are an excellent example of a very pricey business. First the owners have to lease expensive property, then they have to build a kitchen, then hire a staff, then order the food, manage the inventory, and then shell out more bucks for advertising, and then pay stiff fines to the FDA for spreading mad cow disease. You don't find eighteen-year-olds starting up restaurants across the country for a couple of very good reasons, primarily centered on the subject of money.

And third, we usually don't look to invest in money-losing businesses, including all the operations that have a great story to tell but can't promise earnings anytime in the foreseeable future. We recognize that many early-stage companies can't and shouldn't try to turn a profit right away; that's why we're usually content to wait for them to do it first, or at least to get a lot closer, before we become a part owner. In the odd case in which we do invest in an unprofitable enterprise, it is invariably more than just promise: It is growing dynamically, managed on a plan we understand by people we respect. Otherwise, we don't think it's prudent to invest in latest-rage businesses. Of course, when you find a latest-rage company that *does* make money and that is visible to the consumer, whoa there, look closer. Throughout the mid-1990s, online-service provider America Online was an excellent example, rising more than 10,000 percent. Why? It was the latest-rage, consumer-demand business driving into profitability. Loads of pretenders are out there, though. Beware the profitless latest rage.

If we bring all these attributes together into a single bête noire, it looks like this: a very heavy, very expensive manufacturing business that isn't making money and whose products are invisible to the average consumer. Oh yeah, and big tusks and menacing yellow eyes, as well. Stare into those eyes and you'll see a creature that costs too much money to maintain, doesn't earn you back much, winds up forcing its master to take on debt to support it, and (without a large population of adoring customers) is extremely vulnerable to the whims of its few industrial customers. What if one of them pulls out? No, no, better to have two billion people using your razor or drinking your juice than a few Fortune 500 customers carrying your business.

OK, so if the Fool says to look for consumer-driven, visible businesses that make a lot of money, where should we look first?

Buy What Everyone Knows

Peter Lynch's excellent books *One Up on Wall Street* and *Beating the Street* championed the notion that people ought to make investments in the companies whose products they intimately know and love. Our popular "My Dumbest Investment" discussion board at Fool.com supports this advice. There you'll find investors from around the world sharing horror stories of having "gotten in on" things about which they knew little or nothing. Mining companies in the former Soviet Union, Venezuelan bean futures, and sight-unseen real estate in eastern Montana. Investing in what you don't understand—in what very, very few people understand—is like driving north on I-95 with a shade drawn over your windshield.

But The Fool has a modification to Peter Lynch's "Buy what you know" credo, and that is, *buy what everyone knows*. There's a simple reason for this—that *what you know well could prove a very lousy investment*. Some of you are extremely knowledgeable about electric utilities, but if from 1990 to the summer of 1997 you were restricted to buying only what you understood, you badly lagged the market. Stocks grew at an overall rate of 154 percent, or 14.3 percent per year, over that period, while utilities stocks climbed a mere 9.4 percent, or just 1.3 percent growth per year.

So, our suggestion is that you start out buying what *everyone* knows to be great, products that *everyone* uses, from soft drinks and potato chips to blue jeans and baseball mitts to television shows to movie studios. Start by buying the mass-consumer businesses: Pepsi, Microsoft, Gap, Disney, Wrigley, Nike, Gillette, Johnson & Johnson, Gannett, Wal-Mart—you can guess the rest. This is just a starting point, but it's the best we know.

Our experiences online over the past few years have forced us to recognize just how many people in America have lost good money buying low-grade, unknown, broker-pitched companies with few prospects. As such stocks fall from $3 per share to $1.50 to $0.50 and then dribble off into bankruptcy, consider what has happened to the values of the ten companies we casually tossed out above. Take a look at their stock performance relative to the returns of the stock market (measured by the S&P 500).

TEN-YEAR PERFORMANCE OF SOME CONSUMER GIANTS

	1989	1999*	Return
Microsoft	$1.21	$116.75	9562%
Gap	$1.90	$46.00	2318%
Wal-Mart	$5.61	$69.13	1132%
Nike	$6.66	$49.56	645%
Gillette	$6.14	$41.19	571%
Johnson & Johnson	$14.84	$93.25	528%
Wrigley	$17.88	$82.94	364%
Gannett	$21.75	$81.56	275%
Pepsi	$9.80	$35.25	260%
Disney	$9.33	$29.25	213%
S&P 500	353.4	1469.25	316%

*Numbers updated through December 31, 1999. Stock prices are adjusted for stock splits. Returns are for price appreciation only, and do not reflect reinvested dividends.

When you buy shares of companies that everybody knows, whose products or services we run across every day, you put yourself right into the hotbed of consumer demand. And it's not just plain old short-term mania; these companies have profitably served the planet for years, even quarter centuries. It is that enduring demand which drives the sales and earnings growth that will increase the value of the enterprise. Just what you're looking for. With the right investments, you'll be the first family on your block to take a pony ride around the moon, or to buy that bungalow in the Alps, or to help rebuild what was once a charming wharf in your local district, or shucks, just prepare for your retirement.

If investing can be as easy as buying what *everyone* knows, why do so many people buy penny stocks, gold coins, land without access to well water, limited partnerships, banana futures, mutual funds, and commodities that they know nothing of? Usually they buy them because a broker or financial advisor pitched them hard over the telephone or in a face-to-face meeting. If you take nothing away from our chapters about investing in this book, remember that financial advisors and brokers are paid commissions to sell you certain products. Don't be surprised if your advisor at the firm of Harry Watsworth pushes the Watsworth Emerging Growth mutual fund on you! Most of our financial professionals are trained as salespeople. So do your own research, research that need include nothing more than casually naming the consumer giants whose businesses you expect will survive and succeed in the decade ahead.

But that's not enough—buy what everyone knows? Everyone knew moon boots in the 1970s, but that business died. There has to be more, and is. Start by asking yourself these six questions of companies you're examining.

1. HAVE THEY BUILT A CONSUMER BRAND?

The very first question to ask is, do they have products, services, and brands with which consumers across the globe are familiar? We'll try a few out.

> Wrigley's Spearmint gum? Yep. Pharmos drug delivery services? Nope.
> Gillette razors? Yep. Pitt-Des Moines steel fabricating? Nope.
> MTV? Yes. Cambrex specialty chemicals? Nope.
> Levi's? Yep. Huntway liquid asphalt? Nope.

Your first filter is just to drive out any of the nine thousand or so public companies in the United States that your grandfather, uncle, cousin, and daughter can't all access easily in their daily lives. They may not all watch MTV, but they probably all know of it, or at least they all have access to it. Your ideal business is going to be the one that they all know about, that they all use, that they all buy from week in and week out, and that makes money from them doing so.

Find the businesses that have built a global consumer brand you know and that almost everyone around you knows. Once done, move to question 2.

2. ARE THEY THE BEST IN THEIR BUSINESS?

Choosing a best over a second best isn't always terribly easy. There's no question that today Coca-Cola is beating Pepsi around the planet. Nike has really taken Reebok to task. But the battle between numbers one and two can be difficult to call over any ten-year period. Maybe next year a handful of key employees and executives move from one to the other. Maybe a hotshot creative mind joins the second-place business. Maybe lawsuits or other extraordinary circumstances hammer the leader. Figuring out which will be the best over the long haul can be tricky. But distinguishing the top two or three from the rest of the pack typically isn't. In soda, you have Coke and Pepsi. In computers, Dell and Compaq. In casual clothing, Gap and Levi's and Tommy Hilfiger. In any given group, you can distinguish the superior two or three businesses from the rest.

Do so.

We do not think it's a good idea to invest in businesses trying to turn around or trying to become a top-tier competitor after years of slumber. In this category, we suggest that you find the best of the lot, do a few minutes of research into their financial situation (which we'll consider in a bit), and then buy and hold the strongest among them. And hold them for decades. But wait, don't buy yet. We have two qualities nailed down: consumer brand and best of breed. But there are more. Read on.

3. DO PEOPLE BUY THEIR STUFF REGULARLY?

Coca-Cola gains free marketing every time you plug seventy-five cents into one of their big red machines and punch up a Coke. You step up to their machine, press the button with their soda can pictured on it, drink down their drink, and recycle their can. If you're like the average American, you drink a Coca-Cola every other day. Thus, each week, Coca-Cola gets a free series of advertisements with every man, woman, and child in America in the form of the looks you get at their product when you use it. And that relationship with a brand, that loyalty, runs deep. Just try taking your average young woman's breakfast can of Diet Coke away from her. Yikes.

When selling products through to consumers, marketing is often the greatest expense, and thus engenders the greatest risk. To gain free daily promotion from product sales is a wonderful thing. Check out all these Internet companies vying for consumer enthusiasm. They are losing money off the marketing fees, not much else. And it's exactly how they should lose money, if they want to win in the future. They are aiming to build daily interaction with their readers, and a global brand. If they win, it's a huge win.

For this reason, we suggest that you study most carefully those businesses that are frequent servants of their global base of customers. Those that have that daily relationship with their customers gain free daily promotion. Or rather, they make money promoting themselves, via the sales of their stuff. Contrast that with the car companies that pour out tremendous amounts of money to attract buyers for that once-every-few-years purchase.

Compare *that* model to Gap, Coke, Nike, or Johnson & Johnson—where buyers return daily, weekly, or monthly for more stuff. This is one of the reasons Charlie Munger at Berkshire Hathaway calls Coca-Cola the greatest business in our nation's history. It's why Warren Buffett maintains that if you gave him $100 billion in cash and said, "Warren, go out and beat Coke," he'd give it back and say, "It can't be done." Businesses that become brand leaders selling directly through to the consumer daily or weekly are in excellent position to be named Obviously Great.

4. ARE THEY MAKING A LOT OF MONEY FOR THEIR EFFORTS?

This varies quite a bit, and, of course, companies fight through all sorts of changes. At times, giants have to endure huge short-term costs to get out of grimly declining markets and into hip-hop, happening markets. But in general, what you want to find is companies that make more than seven cents off every dollar of sales (after taxes), and you'll generally want those companies to be experiencing (or driving) a consistent rise in that rate of profitability. You want to invest in the giants who really do create economies of scale as they charge into foreign markets or debut new businesses here at home. Thus far, the model Obviously Great Investment is looking like a brand leader that sells to the consumer frequently, with profit margins on the rise.

Many well known companies aren't profitable enough to make this cut. As enormous as General Motors' sales are, its earnings line is strikingly small. In 1999, General Motors had $176 billion in sales yet turned less than $6 billion in profit. The profit margin, the amount of money GM made on each dollar of sales, was about 3 percent. Contrast that with Merck, provider of PepcidAC; they have profit margins above 18 percent. For every dollar of sales, they make 18 cents in earnings. Smashing. We like to see net margins above 7 percent.

5. ARE THEY FUNDING NEW GROWTH WITH THEIR OWN MONEY?

Put Donald Trump and Bill Gates into a boxing ring, and Trump will win
the first two rounds. He'll push the Boy Wonder back into the corner and
beat him mercilessly. But even as the fight moves into just the middle
rounds, Trump won't have anything left. His knees will wobble like tooth-
picks. Gates will skip-rope dance in front of him, waving his mitts flam-
boyantly, playing to the crowd before the big knockout in the sixth.

Donald Trump borrowed $1.7 billion to run his casinos in Atlantic City.
His debt is financed at 13 percent per year—in other words, that $1.7 bil-
lion in long-term debt is demanding annual interest payments of over $200
million. (A bit more than most people have racked up on their credit cards,
though the interest rates aren't terribly different!) And this is all happening
in the middle of a rather glorious bull market helped along by low interest
rates, with the Fed worried about inflation and mediocre sports athletes
bringing in million-dollar annual salaries.

Contrast that with Mr. Gates's business. Microsoft today has more than
$17 billion in *cash,* just sitting there earning interest. The company turned
thirty-nine cents in profit off every dollar of sales last quarter and is sitting
over a burgeoning global network desperately in need of programming improvements. Not a bad seat in the theater, we'd say.

Trump's style of business wins early leads, celebrity, and an ongoing series of buxom babes. By contrast, Gates's style involved not selling any of
his company to the public for eleven years (oft-overlooked in the search for
the "next Microsoft") and the relentless pursuit of earnings growth without
external funding. There is no debt on the Microsoft balance sheet.

If you're going to invest for a lifetime in search of enduring profits, you
probably want to put your chips down on the businesses that will dominate
their industries in the later rounds—the ones that don't borrow a lot of
money or sell a lot of stock to raise cash.

6. HAVE THEY BEEN A SUCCESS UP UNTIL NOW?

Past success certainly doesn't correlate infallibly with future success. But
it *is* an important indicator, which may be pretty Foolish of us to assert in
a world whose ubiquitous legal disclaimers reinforce the idea that past performance is no indication of future success.

Oh yeah? Take a look at the Obviously Great Investments. They've each succeeded for years and years, and that success has carved them dominant industry positions that even further ensure their future success. And our "past success" rule needn't be confined to companies. It works for individuals and groups of people as well, whether we're talking about the San Francisco 49ers, Meryl Streep, Paul Simon, Oprah, or Steven Spielberg.

How do you find how stocks have done over the past five years?

Well, you can often obtain a free copy of the *S&P Stock Guide* from your discount brokerage firm (we'll talk about opening up a brokerage account later). In it you'll find a section entitled "Total Return % Annualized." Go to the "Total Return 60 Mo" column and flip through the guide circling every stock that has compounded more than 30 percent growth annually over the past five years. Certainly, this rate of growth won't and can't continue unabated. We can't have 124 companies owning the whole world fifty-seven times over, twenty years from now. It won't happen! But many of these companies will continue to grow at market-beating rates. As an investor, what you will be doing is climbing on the backs of businesses to carry you to savings growth. This final suggestion is to ensure that you first climb up on the shoulders of giants, and ride

Show Me Some Companies, Fool

We'll do just that. Of the nine-thousand-plus publicly traded businesses in America, you'll be hard pressed to find more than a few dozen that meet the six criteria outlined above. The businesses that pour operational might into the consumer space, plow their cash into gaining competitive advantages, and work tirelessly to satisfy the needs of their customers are few and far between. There are plenty of pretenders. Each of us can list off a few dozen consumer businesses that feign a love for the people but whose products or services eventually lose their luster. A shortsighted and deceitful management team can blow smoke into the mirrors only so long. Eventually, consumer demand sheds light on the charade and the business is rent asunder.

Let's study in a bit more depth a couple of outstanding operations, both of which appear to be engaged in a virtual love-in with the world while roundly boxing the ears of their competitors. Both have generated extraordinary growth for investors and provided superior products and services for their customers. Both of these household names employ thousands of people around the planet; both make an awful lot of money from the daily operation of their business. Travel along with us as we journey from razor blades to running shoes, from blue jeans to Band-Aids, from soda cans to software.

MICROSOFT (NASDAQ: MSFT)

The Consumer Brand

When Microsoft launched Windows98 with all the hoopla of an Oakland Athletics game under Charlie Finley, the company further solidified itself as a consumer brand that Americans love to use and, apparently, love to envy.

The Best in the Business

We probably shouldn't even go near this one, eh! Microsoft has long been accused of simply duplicating Apple's Macintosh operating systems, licensing them everywhere, charging less, and outpromoting its original creators at every turn. Unfortunately for Apple Macintosh fans, this subtitle reads "The Best in the *Business*." Without question, in the world of programming, Microsoft has run away as the leader of the group. By concentrating on providing functional software at the lowest price to the greatest number of users, Bill Gates has made a business out of what others have treated purely as an art.

Repeat-Purchase Business

Microsoft will be moving increasingly into a world of repeat-purchasing business. To date, Microsoft has been relegated to selling onetime software applications with annual or biannual upgrades. With the Internet opening up new distribution channels and with Microsoft's partnerships with NBC and cable giant Comcast, the company will increasingly be getting out in front of consumers each and every day. Where there is promotion, dear Fool, and where there is distribution, there will certainly be product sales. Expect Microsoft to inch down into a daily repeat-purchasing business in the decades ahead.

Profit Margins Above 7 Percent

Microsoft presently has annual profit margins of 41 percent, the most extraordinary of any company with more than $2 billion in sales. By spinning out such substantial profits from operations, Microsoft has accumulated over $17 billion in cash without a single borrowed dollar to pay back.

Zero or Declining Debt

Nope, not a single dollar of debt hangs over Microsoft's head.

Past Performance

What better place to start than Microsoft Corporation, the company whose stock has appreciated at a rate of more than 60 percent per year since its initial public offering (IPO), in 1986. Investors who had plinked down $10,000 at its unspectacular IPO are now sitting on more than $8 million in pretax profits.

Microsoft meets our criteria. Let's take a look at the Gap!

Gap (NYSE: GPS)

The Consumer Brand

From its advertisements with the hip-hoppingest, most happening Fools in the country, splayed all over magazines, to Gap signs on outfield fences at baseball parks around the nation, the company has done an extraordinary job of getting its name out. Whether wee Fools are poking around GapKids or stylish literati are sorting through summer blazers at Banana Republic—a subsidiary of Gap—the San Francisco–based operation has done a brilliant job of getting itself out in front of the world.

The Best in the Business

Who's the best in the business when it comes to casual clothing? Is it Gap? Or Ralph Lauren? Or Tommy Hilfiger? Or the Limited? Each of them has its merits, but to our eyes Gap is pretty much the runaway leader in serving folks of all shapes, sizes, and ages for maximal profit. Rather than expanding internationally too speedily, Gap has worked to nail down the world of denim in America—posting Gap stores on seemingly every block in major urban areas before once setting foot in Asia. Now, whether you think Gap is the best of the casual clothiers or just one of the few best, its performance and its financial standing make it an Obviously Great Investment.

Repeat-Purchase Business

Make a point in the weeks ahead of surveying your friends on how often they buzz into the large Old Navy stores or Gaps around the corner. The responses might startle you. Parents, young professionals, college students, and high-schoolers are swarming repeat-purchasers of slacks and T-shirts. Though buying clothing isn't as regular as bringing a razor to your leg or face, or tipping back a can of caramel bubbly, or squeezing out a slug of toothpaste on a red Reach brush, or chewing gum first thing in the morning (bleck!), nonetheless, the buying is repetitive enough to afford Gap a whole lot of free marketing.

Profit Margins Above 7 Percent

Gap has profit margins of 8.5 percent and has gradually and surely driven those margins higher year after year. Just as McDonald's makes the lion's share of its profits on the soda and french fries, Gap brings home the bacon from the popularity of its unspectacular stuff: blue jeans, T-shirts, slacks, and button-downs. One ought not to worry much about the success of Gap's spring or fall fashion lines. The profits are in the most frequently purchased items, the stuff that's always there, the simple denim that you'll find in everyone's closet.

Zero or Declining Debt

Gap actually no longer qualifies on this score. Whereas in 1997 Gap carried no debt, today it carries over $700 million in long-term debt. Not too coincidentally, Gap has fared quite poorly in the market over the last couple of years.

Past Performance

Gap stock has returned more than 350 percent growth for its shareholders over the past decade, churning out an over–16 percent rate of annual returns. What is notable about Gap's performance is that, because it is in an industry that is severely hurt by any economic downturns, the stock has gotten obliterated over various short terms en route to this substantial, long-term outperformance of the market. But over longer periods, it has thrived.

OTHER PLACES TO LOOK

Beyond Coca-Cola, Microsoft, and the Gap, Fools should take a peek at our online portfolio dedicated to "Rule Maker" investments at Fool.com. There are loads more Obviously Great Investments. From Nike and Tiger Woods to Cisco's Internet routers to Pfizer's Visine drops to Dell Computers and Band-Aids from Johnson & Johnson, great American businesses have been churning out enormous rewards for their *investing* shareholders—to be distinguished from Wall Street's commissioned traders. Join us online, pitch in some of your own ideas, and consider alternatives to three great businesses: Coca-Cola, Microsoft, and Gap.

In your own research, though, just continue to keep your eyes open at your daily and weekly habits. Do you watch numerous Disney films, and is your daughter frequently seen bounding through the living room in her Mickey ball cap? Are you addicted to salty chicken-and-noodle soup from Campbell's? Was your spouse just spotted having the family credit card scanned in for large purchases at Nordstrom's again this week? Whenever some unethical yet seemingly invincible Wise man acts arrogantly—say, claiming before Congress that nicotine isn't addictive—do you turn to your bottle of Merck's PepcidAC for relief?

Once you've located the arm's-length businesses that you return to again and again, mark them down on a page, bring them with you online or to your investment club, get the company phone numbers there, send away for their financial information, and walk through the above criteria step by step. Are they making more than seven cents in profits for every sales dollar? Are they borrowing money to fund operations? Do you consider them one of the best at what they do? And how has their stock done over the past five- and ten-year period—has it beaten the S&P 500? All the information you need is readily and easily available; and looking here, working with others, and eventually buying stock in what you believe in most and holding it for many years to come will enable you, too, to explain to any familiar face you see, "Yes sir and ma'am, I'm a Fool."

A Less-Obvious Obviously Great Investment

It's worth mentioning, of course, that not every Obviously Great Investment conforms to the model. Some of them you can locate just by keeping your eyes open, and not allowing yourself to be distracted by trifles. Such is the case with an Obviously Great Investment like Intel (Nasdaq: INTC).

Hey, you may not know exactly what a semiconductor chip is, or how many transistors the company can fit on its new Pentium IV chip. You may not even use computers very frequently, or even at all. But if you'd just been reading the newspapers at any point over the past couple of years, you'd know that Intel makes the "motherboards" (a.k.a. the brains) that run most of the computers around the world today.

Step back and ask yourself a couple of basic questions such as, "Do I think computers are an important industry?" And, "Do I see significant future growth for computers?" The affirmative answer has been obvious for years now, and we don't see any sign of that changing. Intel has been dominating this market for a decade, and blowing away its competition. Yet, many of us who were aware of the story all along (and you may include your humble authors in this group) have not bought and held positions in Intel stock. How stupid are we? Well, we should be banished from planet Earth. In fact, let's do step off the planet for a bit and take an alternative look at this story from our perch in outer space. For thereby hangs a tale.

NASA launched the *Galileo* mission in 1989, for the purpose of obtaining a thoroughgoing look at Jupiter. The spacecraft acquired the name *Galileo* because it was that Italian astronomer who first observed Jupiter's four big moons in 1610, through his tiny self-made telescope. We've sent smaller probelike spacecraft out there in the past (*Voyager*, before *Galileo*), but none had ever established a long-term orbit to make detailed observations.

After six years of travel, the *Galileo* spacecraft finally first arrived at Jupiter in December 1995. In all, the craft performed some dozen orbits in its two-year mission around the planet. Its purpose was to monitor and study Jupiter's atmosphere and investigate its moons.

But this story's ultimately about computers, not interplanetary exploration. If you drop in to NASA's huge Web site, you can see a stunning "before/after" shot of the surface of Ganymede (Jupiter's largest moon). The "before" shot comes from *Voyager 2,* a picture taken in 1979; it is exceptionally blurry. The "after" comes to us circa 1996 from *Galileo's* significantly more powerful computers, and staring at it, one couldn't wish for a higher resolution; it's crisp as a fresh nacho.

A span of *seventeen* years separates those two shots, and the improvement in resolution was a factor of . . . exactly *seventeen* times.

Impressed? Now ask yourself this: What sorts of computers on board the *Galileo* took the awesome high-resolution shot of Ganymede's surface, anyway? If you said, "Pentiums," go directly to Jail, do not pass GO, do not collect $200. Remember, the *Galileo* spacecraft left Earth in 1989.

If you answered instead, "8-bit machine comparable to an old Apple II," you got it right. The processors aboard that craft ran at a "clock speed" of 1.6 megahertz (MHz), about forty-one times slower than the top speed of Intel's moribund 486 chip. The Pentium that we used to type up this manuscript runs at 333 MHz, more than *two hundred times* the computing power aboard the *Galileo.*

Should this make us feel guilty, or what? Our silly little computer blows away the ones aboard the *Galileo,* and most of us aren't doing much more than word processing or clicking around HTML Web pages!

So what's the lesson for investors? It's obvious! Learn about technology. We are living through the most rapid advance of technology in the history of mankind, and history will show that the financial commentators who constantly forecast doom for technology stocks were imbeciles!

A second lesson to investors is the same one that applies to most Obviously Great Investments: Consider picking up some shares in this company if you haven't already. At any given moment, it probably looks quite expensively priced. But that's been the case many times over the past decade, and you wouldn't ever have gone wrong before by just buying it and holding it. The company's ongoing mission has been to double the speed of computers every eighteen months, then halve the prices.

Sometimes you have to be 370 million miles away from Earth to really recognize how Obviously Great this is.

The Six Obviously Not Great Qualities

It wouldn't be right to shout out rahs and whoops in celebration of all the qualities that we think make for a great business without considering the other side of the fence. How can we know if our garden really does grow the greenest unless we peek over the fence? With that in mind, let's take a look at the inverse of some of the principles we just championed. We believe these qualities make companies less attractive or unattractive for investors.

1. NOT A CONSUMER BRAND: HUNTWAY LIQUID ASPHALT

Neither we nor America gets enthused about the applications of liquid asphalt on roads and rooftops across the land. Chances are, tens of millions of consumers aren't going to begin stocking up on liquid asphalt soon. To us, this means that if any great profit were to be had, Huntway would have a tough time defending it. How so? Well, it's tough to unseat Nike now because so many people love it. But if Huntway Liquid Asphalt began generating overhealthy profits, competitors would jump in. It is considerably easier to compete and ultimately sink a business that has very few total customers. Huntway has lost over 90 percent of its value as a company over the past eight years—during the strongest bull market in our nation's history.

2. NOT THE BEST IN THE BUSINESS: L.A. GEAR

We'll confess it, we never liked L.A. Gear's approach to promotions—loud commercials featuring aggressive dunks and bad sportsmanship. Courage and heroism didn't find their way into L.A. Gear shoes—only attitude did. The success of its business, which sat smack in the middle of the consumer space, relied upon its ability to gradually but greatly expand its base of customers each year. But the company committed itself to short-term wins, never aspiring to be the best servant of the people. Yes, this is a qualitative read. But it was evident pretty early on that Reebok and Nike would sprint away from L.A. Gear, which went through Chapter 11 bankruptcy in 1998 and is now a private company.

3. NOT A REPEAT-PURCHASE BUSINESS: BOMBAY COMPANY

How many times were you planning to buy Bombay furniture from your local mall? Did you plan to refurbish your living room four times over the next thirty-six months? Bombay Company learned a few lessons the hard way. As it desperately tried to race down into knickknacks that you might buy every week, it lost control of inventories on its larger items. And because people weren't about to furnish their den weekly, Bombay had to spend more and more money to promote itself, to remind America that it was out there. Is the net result that this furniture business might not be a good one to invest in for a protracted period of time? Yep. Bombay has lost 90 percent of its value over the last eight years—during the . . . you know the rest.

4. NOT MAKING GOOD MONEY: PLANET HOLLYWOOD

Restaurants are notoriously difficult businesses to run. Once you've leased favorable property, loaded in your cooking equipment, staffed up for service, and built up an inventory of food—which might need inspection—you still haven't gotten the word out about your business. Gasp. Though many are fascinated by the idea of "running their own eatery," most make for very bad investments. Planet Hollywood is a fine example of a restaurant considered to be a "hot property" that then disintegrated. Even before its celebrity owners abandoned associating their names with it any longer, Planet Hollywood ran a low-margin business. It turned less than 5 cents of profit on every dollar of sales, even when it was *cooking*. We look for businesses with profit margins of at least 7 percent, better yet above 10 percent, ideally above 15 percent. During the most sustained roaring bull market ever, Planet Hollywood saw its value evaporate—as it filed for bankruptcy in 1999.

5. HEAVILY LADEN WITH DEBT: TRUMP HOTELS & CASINO RESORTS

Donald Trump has a way with the banking community. Trump has been able to raise big money to fund his Atlantic City casinos, even though profits have been elusive. As of this writing, The Donald owes $1.7 billion, with interest payments of over $200 million per year. At the same time, Trump Hotels & Casino Resorts is valued at about $60 million total. Wow! We avoid companies that have to borrow heavily to finance daily operations. During the year after its public offering, Trump Resorts lost more than 65 percent of its total value.

6. NOT PERFORMING VERY WELL: KMART

Like all the companies in this exclusive group, Kmart's stock has not performed well. The discount retailer has not expanded into great profit, and shareholders have been hammered with a loss in value of more than 70 percent in the past seven years. Too often when investing, you'll hear the legal disclaimer toll, "Past performance is no indication of future results." Well, it's no guarantee, but we believe it certainly is a relevant indicator. A consistently rising stock is a fine indicator of a consistently strengthening business.

Conclusion

There are exceptions to every rule proposed here. Some companies with debt end up doing extraordinarily well, as growth from their financing allows them easily to pay back their creditors. Other companies that aren't making good money today begin making great money next year. Still other stocks that have gotten walloped then benefit from new management, a new perspective, and provide investors with steep rewards. All of these have happened and will happen again. Our feeling, however, is that the odds favor those investors who buy winning consumer franchises.

The Foolish Operating Manual
for Obviously Great Investments

Before you open an account with any kind of broker, before you buy a single share of stock, let's take a look at all you've learned from a slightly different angle: What are the operating advantages of my Obviously Great *portfolio*? We consider the following five notions critical to your success.

1. NO EXHAUSTIVE RESEARCH

The most common reason people give for why they don't invest their own money is that they think it will take an unreasonable amount of time. Capitalism in the new millennium is proving time intensive. Take a casual stroll down any street in any major urban area in America and you'll spot six guys in suits talking to their cellulars, seven managers in a mad midday rush for the deli, and you'll hear the horns, sirens, and shouts of the hordes rushing who knows where at top speed. The age of wheeling and dealing is upon us. It brings a burst of new ideas from every corner. It is exhilarating. It will lead to a speedier flow of spectacular innovations than anyone ever imagined possible. But living in it means that most of us don't have an awful lot of time.

If you think you don't have the time to invest in stocks intelligently, you're wrong. Buying cuts of ownership in our greatest businesses needn't take more than twelve hours a year. An hour a month — that's less time than you spent watching B movies on television last week! The challenging task is to figure out what information is important, what isn't, which activities are necessary to your success, and which aren't, and then to act accordingly.

If you assemble the right model, you will not waste time staring at 9,000 ticker symbols on a green-lit monitor, or living and breathing financial television, or researching brokerage pitches. Furthermore, you really won't have to study the performance of your investments more than once every six months. Ideally, you'll need to look only once a year. Watch the business, not the ticker. One of the more eloquent fellows who post on our Web site goes by the name of Doubting Thomas. He wrote the following:

"In the end, I doubt that I'll look back on my life and remember the good times I had monitoring the price of a particular stock."

Bravo! Investing is meant to support your ideals and dreams, not distract you from them. Remember that once you've invested, you are counting on the employees and management of that business to earn you profit. You are not steering their ship. A number of very active traders actually believe that by watching ticker symbols tick and tock each minute, they're somehow managing the business. They storm shareholders' meetings and preach executive strategies to investor-relations departments' voice mail machines. Perhaps they will never wake up and realize that while it involves owning, investing is not managing. And really, thank heavens for that. If you pick the best companies, you won't have to worry about monitoring the daily operations of the companies you own. Let them do the work.

Finally, it will become clear to you that your challenge isn't to find hordes of new companies to research, or to ram through a dozen newsletters each month, or to scour the financial news for the latest momentum stock. You won't need to subscribe to expensive research products, consider ten different industries, forty different stocks each year, and try to make sense of it all. Instead, your successes will be determined by how well you can save money and how strong are the few businesses you've selected. If $4,000 invested in Coca-Cola stock decades back is worth over $600 million today—well, what lessons can we take from that? Perhaps that finding even just a few great companies and adding money to them each year will make for a smashingly successful investment career.

2. NO ANXIETY

The second most common reason that people resist buying stock is the perceived stress that comes with it. What happens if you lose it all! Your spouse will pack suitcases and head back to live in the old neighborhood, alone. You will wander from town to town taking odd jobs, working as a blacksmith, then a boatswain on the tourist tugboat on the Potomac River. Gasp! What happens if you lose it all and your kids are forced to work full time down at the mall at age twelve! What happens if you lose it ALLLLL!

Please turn back to pages 150 to 151 and look at the Dow graph.

The trend of the average stock is northward. While you may lose half your investment over the first three years, if you selected quality companies or bought the whole market via an index fund, no few sour market years are going to hinder the long-term growth in your savings. There's no cause for stress if you take the market on your own terms. Let the short-term fluctuations horrify the rest of the investment world. You're in for the long haul.

3. NO FOREIGN LANGUAGES

Here's a simple notion that works whenever you have your wallet, credit card, ATM card, or brokerage account number and password handy: If you don't understand what you're hearing, walk away. In any big-money trans-action—from car buying to insurance to stock purchases—if you can't ex-plain entirely what you're doing, why you're doing it, and what to expect from it, don't make the investment.

So much in the traditional money world has been designed to confuse you. Before the birth of the Internet and the advent of Folly, you operated alone against corporate armies trained to extract another few hundred or thousand dollars from your accounts each year. For years now, your aver-age financial-products salesman has known that you are all alone, unedu-cated on financial matters, and anxious just to get the deal signed. Full-service commissioned brokers would love to hear you say, "Don, just don't lose it. I have no idea what it all means. But just don't lose my sav-ings money." Even if his name isn't Don! This clears him to grind or churn your account through active trading, generating a little sugar for himself on each trade.

Until you understand what you're doing, your money should be in the bank walking in step with inflation. Don't try to speak foreign languages to make money, though. You don't need them. This model of saving, co-operative learning, and long-term investments in Obviously Great Compa-nies is predicated on the notion that the average Fool can be methodical and patient and that he already understands the people's attraction to soda pop, blue jeans, running shoes, and online services.

4. No Buy Points

There are really no buy points with these models—no magic moment when you *must* purchase your picks. The aim is to find a small group of the most financially sturdy, most profitable, best-performing, best-of-breed, strongest-brand, most professionally managed public U.S. companies. When you find them, you can buy them and turn your eyes away from the stock market. There are other things in life, and you have years—if not decades—to let the power of market-beating compounded returns work for you.

Now if you buy and hold great stocks, you will have successfully tiptoed through an industry buoyed by overpriced information and conveniently supportive jargon. Many Foolish investors believe the most valuable finan-cial services out there are the ones that are free—the guides and books that sit in our public libraries. With a dash of cogent research, a sprinkle of basic business principles, and a heavy load of patience, investors needn't worry about what the present prices are of the stocks in their portfolio.

In fact, the idea of "buying low" and "selling high" is essentially absurd for investors looking to make money over the next thirty years. For them, the better line is: Buy smart, buy when you can, and buy again when you have more cash you can put away for at least three to five years. Invest it into these cash-strong, rapidly growing, strong-brand, well-managed U.S. companies. And when a decade has passed, go ahead and run the same screen for the next phenomenal group—for which, no doubt, many of your original picks will still qualify.

As mentioned earlier, Warren Buffett has been quoted thus: "What I have done is actually remarkably unremarkable." He didn't buy expensive neural-network software, $500 newsletters, pricey research reports; he didn't read whisper columns in daily newspapers, hot tips in glossy financial magazines, or any of the wonderful and various financial sources fashioned to tell you when precisely to BUY! and when exactly to SELL! stocks. These may be just the resources that will help you get beaten *by* the market. Engage the market on your own terms, and consider doing so worrying far less about the timing of your entry than about the quality of your selections.

5. No Great Expense

Ever heard a money manager on financial television cry, "Yeah, I bought in at thirty-three and a quarter, I sold at thirty-five and an eighth. I scalped a point and three-quarters!"? Never mind that his math is wrong; his use of language seems flawed to us as well. We believe he ought to be using the *passive* voice to describe the scalping since, in actuality, the brokerage firm and tax man will eat most of that. Unless you have more than $500 million to invest, we don't think it's a good idea to furiously trade your selected investments. Leave active trading up to the mutual fund managers, more than 80 percent of whom underperform the market each year. Buying Obviously Great Investments is a play on market outperformance *and* the minimizing of all associated costs.

It is fundamental to our investment methodology that you not spend a great deal of money on research materials (Fool.com is free), that you not pay out large sums of money in commissions or taxes, and that you not get hit with significant opportunity costs—like skipping the river swim with your family next Saturday in order to stem the flow of losses from your options trading.

Investing Foolishly demands that you follow the lead of the Los Angeles Lakers when they dominated basketball in the 1980s. Do you know what their team motto was . . . ?

  a. Win at all costs!
  b. No guts, no glory!
  c. Kill or be killed!
  d. No activity without reward

If you circled letter *d,* you nailed it. No activity without reward. No work without enduring profit. The same should hold true for your investing approach. Unless you can show markedly improved returns by spending more time, and unless you enjoy spending that additional time, a good blend of obvious greats and an index fund are enough for the whole of your life.

Conclusion

What we believe we Fools have identified is a low-commission, low-stress, low-commitment approach to outperforming the S&P 500—the market index that most "professional" investors lose to while still sleeping well at night. That's right, the same people who tell you in their masters tournament advertisements that investing is no less complex than flying a DC-10 blind through snowstorms in the Himalayas have been roundly beaten by the simpleton investor, casually plunging money into great companies each month, quarter, or year. And, yes, the same Wise men who call you during dinner, talking up $3 foreign stocks or trying to sell you on the next sizzling IPO—these same yo-yos who eat away percentages of your portfolios in trading commissions—they have never put up long-term numbers that can compare with those Warren Buffett has posted for four decades running.

Name us Foolish because we don't believe you have to learn how to guide an aircraft through the mountains or answer brokerage phone calls during dessert to invest successfully. As Peter Lynch has noted numerous times, the diligent small investor has a huge advantage over Wall Street—

because the only master she need bow to is herself. As a private investor, she is not motivated to diversify into twenty-five different products; she needn't be in any rush during her decision-making process; and she won't win a single commission payment for selling herself a basket of penny stocks over the phone. (If she tried, people might think she was losing it!)

Fool, if you stick to giant consumer brands at the start of your investment career, they'll provide a wonderful launch to your investment journey, as life shoots you out into worlds thousands of miles from your front door. The possibility exists that you may never want to leave this group of investments; you may never want to alter the simple approach spelled out above. That's fine. We think you'll thrive. But still, you do have more than you think. You have that brain. And you've got other people, and you have plenty of time, and more money coming in from your salary checks. You might very well want to modify the Obviously Great Investments model as you see fit. Heck, we expect to make minor modifications to it in the decades ahead online. Modifications are constantly discussed and analyzed in our online real-money portfolios in Fooldom. The marketplace, like life, is fluid. Figuring out when you have to adapt to survive, then figuring out how much you need to adapt to survive, then determining the happiest means to do so—it seems like a rather Foolish approach. Test our model here, modify it, e-mail us your results, and enjoy yourself.

OK, enough advice already! You feel ready to start investing. But there's one last problem. The final reason that people don't get started investing is purely an administrative, organizational one. They don't get started 'cause they don't know how to open an investment account or think the process will be a hassle. Not so, nay, not so.

Aiming to clear up these misconceptions and get you on your way, we've titled the next chapter . . .

Opening an Account

B Y NOW, EITHER you're willing to get started investing or you never will be. In one sense, you're already off to a great start. You're already well aware of the importance of compounding long-term returns, you've learned the few terms you need to get started and found the right investments for your first portfolio. You may even have spent some months running your portfolio on paper for practice, as a sort of make-believe market. Well, you're now ready to open an account.

Ah, but first a humorous digression. The first edition of *The Motley Fool Investment Guide* arrived at the stores in early 1996, and as tradition in the book trade has it, we did the book tour thang and hit the talk-show circuit. We schmoozed with Charlie Gibson on *Good Morning America,* sat in the shadows with Charlie Rose on his PBS show, did all the financial cable shows you'd imagine we'd do, and got up at god-awful hours to do morning shows in major metropolitan areas (now *there* is a group of people to admire: the journalists, producers, writers, and cameramen who have the gumption to rise at 4:30 A.M. every morning to run our nation's good-morning shows). We sat down for one print interview after another, from *People* magazine to *Computer Retail Week* to the *Contra Costa Times.*

In every instance, we patiently attempted to spell out the investment world in the simplest, most amusing terms possible. And you know what? We were imbeciles. We figured this out later.

You see, we were giving huge numbers of viewers and readers passable investment advice, *without* most of them even knowing how to open an account. Most didn't even know what the phrase "brokerage account" meant!

"Fool me once, shame on you," the saying goes; "fool me twice, and shame on my market research people." We will not make that mistake again. So here we are with our definitive Foolish chapter on opening an account.

Brokerage accounts are really simple. They are little different from the bank accounts that most of us set up at some point during or after high school. In fact, brokerage firms look very much the same as banks, minus the teller windows. You may never even discover this, though; in many cases, brokerage account holders never visit their branch. To open an account, you just call a firm's office, either locally or via an 800 number, and request the forms you must fill out in order to create your account. You then deposit into it some "assets," generally money or existing investments of whatever kind. Upon depositing your money, you receive an account number. Ever afterward, you can call your broker, give your account number, and trade your account. And there's not much more to it than that.

Before opening an account, you'll first need to figure out where. We recommend coming up with a list of three to eight prospects, then calling each one for an information packet. Read them over and learn everything you can about each, just as you would for a company in which you're considering investing.

You have two primary options, either (1) using a full-service broker or (2) using a discount broker. By now, you probably already know how we answer this question. We recommend in most cases using a discount broker.

Full-service brokers will do a heck of a lot for you: generate investment ideas, give you stock quotes, manage your account if needed, provide investment research materials, help you with tax information, the works. Some of our good friends are full-service brokers, and they work hard for their clients. Unfortunately, these are mainly nice people working in a bad system. The new printing press is here, and the scribes don't have much to offer anymore, especially at far higher costs than the discount brokers who've shown up.

As we wrote earlier, full-service brokers who give advice are essentially salesmen, shopping around their brokerage house's stock picks or fund picks and getting paid a percentage (the commission) for every "sale" they make. So you see, your full-service broker may be paid not for how well you do (which is in your best interest, obviously), but rather on how often you trade (often the opposite of your best interest). Highly distressing. This is why we think today's garden-variety full-service brokering will soon waste away as more and more people turn to online financial resources.

The full-service industry will save itself when it bases its incentives on your performance, not your trading frequency. Your broker should be working to give you the best consistent long-term market-beating return possible and should receive bonuses based on a percentage of your long-term profits. Instead, he's getting paid slices of what he induces you to wheel and deal—how dumb is that?

Until this situation changes, you're going to see full-service firms getting chopped off at the knee by the increasing amount of do-it-yourself investing done through discount brokers by people who are making their own decisions. Many today are getting instant, interactive information and advice online, and we highly recommend this! When we write "we," we don't just mean your un-Wise authors. "We" here means the Foolish online community at large. Here are some snippets from the hundreds of thousands of notes and letters we've received from investors in the past year . . .

Dr. Randall Raabe wrote us:

Even though I have been investing for fifteen years, I have left much of the decision-making to "professionals" only to get burned time and time again. Since becoming a Fool, I have made my own investing decisions and have done quite well. My broker, a vice president at [a large, well-known brokerage firm], has even asked what I think about certain investments . . . this is very sad because many other people have placed their hard-earned money in the hands of nothing more than a glorified salesman.

Drew, a medical officer in the U.S. Army, puts it rather succinctly: "My broker, bless his little greedy heart, focused so much on trading me in and out of stocks, I paid almost as much in commissions as I received in profits, and my profits for the year were up 36 percent!"

Bruce Wilton wrote:

I found Fooldom way back in October of 1994. I was inspired enough that I opened a new [discount] brokerage account at Schwab. The purpose of this new account was to give me a place to practice being Foolish while my "real" broker took "care" of my "can't afford to lose it" money. I looked at the Schwab account as a flyer. That Schwab account today shows an unrealized gain of 178 percent. Needless to say I have closed the account with my "real" broker and now Foolishly manage all of my own affairs. Fooldom has allowed me to quit wondering how to pay to send my daughter to UCLA in September.

And Joe Devenny wrote:

> I kept trying Wisely to make money with brokers or with newsletters that were outdated by the time I got them. It was a real struggle and there were such gaps in information. It is fantastic to be able to share information with such a group of dedicated, Foolish people. I don't know any of them and I've received a thousand times more from them than from any broker I have dealt with.

That said, some people just might not be suited to making their own financial decisions, so a market will always exist for hand-holding. And we reiterate that some brokers are truly wonderful people adept at doing just that. One reader wrote us:

> Last summer, my father distributed his stock holdings to his four children in equal amounts, and since that time I have obsessively studied investing in the stock market. The broker I use is the same my father used . . . Merrill Lynch . . . and a guy who has given me uncounted hours of explanations on terms, advice, and on occasion, a tip. Overall, his advice to me has remained constant: Stick with the blue chip stocks. As it turns out, I can't stick with anything and besides, the first time the market dropped over a hundred points I freaked out and started hammering at the phone, yelling "SELL SELL SELL!" Against his advice, I sold virtually all of the blue chip stocks I had. And of course, they came back. Sigh. My ML guy mentioned that I traded too frequently, and that it was hurting my portfolio. He said I had good instincts, but little else.

There are great brokers out there—but again, they operate in a still quite broken system.

That you are reading this book suggests you're probably best suited to a discount broker. For some, waiting is best, until they feel more experienced and levelheaded than the new investor mentioned above. For you, perhaps a good and caring full-service broker is a better way to start. Of course, we hope our book has already caused you to focus so effectively on the long term that you would never make the new investor's mistake described above. If this is the case, and you're ready, you're ready for a discount broker.

Charging a fraction of what full-service brokerages charge, discount brokers are significantly cheaper than full-service brokers. How do they do this and make money? They just keep their costs down by not offering things like advice, research information, and the rest. They also operate online sites that enable you to manage your own account online—that's very cost effective for them.

There are lots and lots—seriously, lots—of discount brokers. There are so many, in fact, that it can be quite bewildering to figure out which to use, if you're a newcomer.

If you're a buy-and-hold investor who doesn't trade frequently and doesn't hyperventilate about whether your order is executed within 12 nanoseconds or 12 minutes, the broker you choose won't affect your blood pressure or the amount of money you end up with over your lifetime. Not to any serious degree, anyway.

But maybe you're planning on being a very active trader, in which case the slight differences in costs and services between the competing broker-ages will add up. Some discount brokerages are targeting their service toward a more active trader. Some are offering packages of services, in-cluding options trading, that a totally Foolish investor wouldn't be inter-ested in.

What we Fools would consider the core service accounts with little or no annual fees, minimal fees per trade, satisfactory customer service—will be more or less standard across the major discount brokerages. So, to state our position once again: If you're a Fool, it probably doesn't make much difference which discount broker you choose.

WHAT YOU SHOULD LOOK FOR

The following is a list of 10 factors to consider when selecting a discount broker. These factors are not presented in order of importance, as the im-portance will differ from reader to reader. (Unless two readers are identi-cal clones. Aieeeee!)

1. Rates Many of the advertisements that you'll see for discount brokers focus on the price per trade. While choosing the brokerage that provides the absolute lowest price per trade might be attractive—and might even make sense—it is likely that you'll find that there is some tradeoff between service and price. (You've probably discovered that once or twice before in your life.)

Online brokerages can be put into three general categories:

- Super-cheap brokers that charge from $4 to $12 per trade. Best used for those who plan on trading very frequently, but satisfactory for buy-and-hold investors as well.
- Mid-priced brokers that charge between $12 and $20 per trade. These brokers justify slightly higher prices with more well known brand names, and possibly additional services.
- High-priced brokers that charge more than $20 per trade, typically around $29.95 per trade. (They think $30 trades sound too high, so they knock off a nickel—but we're not fooled.)

2. Other fees   Beyond the price per trade, you'll find that brokerages may charge other fees, including fees for transferring assets into the account, fees for closing an account, IRA custodian fees, wire transfer fees, account inactivity fees, annual fees, and fees for not maintaining a minimum balance.

3. Minimum initial deposit   If you're just starting out as a new investor, you might not be rolling in dough. Fair enough. In this case, you'll want to focus on the account option that best serves your needs: an account that has a minimum of $1,000 for initial deposits or even less. There are plenty of discount broker accounts now that have no minimum balance requirement—though you'll want to read the fine print to make sure.

IRA accounts will typically have lower minimums, and in some cases there is no minimum balance.

4. Customer service, site performance, and interface   Check out each brokerage's Web site and make sure the interface is intuitive and pleasing. This probably shouldn't be too difficult because it's entirely subjective, and by now all brokerages have had plenty of chances to test-market their sites on lab rats, robots, and occasionally human beings.

You also want to know what kind of customer service the brokerage has. So test it out: e-mail them a query, and see how long it takes them to get back to you. In addition to their timeliness, was the response informative and courteous? Customer service says a lot, in the financial *services* industry.

Also, checking out The Motley Fool Discount Brokerage discussion board should give you invaluable insight as to the praise and complaints that are being made regarding each of the major brokerages. It's an active board, with many strong opinions. Understand that those with complaints are more likely to post their thoughts than satisfied customers.

5. *Traditional banking services*   It's possible now to do everything for which you once needed a bank through a brokerage. Banking features available include:

Money market sweeps
Checkwriting and bill payment
Visa cards
Direct deposit
ATM cards

If you're using your bank in a way that has you going in to your local branch (say you're frequently depositing cold, hard cash into your account), it may not make sense for you to shift all of your banking to a brokerage account. Also, using broker-sponsored ATM cards at the local bank's machine may result in a pile of fees.

However, the higher rates that your cash will typically attract in a brokerage money market account versus the typical savings or checking account could make up some of that difference. Also, if you meet certain minimum account levels, some brokerages will reimburse you for fees imposed by ATM machines. Check out your banking area for more details.

6. *Research*   There's plenty of research available for free and for pay all over the Web (er, did we say Web, because we meant to say Fool.com). Some of the offerings include analyst reports, real-time quotes, and detailed financial data. These offerings are marketed by brokerages as a real plus, but of course there's tons and tons and tons of data, tools, and free research all over the Internet. It is unlikely that any brokerage can offer you proprietary tools that will significantly influence your choice.

7. *Mutual funds*   Once upon a time, the discount brokerages weren't offering mutual funds as an investment alternative—but that is changing. The selection of mutual funds at brokerages can differ widely. Though as you know by now, we're not big fans of managed mutual funds, your opinion still may run counter to ours. If so, and you have a particular mutual fund family that you're set on using, make sure that the brokerage you're selecting offers that family of funds.

No-load mutual funds can be purchased directly from mutual fund companies, so unless you're a mutual fund trading addict, the availability of thousands of mutual funds in one location probably shouldn't affect your choice either.

8. Investment product selection   Beyond equity mutual funds, there are a number of other investment vehicles that you may wish to use. All the brokerages will offer the stocks on the major exchanges. However, if you're somebody interested in risking your hard-earned moolah on over-the-counter (OTC) bulletin board stocks, you'll have to see which brokerages offer them. Other choices such as options, government bonds, corporate bonds, and the likes are not available through every brokerage. Determine what you expect to need—we're fans of just plain old stocks, especially if you're young—and act accordingly.

9. Other methods of getting your investment choices executed   Sure, the Internet is an easy way to invest, but what about when you don't have access to a computer? Check out whether the brokerages you're looking at also have touchtone phone trading, and how that works. Sometimes you just might want to place an order through a real, live individual, and many discount brokerages offer that possibility, too.

10. Other freebies and perks   Beyond the low costs, some brokerages will give you frequent flier miles, books, months of Internet access, or just plain old money for you to open up an account. The reward for opening an account can go as high as $100, so keep that in mind. With the cutthroat competition going on these days, these offers are remaining pretty attractive. We wouldn't suggest making too big a deal about the freebies. After all, they are one-time things, and $100 probably isn't going to be worth the hassle if you soon find that you've made the wrong choice and have to move your account elsewhere. Still, free money is free money, and if you find yourself deadlocked on which brokerage to go with, cash (or some other perk) is a persuasive tiebreaker.

If you're only making five, six, ten, even twenty trades in a year, the difference between paying $7 per trade and $20 per trade isn't significant. Better to make customer service a priority, and not sweat about whether you've made the right choice.

After all, how much did you ever worry about which bank to open your first checking account with? The differences are about the same.

Having chosen a broker and having gotten your account set up, you may be wondering how entering your first trade works. If you're an online junkie, you can do this over your computer, and chances are you already know how (or can figure it out!). The rest of us typically place orders to buy or to sell over the telephone, either by voice or Touch-Tone. If you're near a branch, you could certainly do it in person, though you may be perceived as Mr. or Ms. Dramatic. Anyway, you merely indicate what you want to trade and how much. Most often you'll just trade at the "market price," which means your broker will immediately execute the order at the current market price. You can put in your order in a variety of ways, including asking for the trade to be made at a specific price, a minimum sell price, or a maximum buy price. Talk to your rep for specifics of what they offer. Most will send you an explanatory brochure. However you decide to make your first trade, you'll normally get this transaction confirmed orally while still on the phone, then a written confirmation in the mail.

And there's not much more to it than that!

Direct-Purchase Plans

It is possible to skip right over the broker if you care to do so. A whole bunch of large companies—over one thousand, now—actually sell their stock directly to people like you via direct-purchase plans, called "dividend-reinvestment plans." That phrase has a horrible acronym (DRiPs), which we're going to attempt not to use a single time through this section. (We challenge you to find a single other printed source with information on these things that does *not* say "DRiP this" and "DRiP that." Yuck. These plans are definitely not for drips—they're an exceedingly Foolish idea and make a great deal of sense. Consequently, don't expect your broker to like them very much.)

Small investors use direct-purchase plans to buy stock directly from companies in smaller amounts. We first suggested this idea in the context of our chapter on Coca-Cola. Using a plan like this for building up a holding in Coca-Cola makes a ton of sense, especially if you're just starting out saving and don't have large amounts to save. The plan will get you around ever having to pay a commission; commissions would otherwise quickly eat up any amounts you could save. If you were trying to put away $40 a month into your Coke stock and it cost you $40 every time you made a trade, you'd have long-term savings of zero bucks. Youch. With reinvestment plans, you buy stock while avoiding the middleman's cut.

Not all companies have direct-investment plans, but most big ones do. Participating companies have traditionally engaged the services of a "transfer agent" to handle their plans. You can use these transfer agents, who serve as clearinghouses for a huge number of these plans, or you can increasingly go through the companies directly. Check with the company in which you want to invest.

Many of these plans do require that you purchase a first share of stock to start, which you'll generally have to do through a broker. The key is to make sure the certificate is issued to you in your name. If you buy a share of stock as a "book entry" share in "street name," it is held in the brokerage company's name. Don't worry what that means. Just tell the broker that you want *your* stock in *your* name and you want the certificate in *your* hands. Don't worry, your request is not unusual and should be no problem, but since the plan has to be in the name of the registered shareholder, you need that certificate! After you get the certificate, you contact the transfer agent for the company. They send you a form to register in the reinvestment plan, and you are on your way. Almost.

Bear with us here, we're almost done. (You think we *like* having to write sentences with "register" and "reinvestment plan" in them?)

These things are called *dividend*-reinvestment plans because they were initially created by companies for shareholders to reinvest their dividends automatically, those who wanted to do so. It meant you didn't have to pay any attention to your $12 payment from General Electric, for instance—GE just turned your dividend into more stock. Later, the plans evolved into an opportunity for you to buy new shares (whole or fractionally) directly. Some companies today offer plans for new investment requiring as little as $10 a month. Very, very Foolish.

Depending on the rules of the plan, you may have to send the check yourself, or maybe they'll even take the money out of your bank account on a regular set date. Is it all free? Sometimes. Again, the plans differ. Some have buried fees and aren't really cheaper for larger purchases than a deep-discount broker. Most plans don't charge you anything. Some charge a modest amount per transaction, usually a certain amount per share and a minimal transaction fee.

George Runkle, one of Fool HQ's specialists on these plans, expresses strong preference for plans that let you invest regularly (monthly or even weekly) and automatically take the money out of your account. For many people (perhaps you, for instance), if it isn't done *automatically,* it may not get done. Try to use a fixed amount invested on a regular basis.

Let's say you invest $100 a month in a certain company, come rain or shine. In months when this company's stock is the most popular investment on the planet and is way overvalued, you purchase fewer shares (2.50 shares with Pfizer at $40). In other months, when nobody knows this company exists and the stock price stagnates, you buy more shares (five shares of Pfizer at $20). In theory, your cost-per-share basis is very low.

Some investors take another tack; they use their own discretion, making all the purchases themselves. Every month they decide whether each of their stocks is a "buy" or not. If the stock is overvalued, they pass on investing. If they consider it to be undervalued, they throw more money at it. While you can theoretically do really well this way, you'd have to be a savvier investor who wants to take the time to study and research your companies. And from a savings standpoint, do you have the discipline to decline the *automatic* approach? You make the call!

A minor downside to using these plans (you were just waiting for this, right?) is that you can't sell your shares nearly as quickly as if you'd just held them in a brokerage account. You have to fill out paperwork and mail it in to terminate your plan, ending your days of part ownership. If you've picked the proper companies (the sorts you've read about in the past couple of chapters, for instance), you really shouldn't have to sell anytime soon. That's the whole idea of using a div-reinvest plan (there we are, inventing hip phrases to get around that hideous acronym—hey, we kinda like that one!). You're buying stock in companies that are great for the *long term,* using their shares as your savings vehicle because you're highly, highly confident they'll outperform your old bank account.

Finally, how do you find companies that sponsor div-reinvest plans? Many books (including one self-published by The Motley Fool) list participating companies; any library or bookstore will carry them. However, the print medium is unable to update itself very quickly, so for the latest information you can check into Fool.com.

PART IV

AN INVESTING LIFE

Buy What You Are

A VERY WELL KNOWN route to take with your next investments was originally and most eloquently presented by Peter Lynch in his superlative book *One Up on Wall Street*. Lynch preaches purchasing stock in companies you know that offer products and services you like within industries you follow. This is time-honored Foolish advice, and we've mentioned it already in various ways at various points in this book. Think back to the motorcycler who failed to buy Harley-Davidson; Harley-Davidson should absolutely have been *the investment* for this fellow to make. It just makes sense to buy what you know, to buy what you are. To do otherwise would be to put yourself at a significant disadvantage. Buying what you *don't* know, what you *aren't*, is like putting the apple on your head for the rookie knife thrower twenty yards away.

Let some nicer person give him practice.

Buy what you are. Indeed. The greatest blunders we make as investors occur when we try to reach at ideas that sit outside our circle of expertise. We hear there's money to be made drilling for oil on the Shandong Peninsula in China. But whether or not there is, we have no real understanding of oil exploration, and we couldn't possibly tell you how many companies are out there drilling already and whether it makes sense to purchase shares of a smaller, speculative company when (for all we know) the only companies really capable of making money out there are Chevron or ExxonMobil or Schlumberger. Silly, silly.

Conversely, buying what you *do* know is putting your natural advantage to work in the stock market. Are you a marine biologist? You're going to know a lot more than the average Fool about the fishing industry, about diving equipment, about what works and doesn't in offshore drilling, about underwater photography, about beachfront real estate, and so forth. Are you a high school teacher? You have the advantage when it comes to books, educational software, the school's computer and networking system. *And* you have immediate access to perhaps the largest gold mine of all—adolescent buying habits. Are you a homemaker? Wall Street's high-paid analysts would love to have your experience with household products, foods and drinks, athletic equipment, your and your spouse's weekend activities, and (of course) the often unrestrainable buying habits of your adolescent children.

Square in the middle of your life, *at the very heart of who you are,* lie your advantages as an investor. As you move beyond buying what everyone knows, or buying the index fund, discipline yourself to look past the drilling operations in Shandong. Push forward into further exploration and learning. Start by looking at three key facets of your life as you take up the approach of learning to buy what you *are.*

Your Necessities

Of this we've spoken before, but let us restate. In and around your daily needs—food, drink, sleep, shelter, and human affection—lie superior businesses waiting to compound growth on your savings. Search for brand names and the stuff you love. Scan your bedroom, dig through your closet, sort through your vanity stuff, rifle *through* (do not rifle) your medicine cabinet. Don't forget the trip downstairs to the kitchen to pop open the fridge (and guys, again, let's finally get rid of the empurpled tuna sandwich back behind the jar of pickles).

Companies that provide the stuff you need to survive, week in and week out, make for such great investments that deviating from this category almost doesn't make sense. Forget the unknowns. Just follow, say, your repeated purchasing of Campbell's soups with an investment in the company. Campbell Soup Company has risen from $6 per share in 1988 to $25 at last check. Even though the dominant soup maker has executed poorly over the last few years, $10,000 invested in Campbell in 1988 is worth well over $40,000 twelve years later. The company was founded in 1869. Probably it'll be in business for a few decades more, no? You might be interested to hear of some of Campbell's nonsoup products:

Godiva chocolate
Pepperidge Farm

Prego
SpaghettiOs
V8 juice

Great investors focus on those bestselling items which are the things that people really *need*. Which are the things that *you* really need? It doesn't take an expensive MBA degree or "hot tips" from a high-priced financial newsletter to answer that question.

Your Hobbies

Next stop on the Fool Train is Hobby Land. Baseball, hiking, badminton, needlepoint, mountain biking, card playing, river floating, computer gaming, billiards, snowboarding, amateur mechanics, microbrewing, moviegoing, Ping-Pong, foreign travel, stargazing, deep-sea fishing, hanging out at Fool.com. Most of your hobbies are directly or indirectly supported by the daily machinations of one or more public companies. By opening your eyes to these businesses as potential additions to your core portfolio, you'll further increase the odds of becoming Total World Leader via your stock market riches earned in the decades ahead.

You probably know that the world of hobbies is more fickle and fluid than that of necessities. Campbell's soup outlived the Hula Hoop. Coca-Cola has considerably more staying power than the latest, greatest computer game. Take, for example, Maxis Corporation, maker of the extremely popular Sim series of computer games. At the height of its popularity, in 1995, the company's stock ran from $20 a share to $50 during the summer. From there, it proceeded to shed 90 percent of its value, down to $5 per share, before being bought out by Electronic Arts at $11, in the summer of '97. Hobbies are not changeless. Coca-Cola is nearly so.

If you invest in your favorite pastimes (and we think you should) just be aware that what you love today, you and others may no longer be spending any time at tomorrow. Many of these leisure businesses live short lives as growth stocks. The companies that make Rollerblades, snowboards, regional dark beer, cool new software games, and fly-fishing rods have shown great two- or three-year runs, but over decades have mostly failed their shareholders. This is not always true. But the longer you plan to hold a stock, the more certain you should be of its company's staying power. Some hobby businesses have thrived for years. Disney has been eating up our leisure time for decades and making its shareholders a lot of money in the process. Consider buying what you play around with on the weekends, but watch this one a little closer; move a little more cautiously.

Your Job

The final rock to overturn is the one under which rests your place of employment. After a weekend of semileisure, most Americans peel themselves out of bed on Monday morning at around 7 A.M., sort through their closet, dig through their bathroom cabinets, poke around in their refrigerator, and then hustle off to work. They spend something on the order of fifty hours each week working. If we assume eight hours of sleep each night, that means that people spend 45 percent of their waking hours at work. Wow.

All that time means that you do know, and you should know, more about your professional life, your business, your industry, than anything else. We're not going to dwell on whether that's a good or a bad thing. (It's probably both.) It just is the thing. Given that, extraordinary investment opportunities are probably out there all around you. We were reminded of this again recently when a young woman from Oracle's software sales department dropped by Fool HQ. Over lunch, she confessed—nay, celebrated—that she had Microsoft stock in her portfolio, right alongside her employee stock from Oracle. She was holding the two strongest, fiercest competitors in the software industry in her portfolio—one that she worked for, one that she worked against. And she's probably making a fortune. Take a look at their performance since 1990:

	12/29/89	12/31/99	Annual Gain	Total Gain
Oracle	$2.31	$112.06	47.38%	4754.04%
Microsoft	$1.21	$116.75	57.87%	9562.07%

Whether you're working in technology, oil refining, finance, automobile manufacturing, media, botany, or at a bakery, you know your industry in a way that Wall Street never can. Capitalize on your advantage. If it means owning a slice of your competitor because they're equally or more productive and profitable, do so. If you see a company in your professional space that is in serious financial trouble, purchase *The Motley Fool Investment*

Guide or come to our online area, learn how to bet *against* stocks by shorting them, and then put some money down on the "Don't Pass" line.

You probably spend from one-third to one-half your waking hours at work. You know your business better than most. Consider using your expertise to add to your core holdings, fellow Fool.

When you invest in your necessities, selectively in your hobbies, and intelligently in the companies in your professional space, you dramatically increase the chances that you'll improve upon the returns of your core holdings (the Obviously Great Investments or index fund, or both). Ever since the debut of our Ye Olde Printed Foole investment newsletter, back in those antediluvian, pre-online days of July 1993, we have preached over and again one basic idea: *DO NOT invest in what you don't understand, don't use, and aren't familiar with.* It's a simple credo. It's another one of those Foolish maxims that should have been taught in eighth grade but wasn't. It would've saved tens of billions of consumer dollars. It still can.

Before we close up "Buy What You Are," it behooves us to consider one additional aspect of personal investing: What about stuff that you are *not?*

Ethics in Investing

Some people call it "socially responsible investing." That rather sanctimonious phrase has always turned us off. "Green investing" is another term some use; others go with "ethical investing." It's a self-imposed, selective approach to investing, one that has ultimately kept millions of potential investors around the globe from buying into certain public companies, whose corporate activities they deem immoral, damaging, or exploitative.

Now, in Utopia (from the Greek *ou topos*, meaning "no place"), we could simply tell you to invest without concern. You'd be living in the perfect society with perfect laws and no need for regulatory bodies. You would know, in every moment that you invested, that your company was maximizing the growth of wealth for *every* constituency: customers, employees, management, shareholders, and society. If ever one group was temporarily over- or undercompensated, the whole structure would tilt immediately to correct it (probably slightly too far in the other direction, briefly, in order to create total equity). Doesn't it sound great?

Ou topos—no place.

No such world has ever yet been, unless St. Thomas More's legendary traveler was telling the truth. And most important, no single life has ever been continually, uncompromisingly painless. With no Utopia in our personal or professional lives, we certainly shouldn't expect one in our investing life. At the most basic level, we all just have to do our best, make the best of things.

The whole concept of ethics in investing has had much ink spilled over it, with many zealots poking at one another and many very bad mutual funds springing up trying to meet this need in certain people to feel good, or true to themselves, or true to others, or whatever. The issue is deadly serious, which is why we feel it's important to touch on it here and now. In fact, our own Foolish answer, our own Foolish approach, generally causes us to see through much of the rest of the arguments for the hot air that they mostly are. Because here's our advice for now and evermore about how to treat Philip Morris, or the big chemical company, or the paper products manufacturer that just paid to fell another forest:

Buy what you are; buy only *what you are.*

Here's the deal: If you don't like Philip Morris, don't invest in it. If you think companies that do business with Libya are bad, don't invest in them either. Never lose sleep over an investment that you made tentatively, in an enterprise you don't truly support. Blow it off. Buy something else. Buy what you are. Buy only what you are.

For different people, this means different things. One person buys Nike because it's profitable, makes great shoes, and puts up advertising campaigns supporting racial tolerance and the great American melting pot. Another thinks it's evil to hire Malaysian kids of elementary school age to make the shoes that Michael Jordan wears, when they're paid just a fraction of our minimum wage. Whatever we believe, we can see both sides of that one; if you're squarely on the side of one or the other, act accordingly! If Nike is truly doing something wrong, it'll pay for it in the long term. The chickens always come home to roost. If Nike is truly doing something right, it'll benefit in the long term. Your own beliefs, leading to your own actions, will eventually benefit or penalize you as history plays out and you see who's right. That's the way it should be.

You know what makes us smirk, though? The "socially responsible mutual funds." When you buy such a fund, *WHO* are you buying? Are you buying what *you* are? Of course not—you're buying what someone else is.

One person's evil weed tobacco company is another person's favorite product company. Listen, when you buy a mutual fund, you're consigning over the destiny of your money to a stranger you'll most likely never meet. If you take ethics in investing at all seriously, we fervently argue that you're being most *irresponsible* by saying, "I'll buy that pleasingly named fund." You're effectively cutting loose your own beliefs and substituting those of someone else, who's probably just "target marketing" to you.

Do keep in mind as well that most big mutual funds (including virtually all index funds) own Philip Morris, so if you're a fund investor who would never buy the company on your own, you probably own some without knowing it. The point is the same: True ethical investing is done on an individual basis, dear Fool, through buying what you are—buying only what you are.

Finally, do remember that a company like Philip Morris also makes Kraft cheese. And Jell-O. And Miller beer. And Post Raisin Bran. And Oscar Mayer frankfurters. Many people who are outspoken opponents of investing in Philip Morris are repeat purchasers of many of Flip Mo's products—they've given thousands of dollars to the company for decades. Now, which do you think helps Philip Morris more—your purchase of a few shares of its stock, or weekly purchases of its food products? The latter, of course; you're creating profits that will ultimately drive the stock price. So if you do opt out of a company with which you have ethical disagreements, make *sure* you know the company well enough not to be helping it even more in another way.

In the end, each of the components in this chapter is really just about the same thing. You are who you are. You'll buy what you'll buy. You should therefore tend to consider investing in the companies that you buy from, out of necessity or as a hobby, or the companies you know and work with. By doing so, you'll also be supporting with your *investment dollars* the very same companies you're supporting with your *consumption dollars*. Makes sense. Makes so much sense, in fact, that we feel strongly you'll also wind up earning far better returns investing this way. And you'll feel right about what you're doing. You'll be in sync. You'll be a true Fool.

Where Do I Fit?

WHETHER YOU HAVE sixty bucks or $600 million to invest today, if you're debt free and treating the money as hard-core savings, have we got an investment for you! The stock market, as you well know. But as we wrote in the last chapter, one man's evil weed tobacco stock is another man's favorite product stock. Correspondingly, one man's small-cap is another man's runaway winner and guarantee of early retirement: It largely comes down to how much each put into it and how the rest of their money was allocated. This begs the question as to how one should allocate one's dollars. Surely, the novice investor who's just shed her debt should invest differently than Hillary Clinton. (Indeed, Mrs. Clinton may have a trick or two to teach the novice—to teach all of us!) That's exactly why we've fashioned this chapter into a ladder, with each rung representing a slightly different investment style based on the appropriate level of assets and savings.

So climb the ladder with us, and hop off when you find your rung.

All suggestions about allocation are extremely general, since the same guidelines don't work for every individual. We each have different amounts of attention to devote, different thresholds for pain, and different time horizons. No single perfect, uniform answer exists. So please take our general principles in the spirit that they're offered, as loose guides to get you started thinking about how to apportion your investment greenbacks. While exactly how you grip your rung of the ladder will ultimately be up to you, rest assured that you'll eventually find a silken motley glove that fits your hand perfectly. You just need to spend some time looking for it on your own, beforehand.

So, to the Ladder of Foolish Allocation! (Sounds like a poor parody of something from *Ghostbusters* . . .)

The Ladder of Foolish Allocation

RUNG 1: FROM $0 TO $500

Before you picked up this un-Wise parchment, you probably thought you didn't have enough money to get started. We expect that, hands firmly gripping the first rung (this would mean, we suppose, that you're lying facedown on the ground—sorry about that), you've since realized that it ain't necessarily so. In fact, of all those waiting to ascend the ladder with us, *you have the most to gain from investing*. Turning $10 million into $20 million in one's lifetime isn't nearly so fulfilling as growing today's $300 into $1 million by retirement. Unfortunately, most first-rungers don't realize that the stock market is well within their reach, if they even have any idea what the heck the thing is.

In our section on direct-purchase stock plans, we walked you through the process of buying shares straight from the companies—without need of middleman assistance. This eliminates your commission fees and, allows you methodically to add new savings at the end of every week or month, making you part owner of some wonderful businesses. Here is a short list of companies that we think would make for an excellent first investment, that offer direct-purchase plans with little or no administrative fee, and that fit our criteria of profitable, global consumer franchises:

American Express	Johnson & Johnson
Avon	Kellogg
Coca-Cola	Liz Claiborne
Gillette	McDonald's
Harley-Davidson	Pepsi
Home Depot	Pfizer
IBM	Wal-Mart
Intel	Disney

With your couple of hundred bucks, we suggest that you buy into just one of these, almost completely avoiding all additional fees. In these early stages, you needn't spend any significant time analyzing or even tracking your investment. Use the time instead to get out and make a little money, via your favorite trick dog or otherwise (a real job comes to mind). Your financial focus needs to be on building up your savings, not obsessing over stock price movements. Just buy one big company through its direct-purchase plan, and keep saving!

With more than $500—rise to thy knees and grip that second rung.

RUNG 2: FROM $500 TO $5,000

With more than a grand, it's time that you considered opening a brokerage account. We've already talked about how to do that, and while we haven't suggested any specific names, these days you can find any number that offer to transact for you at less than $10 a trade. Your goal on rung 2 is to keep the cost of trading commissions at 2 percent or less. Thus, if you just came into an additional $500 that you can afford to sock away for the long haul, dump it all into a "What You Are" company, or an Obviously Great Investment, and pay the freight ($10 ÷ $500 = 2%). As you inch toward the third rung, trending up toward $5,000, naturally you can add more stocks. At $10 per trade, you could transact again once you hit $1,000, either adding to an existing position or buying a third stock. Same thing every five hundred dollars you save up. Just calculate your commission payments as a percentage of each investment, and keep the total at 2 percent or lower.

On this rung, your best bets remain big-name winners, companies like Microsoft and Coke that for decades have shown extraordinary growth and have dearly rewarded their shareholders. Here as well, you shouldn't be scrutinizing or fretting over your decisions. If your $2,500 doubles over the next five years, great. That said, the $1,800 you'd wind up with in after-tax profit (assuming a 28 percent tax rate) should easily be dwarfed by the savings you rack up through hard work at your job (and controlled spending habits). Plus, don't forget, you might make more than $1,800 over the next few months pocketing pennies from foam cups *alone.* Get this money into proven and solid companies, and keep accumulating!

Once beyond $5,000, stand, dear Fool. Wrap your fingers round that third rung.

RUNG 3: FROM $5,000 TO $15,000

If you've grown your savings to between five and fifteen thousand bucks—or if that's where you're starting from—now is as good a time as any to celebrate with a full weekend off from work. May we suggest a ball game on Saturday, followed by a shrimp-and-steak dinner with close friends that night? Then, on Sunday, have a picnic and take a trip to the waterfront with water wings, inner tube, or surfboard, followed by a whole evening of obscure foreign movies on the VCR (it's time to start putting on airs).

Congratulations. Now, let's get your remaining money invested.

On rung 3, you should begin splitting out your savings between the Obviously Great Investments and your own choice of "What You Are" stocks (for those who want to pursue their own investments), index funds, or some combination thereof. Particularly as your assets move into the five figures, you can afford to diversify and should. (That never means, by the way, overdiversifying—don't make the same mistake the fund managers must make.) At most, you might have ten stocks in your portfolio. Could it be very long before you're at the fourth rung? We doubt it.

RUNG 4: FROM $15,000 TO $50,000

Ah, the fourth rung. You step up onto the ladder and grip the thing, and doesn't financial independence feel good? Welcome, fellow Fool.

If you've pulled yourself up by your own bootstraps to reach this point, you're expertly prepared to make your own decisions. You are a total Fool.

If, on the other hand, this was your current savings level when you began reading this book, chances are pretty decent that you've used the help of someone else to get here (broker, fund managers, financial planner)—y'know, one o' them financial pr'fessional types. If you love this person or people and you've verified that they've been providing market-beating historical performance, you can't be faulted for staying the course. If that's what you want to do, we certainly understand; just recognize how unusual your situation really is. What good fortune has found you!

But if you haven't been getting great performance from your funds, or if your due diligence turns up a broker who spotted you 5 percent less than the index fund last year, it's probably time to take action. At minimal cost and on your own, you could at the very least just put your money into an index fund. But if you're feeling a bit more Foolish, what about investing your discount brokerage account this way? Let's assume you have $40,000 to invest:

	Dollars Invested
Obvious Greats	
Gillette	$5,000
Intel	$5,000
Microsoft	$5,000
General Electric	$5,000
Pepsi	$5,000
Johnson & Johnson	$5,000
What You Are	
Biogen	$5,000
Pioneer Hi-Bred	$5,000

You own eight stocks, having paid $80 in commissions to get into them (that's just 0.2 percent of the total account). What you've wound up with is a stable full of great companies. The informed reader notes here that you work in or with the biotechnology industry. Not a bad position to be in; just avoid the promotional penny stocks.

The allocation presented above represents just one of dozens of variations on the theme. It puts 75 percent of your money into Obviously Great Investments, and an additional 25 percent in your specific field of expertise. This allocation suggests a more cautious investor, one who's not terribly confident of making his own investment decisions yet, and so he's putting only $10,000 into the category in which his own decisions, his own guidance, count for the most. The others are fairly brainless great picks for long-term performance.

Your approach may differ.

Anyway, once you eventually catch a 25 percent gain off that allocation, it's another big step up, to the fifth rung!

RUNG 5: FROM $50,000 TO $250,000

When your smartly shod feet touch down on the fifth rung, hi-ho, it's time for another celebration. Let's go with a balloon ride this time—ever been up in a hot-air balloon? If not, it's time you did! Listen, you get to spin round the sun only so many times before it's all kaput and you're buried and you evaporate. So get out there and LIVE, baby, LIVE.

OK, with fifty grand up to a quarter million, good investment decisions become worth even more. Any single stock in your portfolio might turn in a great run over a few years and make you $50,000 or more *on its own*. Keep in mind that as you're now dealing with pretty hefty numbers, you shouldn't sweat it when you look at your brokerage statement and see that you lost $20,000 last month. Off a $200,000 account, that's just 10 percent—no shabby percentage or amount, we grant you, but that's going to happen at inevitable and infrequent intervals. Back when you had only $20,000, a loss of $20,000 would've been, well—would've been pretty hard to do. Oh, and pretty disastrous, too. But now, it's all in a week's work $20,000 down *or* $20,000 up.

To construct a fifth-rung allocation, let's say you have $180,000 saved. Why don't we begin just by going back to the index fund for a sec? It alone will grant you extraordinary profits compounded over time. Let's start the market plodding ahead for you next year at its historical average of 11 percent. Your indexed account would generate $19,800 in pretax profit. Splendiferous. Even better, of course, are the long-term numbers. Take a look-see:

Your Portfolio	Growth Rate	Tenth Year	Twentieth Year	Thirtieth Year
$180,000	11%	$511,000	$1.45 million	$4.12 million

And that's just sleepy, market-average growth, which you can get without management fees and without doing any research. Just average returns with no effort, *without adding any new money,* and your $180,000 grows to over $4 million in thirty years. Celebration time again.

But the index fund average is just that—average. By now you know we believe that people who are truly interested in this subject and knowledgeable about one or more industries should invest in the best prospects within those industries. (For all the rest, there's the index fund.) So if this describes you, your allocation on the fifth rung might look something like this:

50%   Obvious Greats
35%   What You Are
15%   Rule Breakers

"Rule Breakers?" you may be scratching your head. These are earlier-stage, high-growth, dynamic companies that are breaking the rules of business as they've been set forth in their industries. Much more on these in the third book in our series, *The Motley Fool's Rule Breakers, Rule Makers* (also available from Simon & Schuster). All we're trying to get across here is that when you have enough money to be comfortably invested even through a really bad market, you may want to start moving some of those dollars into higher-risk situations that hold lots of promise and that you know well. You may want to start breaking the rules.

Again, we don't think there is ever any need for you to own more than fifteen stocks, with ten to twelve being more our ideal, so the above valuation for a $180,000 account could include six stocks in the first cluster, four in the second, and two in the third. Our final suggestion is that up here, on the fifth rung, you not let your brain atrophy. The world still needs you at work and helping out in the 'hood. And your portfolio should always hunger for more savings.

RUNG 6: FROM $250,000 TO $2 MILLION

Welcome to the sixth rung—home to older doctors, lawyers, Silicon Valley executives, M&A investment bankers, and the sixth guy off the bench for a National Basketball Association franchise. When you have this much money to invest, surely you shouldn't be doing so without the help of skilled professionals on Wall Street. Or should you?

(Getting the sense you're about to read a thinly veiled diatribe that really doesn't relate specifically to the sixth rung? Hey, if we don't say this stuff, who will?)

Would you really want someone managing your money whose rewards were based upon the number of trades she made, not how well your account did? Curiously enough, that principle still drives the majority of the compensation directed to the retail wings of full-service brokerage firms. Hey Fool, do you really *want* your account to generate fifty trades per year? Probably not. But your broker does. Ahhhh, perhaps your broker is now calling herself a "financial advisor" and offering to manage your account for a fee equal to 1 percent of your total assets.

Notice this isn't a flat fee, it's a percentage of total assets—a clever way to pull *more* money out of your account! Hey, if you're up on the sixth rung, sittin' pretty with $800,000 in savings, you should expect to be treated like royalty in the offices of the financial advisor. Play hard to get, or hard to keep: You may wind up with free food, free sports tickets, free apparel—you might make thousands in freebies as they try to lure you in! The truth is, the financial advisor couldn't be happier to lighten your $800,000 load by a cool $8,000 this year. Unfortunately, plain honest statistics reveal—no matter how much or how little you're paying her—she's probably still going to lose to the market's average return. Had you just purchased an index fund, buying the entire market and earning its virtually identical return, the charges against your $800,000 would have toted up to a bit less than $1,600. Hmmmmmmm.

You may buy that index fund if you like. We won't dissuade you if that's your style. But the primary aim of this half of the book is to make it clear that not only is the stock market not difficult to follow or to comprehend but also it's not *that* difficult to beat, if you take the long-term mentality! Here's an $800,000 portfolio that we expect to toast the market over the next twenty-five years.

	Dollars Invested
Obvious Greats	
Pfizer	$40,000
Gap	$40,000
Microsoft	$40,000
General Electric	$40,000
Coca-Cola	$40,000
Amgen	$40,000
Cisco Systems	$40,000
Index Fund	$280,000
What You Are	
Capital One Financial	$50,000
Morgan Stanley	$60,000
American Express	$60,000
Wells Fargo	$70,000

The account includes twelve stocks with total combined sales of hundreds of billions of dollars, strong profitability, a lot of familiar name brands, and four fine financial stocks that reflect the buyer's area of interest. So long as this investor is concentrated on portfolio performance looking out further than a decade, buying and *holding* (not sweating the declines, not wasting any money "trading"), he'll wallop the Wise Men on Wall Street.

RUNG 7: FROM $2 MILLION TO $15 MILLION

Reach . . . reach . . . a little higher . . . reach . . . UP. OK, there you go! You've hit the seventh rung, a multimillionaire. By now, if you're not already living in your *exact* ideal climate, you're at least checking house floor plans somewhere in that region. Or perhaps you're preparing to transition into politics, where you could blow much of your awesome investment portfolio running a smear campaign to oust Arnie Peeswell from his coveted seat on the school board (having invested all his life in savings bonds, Arnie is in no real position to defend himself). Everybody's got to start somewhere. We do encourage you to start new things at this point, by the way, rather than just concluding all your existing ones and disappearing from the scene.

Should someone with, say, $5 million in savings be concentrating much of his time on money and investing? Really, no more or less than the average investor, we think. We want to restate that no matter how much money you have, we don't think you ever need to hold any more than fifteen stocks. With billions of dollars, Warren Buffett has concentrated the majority of his holdings in half a dozen positions; at various points, his ownership of Coca-Cola stock has been in excess of 25 percent of his entire investment portfolio! If you love tracking business so much that you'd like to hold ownership positions in twenty-five companies, well, certainly, pursue your passion. But if that's not you, diversify among ten to fifteen good companies and no more. After the tenth strong one enters your portfolio, all that matters is the quality of future holdings. You're covered on quantity.

RUNG 8: FROM $15 MILLION TO $500 MILLION AND BEYOND . . .

A couple of quick suggestions. You probably can stop teaching tricks to your dog, and just let him be a dog. And forget about swiping your friends' books anymore. When you have this much money, don't invest in mutual funds, *become* a mutual fund. Here's where you might break our rule about never investing in more than fifteen stocks—buy all thirty of the Dow Jones industrials and become your own personal Dow fund. (We made you an index fund—wasn't that good of us?) Certainly, we can see taking on a financial advisor to help you with extraordinary circumstances: trusts, charitable contributions, wills, and the occasional tax loophole. But even now, all the way up at the top of the ladder, your investments demand no greater scrutiny than when you stood on the first rung. You are a mutual fund, an index mutual fund. You will buy and hold yourself, you will compound, and you'll *like* it.

(Oh, and while you're up there on rung 8? Psssst! There's this little private company called The Motley Fool that might be willing to part with some equity—who knows?!)

Become a Partner

GIVEN THAT WE AGREE on the importance of finding great companies and staying invested in them, we should certainly go on to consider the notion of partnership. A comparison here to another great form of human partnership—marriage—seems appropriate!

Some people say you shouldn't marry your stocks. That may certainly be true for those who've spent no time or thought figuring out what to marry (having been sold "their spouse" by a broker, for instance, the investing equivalent of getting a mail-order bride). But if you've worked hard to locate the right investments for you, we don't see why you *shouldn't* marry them! Indeed, the more that your investing resembles a good marriage, the better off you'll be. That means staying committed, not flirting too much with lesser options, and sticking it out through the occasional hard times. Really, the main difference between marriage and buy-and-hold investing is probably that when the latter is done right these days, it'll outlast most marriages!

When we listen to talk radio in the idle moments of a long car ride, we sometimes come across one or another show featuring relationship counselors. The greatest emphasis these people put is on good and open communication. Consider that the two most frequent causes of divorce are (ah, those age-old institutions) love and money. But what lies behind them both? A shared failure to communicate, prior to their becoming big problems.

We should probably back off this now, before we go too deep into the realm of self-help. After all, we'd be completely insane to steal the thunder here from our next book, *The Motley Fool Guide to Love and Self-Renewal*.

So let's apply these thoughts now to investing. Good communication characterizes public companies that routinely, honestly, and effectively share information with their shareholders and the public at large. As you become a partner, you should specially favor such companies, tending to avoid those not fitting into this group. While there are many ways that companies communicate today (their ad campaigns, their TV interviews, their Web sites), we want to focus this section on the one we consider the single most important. The best way to judge a company's ability to communicate is through its quarterly conference call.

Every quarter, companies report their sales and earnings. And concomitant with those announcements, public companies hold conference calls in which they announce their results and answer questions. This question-and-answer session forms a superb, live, human complement to the numbers and text of the corporation's financial statement, making for a must-visit for shareholders who want to become partners. The act of listening to a sixty-minute call a few times a year, or reading a written summary of one, or (these days) watching it via an Internet Web cast, is among the best uses of an individual investor's research time. You'll effectively have gained access to an informed and open discussion involving a company's management and its savviest observers, providing you valuable insight into the corp's present conditions and, importantly, management's perspective on the future. When else can you actually hear these people *talk*?

Traditionally, however—and here's the catch—individual investors have been *excluded* from live or taped versions of these calls. Even today, many companies have continued to send out call invitations to just an exclusive list of Wall Street analysts, perhaps with a smattering of journalists from traditional media outfits thrown in. Who's missing in this picture? Try *the actual owners of the business*—the non–Wall Street *shareholders*, spread around the nation from our cities to our 'burbs to our cow pastures. Something quite wrong has been going on here.

After all, the Securities Exchange Act of 1934 (which created the Securities and Exchange Commission) set disclosure requirements for companies. No longer could publicly traded companies hide their balance sheets from the public's knowledge or only give large investors the straight dope on what was going on. This made sense, as the owners of shares in these companies were in fact owners of the companies. To deny individual investors access to information about companies they owned while at the same time giving it to a "professional" class of investors was not only unfair—after 1934, it became illegal.

Let our bright, Foolish trumpets sound from hill to valley: We believe fervently that *all* shareholders are entitled to timely full disclosure! The privileged sharing of privileged information is obviously no different from insider trading, except that the insiders here are analysts, not company officials. No matter. By too many companies, individual investors have been unfairly treated with regard to the distribution of sensitive information that affects their investment. And these are part owners, dear Fools! That's the irony. Imagine if you were prevented by a real estate agent from seeing the results of your own house inspection, for instance. It's ridiculous. You simply can't be an effective partner if your other half won't talk to you.

Because we have felt so strongly about this, in 1996 we hired a full-time staffer to spearhead a public effort to open up access to company conference calls. On a daily basis we aggregated and then publicly posted whatever conference call phone numbers were available that day. Our team then connected to several of these, composing synopses of the proceedings to be published online in full public view—an objective permanent record that any investor could access on our Motley Fool online site. This effort to open up doors for individual investors who had previously been disenfranchised by old-school attitudes provided us some worthwhile and memorable experiences.

Take, for example, the 1996 case of Xilinx (Nasdaq: XLNX), the San Jose manufacturer of computer chips and integrated circuits. After having given Fool HQ the number and code to access its upcoming quarterly call, Xilinx proceeded to reverse its decision, saying it had "made a mistake" and "could not allow access" to the call *or* the taped replay. Lori Owen of Xilinx explained at the time that company policy allowed access only to XLNX's largest shareholders—effectively shutting out anyone who is not a professional money manager, whether an owner of a piece of the company or not.

That news was published on The Motley Fool and up online for only forty-five minutes before Xilinx reversed its decision again and granted Fool HQ full access to the call; its fax machines and phone lines had been flooded with upset investors. The online medium, which will continue to shape so many positive changes going forward on Wall Street, had struck one of its first blows for freedom of information. It's now easier than ever to become a partner with Xilinx.

Starbucks, too. In 1998, we read an explanation in *Investors Business Daily* newspaper as to why that company wasn't opening up its conference calls to its individual investor part-owners. The company spokesman's reason? That the coffee business was too complicated for average investors to understand. Starbucks Coffee! That weekend we encouraged our national radio audience to e-mail Starbucks, explain that they DID understand the business (else, why else had they bought the stock?), and that they'd like to hear the next conference call. Within two weeks, every person who'd e-mailed Starbucks got an e-mail back thanking them and letting them know the policy had changed: Starbucks's next conference call—indeed, every one in future—was now open.

Other companies have continued to make it difficult to become a partner, usually defending their closed-door policies by basically stating that individual investors couldn't understand their operations. The response we got from Jim Foltz, National Semiconductor's (NYSE: NSM) director of investor relations, was typical of these old-line attitudes: "The biggest problem with individual investors is that they neither have an interest in nor an understanding of our technology; they generally just want to be disruptive. If we were to let them in, institutional investors would drop off the call." We pointed out that National Semi could offer the call publicly as a tape replay, denying individuals the opportunity to ask questions but still enabling them to listen. The answer was still no, but this time the reason was: "The news media takes comments out of context. If institutional investors knew that media were on call, they would not participate." Foltz did point out that his company provides its financials and other investment info on its Web site. National isn't alone, but we hope that by the time you read this, it and all the others (are you on board with this yet, Electronic Arts?) who would restrict the flow of information will have changed their disrespectfully silent tunes.

Taking a completely different approach have been companies that freely invite interested parties to participate in their conference calls or listen to taped replays. These include impressive investor relations departments at companies of all different sizes: Sun Microsystems, Home Depot, Adobe Systems, Canandaigua Wine, Genentech, Microsoft, Jabil Circuit, and Ford. Indeed, Ford has in the past provided conference call listeners an accompanying thirty-one-page fax with press releases, charts, and slides reviewing its earnings.

It's obvious which way the winds are blowing. Eventually, every public

company will have to (and most should want to) broadcast their conference calls and annual meetings over the World Wide Web. In fact, in 2000
(finally!), the United States Securities and Exchange Commission passed
a new rule requiring that companies no longer provide *any* material information to favored institutional shareholders and Wall Street analysts without simultaneously giving it to the public as well. Three cheers from Fools
everywhere to the SEC's chairman, Arthur Levitt, for standing up to Wall
Street on this one. We hope and expect that the passage of this rule will
soon force all future conference calls to be open to the public.

It's all getting easier and more enjoyable to become a partner, largely
due to the spread of information and a continuing atmosphere of openness
and inclusiveness abetted by the Internet. On the other hand, companies
that don't operate openly and honestly will look more and more like appa-
ratchiks, and are not worth your investing dollar.

Thus, your mission is simply to locate the right companies to marry, call
them up and get their info, ask them when their conference calls are and
how you can participate, roll up your sleeves, and get ready to make use of
better information than you've ever had before. It was Martin Luther of all
people who wrote, in one of his lighter moments, no doubt, "There is no
more lovely, friendly and charming relationship, communion or company
than a good marriage."

Getting Help Online

For MANY PEOPLE, computers remain intimidating, unhelpful devices. The computer really is not terribly different from using a typewriter, except that once you get online, other people start typing back into your typewriter. It's great fun, actually. It can be incredibly educational.

We run a pretty enjoyable online forum for people who are looking to learn what to do with their money. What makes it educational, fun, and useful is not ultimately the efforts of the men and women who come to work at Fool HQ every day. No. The beauty of the online area, as we mentioned earlier, is that people are helping other people. The majority of the work done every day at Fool.com is done by our readers, and we'll give several examples. These examples and this chapter are designed to help you understand how mass communication on the Internet, much of it through The Motley Fool, is reforming and revolutionizing the financial world today. So even if you don't currently have an interest in or access to computers, you should know what's going on. Chances are you will be logging on and participating at some point very soon, anyway.

After only a few years in existence, Fool.com has become the best-known online site for average Americans looking to learn how to invest and stay informed about their money. Every day, thousands of messages are posted to our online message boards about the stock market, individual stocks, mutual funds, mortgages, quitting smoking, losing weight, divorce, living below your means, Christianity, retirement plans, cars, credit cards—you name it. Our message boards represent nothing more than an open conversation arranged chronologically, involving anyone who would like to contribute a comment. It's kind of like an organized form of talk radio except that it's text based (which makes it smarter and more useful), better organized (you can return every day to a particular topic that interests you), and anything put up on the online site stays there permanently—so you can go back to material you've already seen and found useful (unlike TV, for example). You will learn a tremendous amount.

And here's why people are using our site and a few other good ones, day in and day out. Here's what they're actually doing . . .

They're cooperating. They're working together to understand companies and businesses, to value stocks, to recognize and act upon key news, and even in some cases create that news.

One company, Structural Dynamics (Nasdaq: SDRC), was rumored a few years ago to have a large deal brewing with Ford Motors. Our Midwest readers scoured every information source they could find and discovered new job listings for the company at a Detroit site. That excited them. What excited them more was their subsequent discovery that the address of that site was right next to a Ford plant. And that "rumor" turned out to be dead right; the deal was thereafter announced. The stock rose five times in value that year.

We could go on about this. There are dozens of examples. But to generalize about all of them, the message is clear: You can get *tons of free* help with *whatever* financial question you have by coming online. With everyone's computers hooked together, isolation is disappearing. To resound a clarion call heard earlier in this book: You have more help than you think.

This is excellent news for consumers. You see, for many businesses, isolation has been a strong weapon. Take car dealerships, which we wrote about earlier. Let's do it again, though. Every four or five years, many of us go to buy or lease a new car. And very few of us enjoy the process. Why? Because most people can't stand bartering. They go into the showrooms, look over several contraptions, take one or two out for a test drive, then sit down with the salesman. The old ritual begins . . .

"OK, I like the blue one. So how much is it?"

"How much would you like to pay for it?" the line comes back. We hate that line! Talk about making a customer feel isolated and vulnerable. Who could like these businesses?

When you buy a car, you're isolated. When you sit down with a financial advisor, you feel isolated. When you hire a lawyer to draw up your will, or take a broker's cold call over the phone, or buy a house, you feel isolated. But in a world with high-speed national data networks featuring online sites that attract the consumer mass market, consumers who were once isolated and taken advantage of can now benefit from a word of mouth that doesn't come from their neighbor Janice next door, but rather from a hundred Janices from everywhere. Isolation is disappearing.

Let us close with an additional example, to make it crystal clear what a new world we live in today. In our "Obviously Great Investments" chapter we included a mention of Intel, describing its technological advances as a way of showing how profoundly computers are changing business and society, and how crazy we've all been (ourselves included) if we haven't just bought and held the stock. To demonstrate the company's amazing reach, we ended that chapter by examining the use of computers in space exploration, concentrating on the *Galileo* mission to Jupiter. Now we'd like to share with you the postscript to that story, because it's a great example of why the new medium blows away all the others.

That report was initially published online, and within fifteen minutes of putting it up, we received a note from a technical editor. "You spelled the abbreviation for 'megahertz' as 'mHz' when it actually should've been 'MHz.'" The guy was right. We went back and revised the article right away. How quickly the online medium can repair an error! (Newspapers may or may not print an erratum notice, often days later, in an out-of-the-way corner somewhere. Television? Hey, we can't remember the last time we saw a correction on television.)

OK, so then a few minutes later the next note about the report came in. It was from a Mr. John Hammer of New York. Mr. Hammer corrected another inaccuracy in our report. Writing of the *Galileo* mission to Jupiter, we'd written that the gorgeous and icy Europa was Jupiter's smallest moon. Mr. Hammer wrote, "Actually, Europa is the smallest of Jupiter's four Galilean moons—those first seen by Galileo and easily visible by an amateur with a small telescope. Jupiter has more than 26 moons; that makes Europa #4 of 26, and coincidentally one of the largest in the entire solar system."

Right on. And you know what? Mr. Hammer just so happened to be the director of education of the New York Hall of Science! (We did our homework on that one: Located in Flushing Meadows–Corona Park, the hall offers 230,000 annual visitors over 160 interactive, hands-on exhibits on physics, microbiology, and technology. Mr. Hammer informed us that the hall has the highest visitor density of any museum in New York City, and possibly the highest of any museum anywhere—visitor density being the number of annual visitors divided by square feet of public space.)

But that wasn't all. You see, within another couple of hours, an additional e-mail arrived. It began like this:

Dear Fools,

My wife and I read your Fool Wire today—and were duly impressed with the comments you made about Galileo and the Europa encounter. I read your remarks with particular interest since I am a scientist on the *Galileo* mission and conduct the atmospheric and auroral observations using the ultraviolet spectrometer.

As the French say, *"Sans blague."* No joke. And Mr. Kent Tobiska went on from there to offer Fool HQ a glossy photo of the high-res image of Europa once it finished downloading (at 20 to 40 bits per second, versus the 28,800 per second that, at the time, represented the standard transmission speeds on Earth!). Of course, we jumped at his kind offer. Today, that photo proudly adorns our reception area at Fool HQ, seen by the thousands of visitors who annually make pilgrimages to the ol' corporate headquarters in Alexandria, Virginia (all we ask is that you bring candy—but no Mounds bars!).

Is that a "ton of free help," or what?

That's why we love the online medium. In fact, we've since resolved to include hundreds of inaccuracies in our future writings on technical subjects, just to discover how attentive, brilliant, and well-placed some of our readers are.

We'll close by making the same points we made at the beginning. Computers are very simple gadgets that many people still don't feel comfortable using. In most cases, that's because those people have never taken the time—say, two hours out—to sit down in front of one and plink around a little bit alongside a friend or family member who has some familiarity with them. Take the time to do so, because it will greatly improve the quality of your life. There's simply never been anything before like the help you can get online.

In fact, if you have questions about getting started with computers or using Fool.com, drop us an e-mail at help@Fool.com.

The Ten Most Common Investing Mistakes

W E NOW REACH the end of "An Investing Life," following "An Introduction to Investing." If you're the type who likes helpful restatements and summaries of the major portions of a book, read on. Just as we closed the personal finance portion of the book with "The Ten Most Common Financial Mistakes," we're going to close the investment portion of the book with "The Ten Most Common Investing Mistakes." There are other common ones besides these ten, but if we could all just prevent ourselves from making these, the world would be a much safer place to invest!

#1: Buying What You Don't Understand

Baptisms by fire are common on the stock market. Poll the populace and we feel quite sure you'll discover that most people had little to no understanding of what they first invested in. Your third cousin Al is intent upon launching a mobile-telecommunications business. And he swings for the fences. So you plink down $5,000, without thinking at all. Uh-oh! Or maybe, last Thursday at the company barbecue, that new hotshot in the marketing department tossed a tip out at the punch bowl. "You just gotta love FLYR," he says, talking in ticker symbols. "The potential leverage they'll have over the airline industry? Gimme a break. No-brainer!" The price? Just $8.25 per share. The business? Something to do with airport security. Uh-oh—you don't really know!

The pathway to superior investing is unfortunately often littered with speculations in low-grade, cash-burning, promotional operations that are largely unfamiliar to their shareholders. But any investment in something that you don't understand is a mistake even if it beats the market for you. Allow us to make our point by going to an extreme. One of the worst decisions you could make right now is to plunge your savings money into the Coca-Cola Company only on the basis of your reading of our "First Federal Bank" chapter. Sure, you know our thoughts on Coke's business and on the prospects for their stock over the next few decades. But whoa there. We're just two guys. Would it be particularly smart to rely solely on our ramblings when

a. We have more than three hundred staff members and over two million readers at Fool.com talking about investing *right now*

b. Your local library doesn't charge you a dime for perusing the loads of information and analysis available on Coke's business

c. You can call Coca-Cola directly at (404) 676-2121, obtain its financials, and ask questions of your investment club, mother, or folks in an online investment forum to gain further insight

Mind you, we think our analysis of Coke is pretty sound. Yet, should you just buy shares of Coca-Cola without any of your own exploration? Nope.

The salient point here is that the story of your journey into the world of savings and investing has as its antagonist anyone who tries to rush you. You're the heroic figure in this ever-unfolding financial drama—slated as a made-for-television movie in 2010. What a shame it'll be if the film accurately depicts you acting on other people's opinions, making hasty decisions, and suffering the unpleasant consequences of these misdeeds (frequent nausea, caffeine addiction, and inattentiveness). Nobody's going to root for you in that movie. Instead, read this book again if necessary and soak up the best lessons a second time. Soak them up slowwwwwly. Becoming accustomed to this sort of deliberation will benefit you as an investor; it's the direct opposite of what most people do, which is to rush to act quickly on the recommendations of others. And by "others," we mean anybody or anything: a full-service broker, an online investor, your magic eight ball, your great-aunt Leona in the middle of her hot streak, or the CEO of the company in which you plan to invest.

Without exception, verify the financial information and analysis you are presented. Information is everywhere to be had, combined with our ongoing communications revolution (online and off); you have an endless number of checkpoints, loads of opinions, and plenty of data to support or dismiss anyone's claims.

Onward!

#2: Focusing on Your Short-Term Performance

It's unfortunate that no matter how frequently the principles of compounded growth are made evident, with the mightiest profits coming on the back end of an investment life, some investors continue to believe that profits on the front end, profits *today,* are meaningful. Which is a shame. Because, in many cases, that impatience results in flawed logic, poor investments, digestive complications, and pacing around the den past midnight.

It ain't worth it.

The stock market isn't going anywhere. And barring the absurd, you have plenty of time to research your stocks, trying to locate the best entry point. Whether you enter the market today or in six months or in a year will matter very little to your long-term aggregation of wealth.

Remember that 20 percent of $1,000 is $200. And 20 percent of $100,000 is $20,000. As time expands your base of capital, each later year of growth will provide substantially more dollars. When Anne Scheiber first started investing in 1944, her $5,000 earned her less than $1,000 that year. In the final years of her life, she was generating more than $500,000 in annual dividends, and an average market year brought her more than $2 million in paper gains.

The tomorrows build wealth, not the frenetic activity of the todays. What your portfolio does this upcoming week is several orders of magnitude less important than what it does between the years 2005 and 2010, or better yet, 2025 and 2030. And since what matters financially comes ten and twenty years from now, why not take the next six months just to ask people questions beginning with the words "I'm new at this"? Not a bad idea, if we may clap ourselves on the back; the private investor's biggest blunder is to start investing before asking enough simple questions.

#3: Finding Yourself Becoming Enduringly Bearish

Message in a bottle: As of this writing, the Dow Jones industrials has moved past 11,000. For five or six years now—and really as far back as the 1987 market crash—a gaggle of alarmists have been predicting the Big One. They have moped from one side of the television set to the next. They have wailed on off-hour radio. They've clamored in the financial press. They've sold millions of dollars worth of newsletters and 900-number phone services. However, they have yet to present a convincing, numerical case for their melancholy banter. And they've just been horribly wrong: It's been a great market.

Consider that at the enduring rate of 11 percent growth per year, the stock market on average doubles in value every seven years. Now you'll understand why the pessimists always pop up on financial television wearing *cheap suits*. If you bet *against* the stock market you can expect to lose all of your money, all of your shirts, and hopefully all of your newsletter subscribers every seventh year. And particularly cruel torture awaits those bears who decide to bet against fundamentally strong, industry-dominating companies. The Coca-Cola Company has grown in value at a rate about 16 percent per year since 1919. On average, every four and a half years, Coke investors have doubled their money. That, of course, means that the investor who bet against Coca-Cola has given it all away every five years this century.

To depict that madness, we'll tell the following tale of faith and cynicism.

The year is 1919. Coca-Cola is going public, and at the starting gate stand an optimistic young woman and a steely-eyed, trained professional. Put your money on the professional, right?! The young woman, we'll name her Joy, is looking to gradually build wealth on her savings throughout her entire life. She's fresh out of college, headed to nursing school, relieved that World War I is over. Her professional counterpart in this tale has other schemes. We'll name him Sam. He's trained his bulging eyes on a new Ford, a beach house in the Hamptons, and raucous weekly parties with young revelers pitching themselves naked into a four-thousand-square-foot pool.

Feeling good with our money on the pro!

Both of these investors start with $3,000 and add another $3,000 every five years. Now, the crucial difference: Our wealth builder, Joy, is going to buy Coca-Cola while our hotshot professional, Sam, is prepared to bet against Coke (known in the financial world as "shorting it"—and yes, you can make money betting against a stock). At the end of 1999, Joy has $989 million; Sam has $2,629. Oddly enough, given his utterly dismal performance record, Sam is a regular on morning financial television; he was featured on the front page of the *Wall Street Journal* last week; he's the proud publisher of a financial newsletter with twelve thousand subscribers; and everyone from his casual acquaintances to the average fan on the Street thinks he's a stock market sophisticate. And where's Joy? She quietly attends Coca-Cola's yearly shareholder conferences; she regularly commits charitable funds to her local community, is helping to put her seventeen grandchildren through school, just collected an annual dividend payment in 2000 of more than $9 million, and reads the *Wall Street Journal* once a month for pleasure, not strategy.

The numbers tell the whole story. But thinking in visuals for a moment might help. It's very hard to come up with an appropriate analogy for what Sam has done to himself by betting against (shorting) the likes of Coca-Cola, Microsoft, Nike, Johnson & Johnson, Gillette, Intel, the Gap, and General Electric, just because they may have looked momentarily overvalued. Perhaps this comparison will suffice . . .

Envision a train pitching toward Minnesota through the golden, hay-baled fields of Montana at a rate of eighty-five miles per hour. Now, in your mind, position Sam on the track one mile east of that train, in a full sprint west toward Seattle. Wait for sixty seconds. (It won't take that long.) Now repeat that scenario every five years, and you've captured Sam's experience in the public marketplace during the twentieth century. Holding to the train theme, Joy has instead made herself comfortable in the sleeping car, convinced that there will be delays along the way, that the engine will founder at some point, but certain as well that the substantial and persistent vehicular momentum is gliding onward.

#4: Believing the Financial Press Is Expert

Our dearly beloved financial press is in the unfortunate habit of downplaying the power that Brother Time and Sister Logic play in the investing world. To date, the media have shown little interest in speaking to the patient private investor who socks money into stocks for decades and ignores short-term fluctuations in the market. Not that there's much to say to him as it is, mind you, but perhaps that's part of the point. In the media's race to present (or design) the latest controversy and in its obsession with today, the business press largely ignores the variable of time, the keeper of all compounded growth. The great self-sufficient investors haven't created millions of dollars of wealth over the last forty years by buying on the rumor and selling on the news. They buy on the research, their own research, and often don't sell. At the *Los Angeles Times* investors' conference in 1997, an elderly gentleman talked with us about his decades of investing, chuckling that it seemed like everyone from investment firm to financial newspaper to glossy magazine had tried to rock him out of his position in Schering-Plough over the past forty years. "And thank God I ignored them all and held straight through."

Yes, give thanks.

The lesson here is so profound, it runs as deep as the earth's molten core. *If time builds wealth, why are the financial media mainly concerned not with time, but with things timely? Why do they hold in such high regard the brokerage firms that profit off impatience and high-octane trading, religiously quoting their estimates and celebrating their predictions page by page?* If these and other financial organizations are fashioned primarily to serve us, why aren't the many Anne Scheiber tales stamped out in their marketing materials and championed in our nation's glossy financial periodicals?

If the modest leftovers from an average salary can patiently be raised into $22 million over one lifetime, what level of madness attends us when we overdramatize the immediate, when we bind our dreams up in short-term profits or put our faith in those who would have us do just that? The diligent but gradually maddened reader of America's financial journals has suffered through a lot these past several decades. During that period, the media have elevated to the stage a curious and unfortunate creation: the glorified bear-market guru (henceforth Foolishly represented as "gooroo"). Thrusting their chests out and showing their teeth, bear-market gooroos have held the financial press hostage and wreaked havoc on the portfolios of private investors during one of the greatest bull markets of the century.

How did they gain such prominence?

Between August and October 1987, the Dow Jones industrial average fell from 2,746 to 1,616—a head-rattling 41 percent decline from peak to trough. During that short period, $100,000 in stocks turned into less than $60,000. Many investors who'd made the mistake of borrowing money to buy stocks were wiped out. As traders collapsed on the market floor, and banks hyperventilated, and investment clubs dug in, the financial media lovingly embraced the cynical gooroo in accepting the pronouncements of those claiming to have "correctly called the worst three-month period in the history of the stock market."

All of a sudden, America was treated to a new stream of magical indicators and hysterical pronouncements, a new cast of players careening across the stage. Newsletters sprang up across the country crying Armageddon, and the bears found themselves welcome on expert panels and in academic halls. As of this writing, more than a decade later, the bear-market gooroo is gradually disappearing. It took virtually a decade for the media to realize that October 20, 1987—the day after the market crashed 23 percent—was one of the most wonderful days to buy stocks this century. (With great satisfaction, we note that Rule Breaker Portfolio co-manager, Jeff Fischer, opened a brokerage account and made his first investment in stocks on this very day.) Since that time, the Dow has risen a total of 527 percent. The bears who gained notoriety by betting against the stock market have lost the equivalent of their entire portfolio five times over since 1987. Has that story been told? No. But, of course, they've sold a lot of investment newsletters to make up for heavy investment losses.

Here the larger point is not that stock prices constantly rise, because they don't. The larger point is that market pessimists always lose out over time. So why do so many media organizations adorn the money-losing cynics with garlands? Because in the media business, controversy and disaster sell. Train wrecks and fistfights, estranged celebrity couples and five-alarm fires, *and* . . . the collapse of the stock market. The editing process at most newspapers and television stations is heavily biased in favor of matters catastrophic. This, even as most Americans are pleasingly disposed in their daily lives. And though the stock market maintains its northerly course, smoothing out each calamity with time, the financial press still too often champions pandemonium and wretchedness.

When we return to Warren Buffett, who claims not to read financial papers, we're reminded of what matters. Private investors have quietly and methodically grown their savings for decades. No, they aren't half as exciting as Donald Trump or the collapse of Barings Bank or (sigh) the next market collapse. So they don't often gain coverage from Manhattan. But they do seem to be making a good deal of money this century, no?

Again, none of this is to imply that the market won't lean this way and that, or that it won't crumble again, perhaps even tomorrow. At some point, it will. But the average American (median age of thirty-four) has four decades ahead of her in which to invest. Whether the Dow index drops by

30 percent tomorrow is of principal inconsequence to Foolish investors. Regrettably, that sort of hasty decline is of principal *consequence* to the financial media, on the lookout for casualties and collision. And therein lies the inversion of interests, pitting patient reader against desperate writer. When learning is prized over controversy, the financial papers will be worth reading. We're not there yet.

#5: Concentrating Your Attention on Stock Price

One of the frequent mistakes of the novice investor is a preoccupation with stock prices. Our first inclination as investors is often to believe that a stock trading for $3 a share is less expensive and holds greater potential for reward than one trading at $95 a share. That idea's as natural as red roses on the vine. After all, having purchased products our entire lives, we've come to recognize that a hat selling for three bucks is less pricey than a hat selling for ninety-five bucks. Simple.

Unfortunately, this principle doesn't hold on the stock market. A stock price in and of itself is meaningless. Please crisscross your legs, open your palms skyward, hum almost inaudibly, and repeat this to yourself: *A stock price in and of itself is meaningless.* As seems often the case, Oscar Wilde sides with the Fools: "Nowadays people know the price of everything and the value of nothing."

What is the total value of a business?

Harkening back to our chapter "A Stock Primer," we reiterate that the total value (or "market cap") of a company equals the number of shares times the price of those shares. Thus, if Leeza's Lenses Inc. (NYSE: SEE) has 10 million shares of stock with each share priced at $15, the company is valued at $150 million ($15 × 10 million = $150 million). And Macrodata Inc. (Nasdaq: POPS), with 1 million shares trading at $30 a share, is priced at $30 million. In this case, the $30 stock represents a lower-priced company than the $15 stock. The market cap indicates the total value of the business, whether the shares are trading at $3 or $300.

To combat the tendency to focus on stock price, imagine that all of the stocks in your portfolio were trading at $100 a share. Further, imagine that every stock on the market were trading at that price. Now, which companies would you invest in? Would you buy that tin-cup-waving, self-promotional Canadian oil driller, or would you buy Nike? Would you become an owner of the highly leveraged Trump Casinos, or would you buy an ownership position in debt-free Microsoft?

Shielding from view the daily meandering of stock pricing, you will naturally bear down more rigorously on the businesses you are buying. In doing so, you will have avoided our fifth giant investing miscue. Now, on to number six.

#6: Buying Stocks Under $5 a Share

We must present the exception to the previous rule, which now validates its status as a rule. We just told you not to concentrate on stock prices. Now, for a brief departure, we offer this: Do take into account the price of a stock when you find one trading below $5 a share.

In this universe of "companies," you can expect to stumble across some amazing stories. You'll find "businesses" that claim to have already cured lung cancer—they just need the go-ahead from the "damned FDA." Others have designed the oxygen-powered lightbulb. Others have unspecified but substantial housing-project opportunities in the former Soviet Union. Still others have claims on adjacent oil patches in downtown Beirut. In our experience, the larger the story, the lower the price of the stock and the slimmer the prospects that some real business exists beneath it all. We read somewhere that 75 percent of all companies with stocks trading under $5 a share go to zero within a decade. In the meantime, stocks like Pfizer, Gillette, and General Electric keep moving higher and splitting, with prices ranging between $30 and $200.

While we dissuade you from ever investing in penny stocks, we do recommend that any fiction writers among us seize all opportunities to interview the executive teams of companies with stocks trading under $1 per share. There's a great novel in there, somewhere. Probably several.

#7: Not Tracking Your Investment Returns

With the Internet and with a variety of software packages available such as Microsoft Money and Intuit's Quicken, tracking the performance of your investments is easier than ever before. By typing in your positions and updating them each week, month, or quarter, you can distinguish among market-beating, market-meeting, and market-losing performance. Is your financial advisor beating the market, after the deduction of all management fees? Has your strategy to buy ownership positions in predominantly high-technology companies proven gainful? Is Microsoft stock beating the market?

Not knowing whether your investments are thriving or barely surviving from year to year is somewhat akin to not knowing what record your favorite baseball team has or—worse—how your children are doing in school or how old you are. The process of maintaining and updating your portfolio's performance relative to the stock market should be painless— nay, joyous.

Too many investors don't know how their account did the previous year or for any of the past decade. There are entire investment clubs that perform wonderful research, do a bang-up job with analysis, and yet, at year end, don't know how their investments have performed relative to the S&P 500. Much as we purely love the process of researching business and investing, measuring performance is critical. And in too many instances, the numbers bring good humor to the financial industry. Not just a few mutual funds have run advertisements that read "Nineteen ninety-nine was a great year. Our fund rose 14 percent!" This in a year that the market climbed 21 percent. The investor tracking returns knew to sell off that fund for promoting its own mediocrity.

#8: Not Diversifying Your Portfolio

At various times along the way, some of your individual holdings will heat up and swell into overlarge positions in your portfolio. At one time, one of our online portfolios was sporting two stocks which had appreciated so substantially that they accounted for over 70 percent of the value of the portfolio.

We were excited. Prospects looked great for both companies. Research analysts on Wall Street that we respect were championing both enterprises. Everything was right at The Motley Fool. It doesn't take a cynic to note that when absolutely everything seems right with the world, it often isn't. It was at that time, in our fury of glee, that we should have been paring back our positions in both stocks. To have over 70 percent of one's value tied up in two positions makes one vulnerable to a comeuppance—one that we did get.

Our recommendation is that portfolios of greater than $15,000 rarely have more than 15 percent of the total capital initially invested in any one stock. From there, we recommend that you think about lightening any positions that grow to become more than 25 percent of your total portfolio. These numbers are guidelines, guidelines to be guided by individual taste and circumstance.

Let's walk through a brief example, with a $20,000 portfolio. First off, you would not invest more than 15 percent, or $3,000, in any one position. Then imagine that your portfolio took this shape two years hence:

Date Purchased	Shares	Security	In at	Now	Value
8/5/97	305	Lou's Drive-ins	8.13	40.75	$12,428.75
8/5/96	85	Sears Roebuck	28.00	48.88	$4,154.80
8/11/96	45	Soup n' Snails	57.88	84.88	$3,819.60
5/17/96	40	Coca-Cola	60.50	94.88	$3,795.20
1/29/96	90	Maria's	27.88	34.38	$3,094.20
8/11/97	55	Shaving Kits	49.00	31.88	$1,753.40
8/24/97	55	Kudzu Kreepers	44.75	26.50	$1,457.50
4/20/97	150	The Motley Fool	16.25	9.25	$1,387.50
				TOTAL:	$31,890.95

In this scenario, you'll see that although no *initial* investment exceeded 15 percent, one of our holdings has exploded. Lou's Drive-ins has quintupled; our holding in Lou's has swollen to nearly 40 percent of the total value of our account. For most people, a little red light should probably go off here. The brokerage account is overweighted in one direction. Probably time to lighten up on Lou's, even though it's been our top performer. Before closing up this section, check out our biggest dog. Ouch.

#9: Not Being Online

The financial story of the last few years has been the growth in activity on the Internet. Investors from across the planet are tapping into a network of resources that dramatically overshadows the amount of information available via any other source.

The discussion boards at Fool.com service conversations among research analysts, company executives, and private investors far removed from Manhattan. In six short years, we departed from a world where only the wealthiest individuals and the largest institutional investors could gain access to valuable information and research. Today, the greenhorn investor with a personal computer and a modem can click into ongoing conversations about personal finance, business, and investing that are educational and inclusive.

It is a profound misstep for anyone with access to the Internet—either at home, school, or a local library—not to take advantage of the resources and the opportunities available, not to step up and have his individual questions answered online. A mass conversation about savings and investing is occurring even as you flip through these pages. And it's a discussion that is changing the way the money world works, an ongoing transformation that greatly works in favor of the individual.

As consumers band together and negotiate with the big boys on leveler ground, savings money is flowing out across America. If you can access the Internet, you should give Fooldom a spin as well as a number of other sites. Rather than learning by passively reading, you can, with your networked computer, learn through cooperative endeavor.

#10: Spending Far Too Much Time on Investing

It seems only right that we close down our investing don'ts with a recognition that some of us fall into the trap of dedicating too much time to money management. If this notion seems ludicrous to you today, don't be surprised if in three years you are systematically checking your stock quotes each morning and find yourself in regular conversations about Nike's prospects with your athletically challenged third cousin Rupert.

Studying businesses, becoming a part owner of enterprises, and talking about your smartest and dumbest investments is actually a helluva lot of fun. But the very brightest find ways to involve themselves just enough to wallop the market's average returns, to learn much from the ongoing investigation, but never (or rarely) to compromise the other joys of life—their grandchildren, a picnic lunch, handling the wheel of a thirty-foot sailboat in the Gulf of Mexico, sleeping until noon one Tuesday in April.

Don't miss out! In the very dreariest of scenarios, some people even take to trading stocks each day, while passing the daylight hours in torn pajamas, huddled over the glare of a computer monitor, blindly reaching to their left and unknowingly eating a two-week-old tuna sandwich off the wrong plate. Although we find it hard to imagine a scenario where this sort of trader makes money and beats the market, even so, can you imagine this sort of living? Can you imagine eating that sandwich? Can you imagine that taste going unnoticed?

As captivating as the market can be, as much fun as the whole process of saving and investing is, verily it does not take the place of living. The blend of online services, the study of business, and market-beating investing has proved nearly irresistible for some. Our suggestion is that if and when you are alerted by spouse or loved one that you haven't heard a word they've said for more than five minutes, it's probably time to take a very long walk together in the park.

PART V

BEYOND

Your First Few
Months Investing

S PEND YOUR FIRST few months doing what most new investors don't: Relax and be methodical, never allowing yourself to get too excited or dismayed by your performance. Remain particularly free from short-term worry, because short-term worries are just that! A classic mistake is to get too wrapped up in the day-to-day. We turn to the Bible for inspiration here, specifically the worrier's favorite book, Revelation: "The devil is come down unto you, having great wrath, because he knoweth that he hath but a short time" (12:12). Was a truer word ever writ? Confound this Screwtape; think and *act* for the long term.

Of course, the chances are excellent that even if you've made all the right moves, you'll find that (surprise!) things won't go absolutely perfectly. If you were a sports team, yes, it would be nice never to lose a game. And while spending a long weekend at the beach, who wants any rain on a Saturday? But don't get down on yourself should your first stock drop a quick 25 percent.

For a starter, you won't find any such thing as guaranteed good returns in our financial world, especially over the short term. Oh sure, you might come across advertised "guarantees" for great investment performance, but in case you needed to hear this from us (which we doubt), you shouldn't trust *anyone* who's making you such a promise. (Indeed, during the writing of this chapter, what should show up in our e-mailbox but a junk ad for a software package offering *guaranteed* winning lottery numbers?) The probability that the market will rise over the next ten years is extremely high. Any *guarantees*? Absolutely not. Risk is everywhere in our world—no free chocolate bars out there—so don't start pouting or swearing off investing if things don't go your way the first few weeks or months, or even the first couple of years—unless you have only a couple years to live!

You might even have a friend or two who ribs you a bit. "You see, Alice? You need a professional." Last time we checked, very few professionals were recommending using no-load index funds, even though most are losing to them. Take a typical case, like Darin's.

Darin is an air force officer who as a lieutenant began investing with a company that targets military officers for their investment and insurance needs. His friendly professional put him in a growth fund with a stiff front-end load of 5 percent and an additional "custodial fee" of 1.5 percent tacked on. A few years later he got to thinking about his finances and his future and began asking questions. He turned to Fooldom. "I invest one hundred dollars a month to this fund, of which they skim $5 for sales charges and $1.50 for custodial fees. Does this mean that the fund has to make 6.95% just for me to recoup my money?" he asked. You betcha, Darin. In fact, tap into that fund company's Web site and you find a few outperforming funds, many underperforming funds, and nary a reference to the benchmark S&P 500. Oh, and a bunch of footnotes. Down below in the fine print, a typical one reads: "Excluding sales charges. Returns would have been lower had sales charges been reflected."

Fellow Fool, the index fund is the stake in the heart of the managed mutual fund industry. It's also a great first step away from expensive "professional management," for those who are ready to take it.

If, in the course of your first few months investing, you find yourself frequently and anxiously preoccupied about your stocks, we're going to ask you seriously to consider selling them and moving the money into an index fund. Anxiety at an early stage like this could be telling you something. It's saying: "This isn't your style, and you probably shouldn't be doing this." Different people have different tolerances for risk. Stick with what suits you, because you'll be better off in the long run (for several reasons) by staying true to who you are. In time, you may gain enough knowledge and experience that you'll consider again the possibility of investing directly in stocks. But until that day (which for some people simply never arrives, which is fine), stick with funds.

Underneath all the ugly invective and name-calling that we've hurled toward mutual funds over the years, we have but one primary message, which we still believe and encourage you to believe. We have no fundamental gripe with funds—how they work, who manages them, or who invests in them—because all we really care about is performance. If the world were populated with thousands of mutual funds that were all beating the market, you can bet we'd give our books lurid titles like *Have You Hugged Your Mutual Fund Today?* or *Get Foolish, Get Rich, Get These Dozen Great Funds NOW.*

Instead, about the only fund *family* we admire is Vanguard. There are some other good individual funds, of course—several hundred of them, among the 10,000. However, given that locating a successful fund before it demonstrates success is far more difficult than locating good long-term businesses, we preach stocks. We aim to beat funds, and the best way to do that is to skip the stable owners altogether and invest directly in the horses.

Of course, one danger of investing in stocks is that at any given moment, a fleet of Wall Street analysts may decide they don't like your company. This happens to great companies and good investors all the time. For instance, we purchased stock in a superb outfit, semiconductor equipment maker KLA-Tencor (Nasdaq: KLAC), at its new high of $44 in August of 1995. It rose a couple of bucks from there and then proceeded to dive-bomb. Equipment purchases in that industry can be somewhat cyclical, and we had bought at exactly the wrong time in the cycle. This became even more evident to us as we watched a raft of Wall Street analysts downgrade their expectations for the company's business and for its share price—and the shares followed through, all the way down to $17 a year later. In one year we had lost 61 percent of our money! But nothing fundamentally had changed about KLA-Tencor, its industry, or its place within that industry, so we continued to hold. And lo and behold, within six months of the low the stock had climbed back up, to $50, for a new all-time high, to put us back in the black. A few months after hitting $50, the stock was worth $70.

The bleakest hour of all was, of course, the moment it hit $17. Things were *worse than they'd ever been,* and some other KLAC investors in our online area had some bleak things to say. But that was of course the best moment of all to have bought! (We didn't, because we tend not to throw more money at stocks that are way down for us. But we were still very happy to be back above even by the first quarter of 1997. Some smart people did, of course, buy at the bottom.)

The story of KLA-Tencor is not at all unique in our own portfolios, or that of most long-term equity investors. Indeed, we've had some other inspirational comebacks. We bought stock in 3Com (Nasdaq: COMS) in August of 1996 at $46. By mid-December, the shares had struck $80 and we were high-fiving prematurely over our expected quick double. Lo and behold, the stock was suddenly felled in the face of new competition from Intel, combined with a networking industry that had overweening hopes factored into its valuation. During four ugly weeks starting in late January 1997, we watched the stock drop relentlessly from $77 to $33. Two months later, COMS was doing a death rattle as it touched down at $24; what had once been up 75 percent for us was suddenly down some 50 percent from the $46 per share we'd paid the previous summer!

Within five weeks, the stock was back to $50, and we were in the money again. In fact, very little changed during that month in terms of the company's prospects; the news on the wires was incidental and mostly meaningless. Essentially, Wall Street institutional investors and analysts had overreacted and created a selling frenzy of a very good company's stock. Long-term individual investors like us had to sit there and take our medicine, but we never allowed ourselves to get caught up in the short-term mentality. So after the rockets' red glare and the bombs bursting in air, our Foolish flag was still there. OK—we're getting carried away. We'll stop.

To restate the lesson here, in your first few months investing (or the umpteen years that follow) you may encounter situations like these. And we're not here to tell you that *every stock* will come bouncing gallantly back as did the two just discussed. Ours don't always, and every investor will take his lumps. What tends to separate the investments that do rebound from the ones that don't is the strength of the business and the company, the extent to which they're built to last, the importance of the company's contribution to society. That, and you have to identify the reasons they're falling in the first place—are they ephemeral and fleeting, or serious, even peremptory? The two cases above both involved a sudden change of short-term sentiment on Wall Street—that is about as fleeting as you get, dear reader. *Nota bene.*

Such extreme volatility isn't for everyone, but it's a lot easier to stomach if you're a long-term thinker and a long-term investor. That's probably a message that the first-few-months investor can't hear too frequently. Remember, the devil hath but a short time.

Shall we just drill this baby home one more time? OK, let's do it.

Put yourself in our shoes, owning shares of the Gap in early 1996. The story hits the wires, January 17.

Exhibit A

NatWest Securities lowered the Gap from "accumulate" to "hold" today. Sources at the brokerage stated that this was part of a series of downgrades involving the retail stocks due to the weak retail environment.

Of course, we'd like to think that every average investor, even those who are just beginning, would react this way: "Oh yeah, right, I'm *really* worried about the Gap's business prospects going forward. Who cares if some brokerage firm thinks we're temporarily in a 'weak retail environment'? I see, so the world is suddenly going to stop buying jeans forever?" This is the thinking of the Foolish long-term investor, anyway.

Ladies and gentlemen, if you will now please flip your calendar page one month forward, to February 29, 1996, and note the following press release (and yes, this is all real—ain't no make-believe going on here)...

Exhibit B

NatWest Securities Corp. analyst Robert Buchanan raised his rating on Gap Inc. (GPS) to accumulate from hold. In a research report, Buchanan said he is "very impressed" by the company's strong performance in a still-depressed environment for apparel sales.

Now this is not a personal attack on Mr. Robert Buchanan or NatWest Securities firm (neither of which we've ever had any dealings with—heck, we don't even know where NatWest is located). Indeed, in the past each of us must admit to having been fickle about our investments, or sports team, or flower arrangement, or the supper we've just cooked. Whatever.

But listen, that's part of the point, right there. Buchanan and his firm are *very much like us.* Most may tend to put an analyst or brokerage firm on a pedestal, figuring those guys are so much more sophisticated and knowledgeable than we are. Oh yeah? We're all human. This is very helpful to remember whenever you're staring at a major negative story or downgrade brought on by an analyst or a firm.

In fact, you have a great advantage over these people: your perspective. They're all playing the short-term game and losing sight of what really makes money: buy-and-hold investing over the long term. (Of course, as we wrote earlier, the way these guys make money is not so much by successful investing but by inducing their clients to trade, which is greatly aided by a short-term focus, *n'est-ce pas?*)

Look at it again: NatWest Securities hopped off the Gap bandwagon in mid-January, apparently unimpressed by the stock despite the company's strong long-term prospects and powerful financial position. From "accumulate" it went to "hold." Then, one month later Gap becomes presentable once again to NatWest clients, upped from "hold" to "accumulate." Would this be the way you would invest?

We hope not. Because the missing piece to this puzzle is where the stock was during all this. Here are two stock quotes for you:

GPS, 1/17 (date downgraded): $43.88
GPS, 2/29 (date upgraded): $53.50

The phrase used in polite company these days is "bass-ackwards," is it not? (We're not exactly sure; we keep hoping someday to get invited to one of these polite-company parties to find out.) Sometimes numbers speak more eloquently than words.

Such examples occur so frequently that we'd be remiss not to point them out. Certainly, some good companies do have long-term business problems and bad stock performances. And some brokerage firms do make the "right call" from time to time. We just want to make sure that you don't believe those are always the case, or even the norm. You won't tend to hear these stories, because, as mentioned earlier, our media tend to focus only on the here and now (a big story the day of the downgrade, a big story the day of the upgrade, but no story linking the two together and reflecting on this—indeed, The Motley Fool was the only entity that reported on this "story behind the story" when it happened, for instance). The short-term focus leads to short-term guesswork shooting for short-term returns, which generally leads to lots of short-term mistakes. And two big long-term ones: You'll spend more of your life trying to beat the market with less likelihood of doing so.

To close: You got through your first few months. They may not even have been that great. You then stuck it out a full year longer, and now you're through your first year and a half and things are no better. You're underperforming. Hey, we know the feeling. Our online Fool Portfolio (since renamed the "Rule Breaker Port") skewered the market its first couple of years in existence, but in year three we hit a dry spell. It's frustrating, of course, but if you're a Fool you're perfectly willing to make deservedly self-effacing jokes about your own failing efforts when the opportunity presents itself. The ability to laugh at oneself is perhaps the best indicator of eventual success. The key is simply not to lose sight of the big picture! Whether it's a bad month or a bad thirty-six months, if you're sticking to a disciplined plan for saving, and investing your money in good companies you understand, you will win in the only term that counts—the *long* term.

The Fourteen Things You've Learned Here

A s WE MAKE our final march toward the conclusion of this tome, we believe it a good and a necessary thing to restate some of the principles you've learned from your journey deep into the heart of Folly. No, you haven't learned how to make an irresistible swath of Guatemalan bean dip; you're no better a doubles tennis player than when you started; and you know nothing more about the Sumatran orangutan than before turning back these covers. But you have learned the following . . .

1. The Value of Just One Lousy Buck

Your road to golden riches and a villa by the sea begins with just a single dollar bill. One dollar saved puts you thousands of dollars ahead of the average American, whose shoulder bag of obligations has nearly swollen beyond capacity. The elimination of that debt and the first saved dollar is the noblest of financial aims. But for many the battle doesn't seem worth it. *Why the hell save one dollar today—what good is there in that?*

Let's review the numbers one last time to burn the effect of saving $1 per day and investing that money in the stock market into your brain. At an 11 percent annual return, $1 saved each day for the next thirty years will grow into $80,633. Two dollars set aside every day, naturally, returns around $161,267. Three dollars, $241,900. Five dollars a day grows into $403,167 after thirty *average* years of stock market investing.

Our presumption is that everyone in this country beyond the age of eighteen can save $5 per day, or $1,825 per year, over the next thirty years. And if they invest that savings money methodically into the stock market via an index fund, the probable $400,000 reward will certainly enable a giant bash for all Fools round the first human-lit campfire and marshmallow roast on Mars in 2031.

Is not the saving of that first dollar then dramatically underrated?

2. The Price of Bad Mathematics

In the United States, more than $100 billion per year is spent on gambling, which amounts to more than $400 per individual wagered against all odds. You learned that an average casino bet takes from 2 to 5 percent of the money out of the bettor's hands and deposits it into the house account. For every $1 billion spent on roulette, craps, and blackjack, the house claims for itself from $20 to $50 million; the bettor relinquishes it. Thus, this gambler generating just average returns on each wager will lose half of his money after just nine bets.

If that sounds grim, consider the unfortunate soul who, believing that his elected officials actually want what's best for him, methodically buys the lottery tickets promoted by the state on street corners, over the radio, and on television. On average, $10 spent on lottery tickets will yield but $5, marking a 50 percent negative rate of return. This system of entertaining taxation—in many ways similar to what destroyed modern-day Albania—will reduce the total value of invested dollars by 97 percent every five bets. A $1,000 kitty set aside for the daily purchase of lottery tickets will be reduced to $31.25 within five days.

The cost of bad mathematics—particularly that promoted by many of our elected officials—ain't cheap.

3. The Health Risks of Credit Card Borrowing

Bad mathematics is hurting us in the shopping malls of the nation as well. Americans have thousands of dollars of debt per adult, at an average interest rate of 18 percent per year. And it looks like the debt load and the interest rates are headed higher. It doesn't take a graduate business degree to project what will happen if this growth rate continues.

Now, our nation's creditors present themselves as servants to those in need of cash. In their *service* role, they *must* have plans for a 2001 marketing blitz to explain to their customers why they shouldn't let outstanding debt revolve from month to month. Right? (Guffaw.) Whichever companies do encourage individuals to live within their means can expect a lot of healthy business in the years ahead. But even if the borrowing and the interest rates head higher and the credit card companies persist in promoting consumers toward insolvency, you now know that no investment can, after taxes, consistently outperform the 18 percent annual interest rate on borrowed money. There is no better financial decision you can make than to pay down all of your plastic debt.

En route to eliminating any debt you have, you should consider going on a furious refinancing campaign. Most credit card companies will reduce your interest rate if they believe you might switch to one of their competitors. Bargain the rates down, then aggressively pay off all your debt. And hereupon, quarantine any desires you have to live beyond your means. Patience will bring it all within reach.

4. The Dangers of Buying Expensive Things Alone

Hopefully, you will never trek to the offices of a financial advisor, real estate broker, insurance salesman, or car dealership on your own again. Big-ticket buying can wreck your savings account. Because they come so infrequently and because of their great expense, big-ticket items can cost the uncareful consumer tens of thousands of dollars in a lifetime. Those same monies preserved and invested in common stocks will—we kid you not, we ain't toying with the numbers—generate hundreds of thousands, even millions, of dollars of wealth in a single lifetime. If, over a ten-year period, you can save $10,000 on the combination of house, car, and insurance buying, that money invested in an index fund may grow to $230,000 or more in thirty years. It's money that is sitting out there *waiting* to be saved. The problem is that the sellers don't want you to save it. Naturally, they'd prefer to see that $10,000 in their corporate coffers, earning 11 percent growth annually *for them*. And that explains their impatience, their use of jargon, their periphrastic legal contracts, and the cheeriness they exude when you sign on the dotted line without doing a lick of research.

None of this should be taken as a personal criticism of the people involved in these businesses. Certainly not. We happen to have a great real estate agent here in Alexandria, Virginia, a great working relationship with our insurance carrier, and have even conversed with the occasional car dealer in our online forum who aims to create win-win scenarios for his customers. All of us would agree—you should take advantage of the Internet, skim a couple of books on the subject, ask your relatives about their experiences, and take your time throughout. Method, scrutiny, and the assistance of others will save you oodles of money. Don't go it alone.

5. The Neutrality of Your Savings Account

Once you've used mathematics to talk yourself out of ever gambling, once you've reduced your consumer debt to nothingness, once you've systematically landed the best deals on those infrequent and expensive buys, you'll start seeing dollars pile up in your savings account. You've noticed that your neighborhood banking executive has taken to greeting you warmly in the street and has been heard delivering high praise of you from one dinner party to the next.

Dear Fool, we don't want you to fall out of the good favor of this fine gentleman, but the placement into a savings account of any monies you will not need for the next three years is wasteful. After you've paid taxes on that money, the rate of growth will at best meet inflationary growth and commonly lose to it. Inflation eats right out of your wallet. At its standard rate of growth, inflation will reduce the value of your savings dollars by half every twenty years. If inflation grows at a nominal rate of 3.5 percent per year, then $10,000 on January 1, 2001, will be worth just a bit over $5,000 on New Year's Day 2021. If you'll need that money in the next three years, it should sit in interest-bearing CDs or savings accounts, yes. But if you can afford to tuck it away for the decades ahead, it should be in the stock market.

6. How to Make Some Money to Get Started

This book has also aspired to provide a sounding board for a revolution in entrepreneurialism. The world has never so hungered for P. T. Barnumesque antics as it does now, at the dawn of the third millennium. Can you not find it in you to play pitchman to a highly promotional, creative, but generally needless undertaking—for profit? Make your dog a trick dog or bottle your bathwater—whatever. Just remember there's fun to be had with everything. There's even some "fun" in "fun"damentalism!

7. The Directional Path of Common Stocks Is Higher

As you put away money for long-term investment—from your professional life and the entrepreneurial endeavors lately mentioned—you'll want to periodically return to the graph presented on pages 150 to 151. Though many have promoted the dangers of being a part owner in American business for more than a decade now, the numbers continue to undermine their position.

Let's say it again: Common stocks have risen at a rate of 11 percent per year over the past century, as the nation has plowed through the final bursts of the Industrial Revolution into the era of new technology and the Information Age. By championing and mostly defending freedom of thought, word, and deed, America has created an environment that allows business to serve its ruling subjects, its people. U.S. corporations, increasingly the model of efficiency, are world leaders in marketing, technological advancement, and cash management.

Does this mean we can expect the twenty-first century to bring in excess of 11 percent annual growth? No, but we do expect the trend of corporate growth to continue, as our businesses become more international, and gradually more universal. With no science to back up our claims, we expect extraterrestrial life to take to soft drinks, blue jeans, romantic comedies, and—we're going out on a limb here—Captain and Tennille remixes. The future of American business, the growth in imaginative enterprise, and the intelligent allocation of capital seem as ripe with possibility as they must have when Wilbur and Orville Wright put their plane into the air nearly one hundred years ago. OK, expect 11 percent annual growth in U.S. stocks between today and the year 3000.

8. When Not to Invest Your Money in Stocks

But now take a second look back at that graph on pages 150 to 151, and you'll notice that on a dozen different occasions, the stock market fell by more than 20 percent from recent highs. From 1968 to 1974, 32 percent of the value of common stocks was wiped out, as the nation suffered through internal strife, an ill-advised war, the near impeachment of its leader, the stoppage of oil flow from OPEC nations, and financial gridlock from heightened interest rates. The common-stock investor was griddled to a crisp, burnt by a market that had fallen this far and this fast only back in the Great Depression.

Because it is a certainty that this sort of dissolution of value will occur again in the decades ahead, we can't recommend that anyone buy stocks who doesn't have a long-term horizon of *at least* three to five years (preferably thirty), or to anyone who isn't free of all prepayable debt, or who isn't entirely comfortable with all of the tricks, traps, taunts, and trials the stock market can deliver in any given year. The critical necessity that you invest in stocks for your retirement is outdone only by the importance of your not entering until you can take the market on your own terms. The state of your financial standing when investing will as much determine your enduring success or failure as will the performance of the businesses you own.

9. The Strange Motivations of the Full-Service Broker

Somehow we reached the final decade of the century without most Americans understanding the role of, and compensation structure behind, the business of full-service brokering. Because stockbrokers were trained as salesmen and compensated on commission, brokering was totally out of control by 1990, when Michael Lewis published his fine exposé of the industry, *Liar's Poker*.

Commission-driven brokering businesses have been built up on the wrongheaded notion that active trading in the marketplace benefits the individual. As brokers shuffle new holdings into their accounts, their firm takes a commission cut from each trade. And if those commission payments aren't enough, coupled with annual, short-term capital gains taxes, frequent trading becomes a wrecking ball for most private investors. At the rate the financial world is changing, the commission-based system may not survive much past the year 2000. When it does eventually get packed away, stockbrokers can focus their energy back on researching great investments and creating substantial wealth for their clients—the reason most of them probably got into the business to begin with.

10. The Submediocrity of Mutual Funds

The great majority of investors who are moving away from the big brokerage firms are still directing their money into mutual funds, even though, according to Lipper Analytical Services, over the past five years fully 80 percent of all mutual funds have underperformed the market's average return. Why? Promotional marketing dollars have outshone the performance truths. But in the long run, of course, the numbers will get to the buyers, and the buyers get wise to the puffery.

What you have learned in this guide is that if your managed mutual fund cannot at least match the returns of the S&P 500, little reason exists for you to remain invested in it. Instead, move your money into the Vanguard 500 Index Fund or the Vanguard Total Market Fund or something similar, where you pay baseline administrative fees for market-meeting performance. If you can't beat the market, buy the whole darned thing!

11. The Merits of Investing Just in Great Companies

The investor with a little extra time, an understanding of basic business principles, and a grasp of numbers can find market-beating investments. From Coca-Cola to Microsoft, from Gillette to Gap and Nike, businesses that are visible to the masses, that are reaching their activities out across the globe, that are highly profitable, and that have shown a consistent interest in rewarding their shareholders have created extraordinary amounts of wealth over the past twenty years. During a decade in which the S&P 500 has risen at an annualized rate of 17.7 percent, consider how rapidly the stocks of the following superior consumer franchises have grown per year:

PER YEAR GROWTH RATE OVER THE PAST DECADE

Microsoft	58%
Coca-Cola	20%
Nike	22%
Gillette	21%
Gap	37%

All of the spoils here went to the investor who, having located a sturdy business, simply bought shares and never traded out of them. And a portfolio that balances the index fund with a short list of top-tier businesses can provide market-beating returns with lower volatility. Investors with access to the Internet who would like to see daily coverage of a portfolio of consumer giants can find it at Fool.com, under the Rule Maker banner.

Our own real-money Rule Breaker (né Fool) Portfolio, which was launched the first day of our online service, contains a few more of these.

Buying and holding great companies places your money with the proven managers of mass consumer businesses, many of which have been churning out market-beating growth for five decades or more.

12. The Beauty of Long-Term Compounded Growth

Which would you rather have, $1.8 million sitting in a bank account for forty years, or a comparatively measly $100,000 quietly invested in an index fund for four decades? The numbers show that you ought to prefer just the $100,000 in stocks. After forty years of average historical growth, the $1.8 million in the bank will have grown to about $5 million; the 100,000 bucks invested, a mere 5.5 percent of its competitor at the outset, will be worth $6.5 million. The importance of superior growth rates over extended periods of time really can't be underrated in a world where so much money is blown on credit cards and numbers games. In that scenario above, if the investor held his stock money for a forty-first year, he would make an additional $715,000 that year, more than seven times his initial investment. Growth off a growing base rewards the most patient among us.

This numerical truth is startling when set alongside the daily banter about stocks and the market. It were as if the only profits to be made always presented themselves in the next week or the next hour. Precisely the opposite is true. This explains how Warren Buffett can live in Omaha, Nebraska, a thousand miles from Manhattan, and earn billions of dollars each year—while mutual fund companies based ten blocks from Wall Street can't beat the market. The country bumpkin investor disciplines himself to believe that there is no real money to be made in stocks over the next five years, just a little to be made in the next ten, and untold sums of money over the next fifty.

13. What Free Resources Lie at Your Fingertips

Never mind the expensive newsletters churned out by television gooroos each year. Ignore the detailed, often outstanding, yet expensive research reports published by our nation's investment firms. And turn your eyes from the newsstand for a second. What sort of free information about your savings money is out there?

While *The Motley Fool Investment Guide, The Motley Fool You Have More Than You Think, The Motley Fool Investment Workbook,* and *The Motley Fool's Rule Breakers, Rule Makers* ain't exactly free (unless you go down to your local library—and even it will ask for its book back), we hope the rewards from reading them will render them priceless. That said, Fool.com is free to anyone with a personal computer and a modem. At our site, individuals can link up with more than two million other people relentlessly in pursuit of better solutions to money management.

Beyond the online arena, really everyone should belong to an investment or money club of some sort. Dinner with three friends once a month to talk personal savings, portfolio allocation, and common stocks is all that's needed. It makes no logical sense to us that people would not convene to share what has and hasn't worked for them—from negotiating for that Ford Fairlane to sorting through insurance options to buying the best computer for your money to locating world-beating stocks.

Finally, the aisles of your neighborhood bookstore and the bookshelves at your local library are flooded with outstanding books on business, money, and investing. In "Appendix II, Books You Should Like," we offer short reviews of a few books we think are worth your while, doubly so if you can read them for free at Borders!

14. Why This Should Be a Family Affair

And finally, we hope you have learned the importance of spreading this knowledge throughout your family. We cannot, for example, think of a single instance where a child should not be taught to handle his or her own finances and to invest in stocks. Parents in our online area have constructed plans whereby half of their child's weekly allowance gets distributed into a stock of his choice, included in his college trust portfolio. Your average eight-year-old has at least seven decades ahead of her before she departs this world, and $200 growing at a rate of 11 percent annually for those seven decades swells into $300,000. That's without adding any money! Get a small fund going not simply *for* your children but *with the help of* your children. Their buying habits are a key through the maze. And teaching your kids this process will generate rich intellectual and economic profit.

But the exchange shouldn't be limited to parents and their bubble-gum-stock-buying children. Sharing knowledge among aunts, uncles, cousins, and in-laws makes enormous sense. Within your extended family, you are bound to find a great variety of experience and professional expertise. Getting the family involved will dramatically increase the number of ideas coming at you. Hey, see just how dog-eared they can make your copy of this book!

Quality of Life

O UR BOOK WOULD NOT be complete without this final chapter, entitled simply "Quality of Life." We've dedicated most of our text—and most of our work these past several years—to teaching about personal finance and investing. But we would be truly un-Foolish if we failed to place all this work in its true context. Other financial books may focus on investing, the stock market, or making money as ends in themselves, some of them to grotesque extremes. Not only do we wish to discuss the *true* end of our journey here, but also the very act of journeying itself.

Like anything else, money must be kept in perspective. It's possible to overvalue it and undervalue it, and numerous examples of both exist.

The danger in overvaluing it involves forgetting that money is merely a medium of exchange. John D. Rockefeller wrote, "I know of nothing more despicable and pathetic than a man who devotes all the hours of the waking day to the making of money for money's sake." John Kenneth Galbraith had similar sentiments, stated in similarly blunt terms. Writing of the stock market crash of 1929 (which he lived through at the age of twenty-one), he offered, "One can relish the varied idiocy of human action during a panic to the full, for, while it is a time of great tragedy, nothing is being lost but money." Both of these American financial figures make points you won't find in your daily financial newspaper or its many advertisements.

On the other hand, some of us undervalue money when we waste it. Your Foolish authors have already made their feelings known about Atlantic City and Las Vegas, as well as your local 7-Eleven's lotto dispenser. Those who've spent anything more than meaningless sums in these venues would do well to listen to the words of Ecclesiastes 10:19—"A feast is made for

laughter, and wine maketh merry: but money answereth all things." It practically can, so long as you retain it.

We have pointed out some ways that money is over- and undervalued. It
remains to identify its *actual value*. Too often, money is thought of merely
as a way of measuring the expense of material possessions, and consequently many of us lose the real meaning of the stuff. Our favorite contemporary preacher, Maurice Boyd of the City Church in New York City,
points out, "Ernest Hemingway used to give things away at the beginning
of a new year. He said he did so to prove that he owned them. If he couldn't
give them away, he didn't own them . . . they owned him. And he lamented
that we spend so much attention on things that cannot feel and cannot love
instead of lavishing our care on people who can feel our affection and return our love."

Please don't do this. Don't equate money with possessions, and possessions with the meaning of life. Hemingway offers the reminder that your
family—especially your children—will end up not liking you very much.

Here's the value of money, and let it be writ in luminous ink across the
night skies forevermore: *Money is opportunity.* It is the opportunity to educate oneself, to move someplace better, to support a large family, to retire
early. These things are all wildly good. To gain the money you'll need for
these opportunities, you combine hard work with saving and long-term investing in the stock market. That is the obvious message of this book.

Learning investing and then doing the investing itself demand that you
sacrifice time that might otherwise be spent in ways more immediately
pleasurable. Time is our very dearest resource, and the actual amount of it
that each of us has in the future is an abiding mystery. Thus, saving and investing in some ways represent risky short-term sacrifices to achieve
hoped-for long-term benefits. But these are the sorts of risks we all should
take! Successful investing buys you leisure and early retirement, which is
another way of saying that it will buy you time.

Those words are echoed by the most Foolish fellow among our nation's
founding fathers. For twenty-five years, Benjamin Franklin wrote and published our literary forerunner: *Poor Richard's Almanack,* a witty com-
pendium of common sense and financial advice. Among thousands of
other epigrams, Franklin wrote, "Dost thou love life? Then do not squan-
der time, for that is the stuff life is made of."

Having identified the meaning of money, we must now discover the
goal, or end, of our journey. It is this: just to give the money away! Because
as you can see, what you're really just doing is donating opportunity to

others. In our own case, we each received money at the age of eighteen from parents who had saved since our birth. That money, invested fully in the stock market, enabled us to take a few years off after college and start our own business, rather than have to work for someone else. Having been given this special opportunity through the foresight and savvy investing of our parents—and their parents before them—we Fools are living examples of exactly what we're writing about. It's made a world of difference in our lives.

Work, save, and plan, and the result will be the creation of wealth that you can use lovingly to benefit others. Create opportunity, then give it away.

That's the true end of the Foolish journey, but we also promised at the beginning of this chapter to talk about the journey itself, and that is our closing meditation.

The journey itself is what most of us are concerned with right now, the next minute, tomorrow, next week. It's the present, the near future. It means a great deal for many reasons, not the least of which is that when one reaches the endpoint, the goal, one generally discovers that all the *meaning* was in the actual journeying. So it better be fun! Additionally, *how* we journey often has as much to do with our happiness and longevity as anything else.

There is a class of investor out there known as the trader. You know about him by now. The trader is someone who watches the financial markets minute by minute, for the purpose of making money by trading in and out of situations that appear profitable and advantageous. Many traders are professionals who report to the trading floors of our nation's financial exchanges or brokerage firms; it's their full-time job. Flipping through television channels you see them occasionally running around the floors of the New York Stock Exchange shouting at one another, wearing colored jackets and tracing out hand signals. The job has a high attrition rate, as the average human constitution can't take the pace in "the pit" for more than a few years. But its passion and frenetic pace have caused the job to be occasionally romanticized in books and films.

Other traders exist besides pit traders. There are money managers spread out across the country who spend their days jiving with the market's gyrations, entrusted with guiding other people's money to victory with the help of the latest-breaking news. It's a big business for these guys, too.

Finally, with the growing ease of use of online trading, a new class of trader is emerging, the day trader. This is the at-home amateur, young or old, experienced or novice, who can generally be expected to have a computer whirring at one end of the room with financial cable TV at the other.

We don't like trading for a variety of reasons. For one thing, trading contributes little to the economy or to anyone or anything else. The trader feeds at the trough of real-time fluctuating exchange prices, scanning for ways to gobble up quick money using a variety of technical tools and techniques. And indeed, we're not even sure it works that well. Many professional traders work to reduce their clients' risk by "hedging," placing short-term bets *against* their clients' long-term positions. The aim isn't to beat the market at all, and indeed, we remain skeptical that one can consistently beat the market by trading. (As you've already seen, high commission expense can sink individual investors on its own even before they begin to worry about tax consequences.) And the success of patient, buy-and-hold investors like Warren Buffett is instructive. Buffett became the world's richest investor by finding a few good businesses to buy, not by spending his time chasing eighths and quarters off gut feelings and market rumors.

While the average person may look in wonder at an acquaintance who's a trader, our own feelings run more toward pity. That's because the biggest argument of all against trading has nothing to do with whether it works, whether it's constructive, or what have you. The biggest argument is that it's a tremendous waste of time. With just one life to live, how many of us wish to while away our hours trying to zig when the market zigs, and zag when it zags? It's the financial equivalent of spending all one's daytime hours walking a dog. Hey, we like dogs as much as the next guy, and we like the stock market too. But if you're spending all day every day holding a leash, recognize that your dog is walking *you,* not vice versa.

A Wall Street manager recently retired early, at the age of fifty-five. His reason? To get to know his grandchildren. He said he'd missed watching his own children grow up, so he wasn't going to make that mistake again. That's tragic.

Back to the right sort of journeying. Let's instead resummon the ghost of Anne Scheiber, the woman we mentioned in our introduction who invested methodically and patiently and died with $22 million. She is the complete opposite of the trader, a woman who spent very little time changing her investments. Scheiber just let the market do its thing, compounding great returns over a long period of time.

Despite our anecdotal references to the Buffetts and Scheibers of the world, you needn't be a legend to succeed here. We get notes and e-mails every day from ordinary people who are making the perfect start to their own journeys. Following a very poor day for his 3Com (Nasdaq: COMS) stock, Gary Estes wrote us:

> We met during your book signing tour in Dallas, on a very slick and snowy day. Y'all autographed a copy of your book for me, which I promptly read. To make a long story short, I wanted to be a Foolish investor. I reshuffled my portfolio a bit, did my own homework, decided to invest in a few of your holdings (the latest being 3COM) and a few of my own discovery, and looked to the long-term horizon. I had a new buying strategy, a way to track my portfolio, a goal to shoot for, and for the first time, a new selling strategy that wasn't based on greed or panic. I even made a bit of money. I bought a Fool baseball cap. (My ex-wife had a field day with that.) [But I still had] doubts, "Was I truly being Foolish with my investments?" I never really knew until today. As I was reading about 3COM's drop in the *Wall Street Journal* and the Motley Fool Evening News, it suddenly dawned on me that my feelings about an event like this had changed! Instead of feeling a stomach-churning, gut-wrenching sickness, calculating how much I had "lost" by not selling at a peak and calling my broker, I now feel almost indifferent. I'm not selling today. No panic. I believe that part of this new feeling comes from being more informed, and knowing more about my investments. And part of this new attitude must be what it's like to be . . . a Fool.

After wandering around our online site for three days, a new reader named Jeff Germanich e-mailed us: "Having never actually been involved in investing, and now realizing that this is what I must eventually do, I need help. I hope you will forgive the really foolish questions I have to ask." Jeff was much earlier on than Gary, but you *can't* make a better first move than asking questions. In fact, neither Jeff nor anyone else should ever apologize for trying to learn. Our staff promptly answered Jeff's questions, as we do for anyone who visits our online site, or e-mails us. A full-time Foolish staff waits on the other end, ready to answer any financial questions that come its way. Just e-mail help@Fool.com

You can see it a hundred yards away, just as sure as that sky-high pop-up will be gloved by the shortstop—Gary Estes and Jeff Germanich are on the right sort of journey. And they're going to get there . . . they're going to win.

Whenever opportunity and journey mingle so closely together, these should set bells off in the heads of most Americans, re-creating our sense of wonder and appreciation for the land that we've inherited. The New

World offered such a powerful opportunity that many of our ancestors—at whatever point, during whatever generation—journeyed here. They shared a few key traits: a restlessness over unsatisfactory circumstance, a willingness to take risk, and sufficient energy to move themselves and their families to a new continent. Ever since, Americans have been characterized as an optimistic people (on occasion disapprovingly).

We can think of few better, stronger, more attractive human traits than optimism. While cynics may wish to equate optimism with naïveté, we consider the word synonymous with hope. In his first inaugural address, Lincoln (who wrote his own speeches—novel idea!) asked, "Why should there not be a patient confidence in the ultimate justice of the people? Is there any better or equal hope in the world?" Long before, another great speaker, Cicero, wrote, "While there's life, there's hope." The reverse of that seems even truer. For those who wish to make some good dent on the world, optimism makes a useful companion. It is also an essential promoter of quality of life. In taking control of your finances, by investing in the future, you are migrating to your own New World, making your own mark. Let us just say bon voyage! We'll be watching out for you, dear Fool.

Folly forever!

Appendix I: Scribes? Meet Printers!

DRAWING VERBATIM FROM Daniel Boorstin's *The Discoverers,* we simply substituted the words below on the right for Boorstin's actual words, on the left. Note the completely on-target, historical (and hysterical) parallels.

scribes and *illuminators = brokers*
books and *manuscripts = investment information*
manuscript books = brokerage research reports
volumes = research
the art of "natural writing" = old-line research
calligrapher's craft = financial world's shenanigans

printers = Internet pioneers
printing and *the printing press = the Internet*
printed book = Web trading
printed section = Web link
the art of "artificial writing" = new-media research

second half of the fifteenth century = first half of the twenty-first century
first half (of the fifteenth century) = latter half of the twentieth century

Boorstin wrote:

It was not dissatisfaction with the work of the best brokers that had stimulated the quest for other ways to reproduce investment information. The original effort was to find how to multiply investment information in larger quantity and at lower costs, but as good as the brokers' best work. . . .

During the first century of the Internet the brokers who were practicing old-line research and the Internet pioneers practicing new-media research competed for the same customers. The Internet did not at once put the brokers out of business. Nearly as many brokerage research reports survive from the first half of the twenty-first century, after the invention of the Internet, as from the latter half of the twentieth century. Brokers continued to cater to the luxury trade, turning out deluxe research for those who could afford it. . . .

For a while there was enough business for both brokers and Internet pioneers. But as the price of Web trading declined, brokers began to have trouble finding work. When it became plain that the Internet was a menace to the financial world's shenanigans, the organized brokers and their conservative allies sought laws to protect their monopoly. In 1534 Francis I [ed. note: curse this political figure, whoever he be] gave in to their demands and issued an edict suppressing the Internet in Paris, but this was never enforced. As brokers saw that the Web trading was here to stay, they began to cooperate. They themselves started using the Internet and saved labor by inserting Web links into their brokerage research reports. . . .

And the rest is history.

As hard as we look, we don't find many scribes around these days.

Boorstin closes his chapter by quoting the English essayist Thomas Carlyle. You can do your own word substitution on this one—it's fairly straightforward:

"He who first shortened the labor of copyists by the device of movable types was disbanding hired armies, and cashiering most kings and senates, and creating a whole new democratic world."

Appendix II: Books You Should Like

MANY OF OUR READERS have asked for a short list of highly readable books on the subject of money and investing. What is not yet apparent is that some of our nation's greatest literary contributions over the past twenty-five years have come from—get this—financial writers. Below are some of our favorite writers and financial thinkers and what they've written. None of them paid for their placement here; we'll charge the next time around.

How the Stock Market Works (New York Institute of Finance), by John M. Dalton, editor. A no-nonsense guide to the mechanics of the stock market, interpreting many obscure Wall Street terms into plain English.

Wall Street Words: An Essential A to Z Guide for Today's Investor (Houghton Mifflin), by David Logan Scott. A good tool for translating stock talk into English.

One Up on Wall Street (Penguin USA) and *Beating the Street* (Fireside/ Simon & Schuster), both by Peter Lynch and John Rothschild. Two of the most frequently mentioned books by folks on our staff when asked about classic books for individual investors. Both books talk about the virtues of patience and about investing in the businesses that you know.

Investing Without a Silver Spoon (The Motley Fool) by Jeff "El Jefe" Fischer. You don't need a lot of money to start investing. In fact, you don't even need a broker, as our resident Direct Investing Plan expert Jeff Fischer explains.

Common Stocks and Uncommon Profits (John Wiley & Sons), by Philip A. Fisher. A wonderful guide to understanding a company's core business and the importance of becoming familiar with the people that run it. Fisher provides a number of ways to better understand what these companies do and why, who they are, and whether you should continue to invest in them.

The Wealthy Barber (Prima Publishing), by David Chilton. More script than manual, *The Wealthy Barber* walks readers through the ranks of personal-finance topics—wills, insurance, mortgages, taxes, retirement planning—with a chatty, real-world narrative.

Confessions of a Stock Broker (New York Institute of Finance) by Andrew A. Lanyi. This book goes into really explicit detail on "how to research" a company and how to understand the company's business beyond just the basics.

The Intelligent Investor (HarperCollins), by Benjamin Graham. This book provides a simple analytical framework for investors as well as a definition of what investing really means, which is to say "investing" shouldn't be confused with "trading."

The Motley Fool Investment Guide (Simon & Schuster), *The Motley Fool Investment Workbook* (Fireside), and *The Motley Fools's Rule Breakers, Rule Makers* (Simon & Schuster) by yours truly. We won't go into great detail here. Pieces of our hearts and souls have been left in these Foolish tomes. We hope they'll make for excellent carrriages for your lifelong journey through investing, savings growth, and the colorful world of business. You can expect more from The Foolish Publishing Juggernaut (TFPJ) in our efforts to reform the financial industry, restoring it as a servant to the people. If you catch us losing our humor, deviating from education, or undermining your efforts to save more and profit off those savings—flame us via e-mail at help@Fool.com.

Ask the Headhunter (Plume Books), by Nicholas A. Corcodilos. While not specifically a finance book, Nick presents a fundamentally Foolish approach to allocating the most precious resource of all: your time working.

Corcodilos puts the onus on the individual to cleverly (even gleefully) navigate the bumpy path to job satisfaction in the Information Age. His approach to understanding the business you work for (or want to work in), knowing your competitors, mastering your industry, and maximizing your value to your employer (and by extension yourself) is applicable to everyone no matter where you are in your life or career path.

Appendix III: Open Letter to the White House

Dear Mr. President:

We write in the hope that you will reassess our nation's position on state-sponsored lottery games. In 1999, Americans spent more than $30 billion on a game that proffers a negative rate of return of 50 percent per wager. As the nation has fretted for years about the possibility of a bear market in stocks—the specter of American business being devalued 20 to 40 percent overnight—the lottery system has visited a bear market on people and their communities *every day of the year.*

Basic mathematics tells us that $2,000 methodically invested into the lottery at a rate of $10 per day will dissolve into $175 in twelve months. In the same fashion, a $10,000 bet will drop to less than $875 in ten years. Our citizens—many of them our least educated—are being persuaded by their state to invest repeatedly in what constitutes the wildest (and Wisest) of investment risks. Indeed, dollar for dollar, the states' expensive commercial campaigns advertising the lottery constitute the loudest message that local government communicates to its people. "The next winner could be you" is the message—not the importance of education or community building or safety on the streets.

We do not request, Mr. President, that you scuttle the lottery system. In an open society, the people do and should have inalienable rights to spend, save, wager, or invest their money as they see fit. However, we are requesting that you use the bully pulpit to discourage Americans from sinking their savings money into a game that rewards so few, hurting far more than it helps. You both could be instrumental in redirecting these wagered billions into our financial markets instead, creating new national savings that would lead to an even more robust and sound economy.

In addition to our call for your support, we request that the Justice Department investigate anticompetitive practices on the part of our state governments and recommend legislation applying antitrust law to their conduct of lotteries. State lotteries are run as monopolies. It hardly surprises us, then, that these games are so damaging and so misunderstood. Monopoly breeds dependence, ignorance, and waste.

We hope that in your service as President you will champion financial education while challenging the shortsighted ignorance that our state lotteries promote. While many amoral activities are legal, we assume you'll agree that American government shouldn't actively sponsor them. The reality of the lottery is that a few people get rich while a million more don't—including some people who over time will lose much of what they have. Society pays for this, in the end, through increases in poverty and crime. This is the untold chapter of the lottery story, the part you never see on the commercials because it has no glamour or pizzazz. We hope you'll paint that picture for America.

Thank you for your attention.

Fool on,

David and Tom Gardner

Glossary

Analyst: A financial professional who analyzes public businesses to determine a "fair" or "intrinsic" value for them. The term is generally applied to almost any professional investor who does research of some kind. There is no specific degree or certification that is required to be called an analyst.

Annual report: A yearly statement of a public company's operating and financial performance, punctuated by pictures of families enjoying the firm's products and/or services.

Annualize: To take an item measured over a certain period and to restate it on an annual basis. For instance, if it costs $10 million every month to run a factory, the annualized cost is $10 million × 12, or $120 million.

Appreciation: Increase in the price (or value) of a stock or other asset. Appreciation is one component of total return.

Back-end load: A sales charge paid for selling a mutual fund or other investment. (Also see *Front-end load* and *No-load mutual fund*.)

Bankruptcy: When a company is unable to pay its short-term debts, it is bankrupt. Such a company often files for Chapter 11 bankruptcy protection, which allows it to continue to operate while it reorganizes.

Bear: Do you think that the market is headed south? You're bracing yourself for a crash or correction? You feel that stock XYZ will soon be taking a tumble? Guess what—you're a bear! Bears are investors with a pessimistic outlook on the entire market, or a particular industry, or a given stock.

Bond: A bond essentially represents a loan. Bondholders lend money to governments or companies and are promised a certain rate of interest in return. Interest rates vary depending on the quality or reliability of the bond issuer. U.S. government bonds, for example, carry little risk and thus can offer lower interest rates. Companies offer higher interest rates. The riskiest companies' bonds are called "junk bonds."

Broker: One who sells financial products. Whether in insurance, real estate, or stocks, most brokers work under compensation structures that are at direct odds with the greatest good of their clients. (Also see *Discount broker, Full-service broker,* and *Stockbroker.*)

Bull: Are your glasses rose colored? Do you see nothing but blue skies ahead for the stock market or a particular stock? Then you're a bull—an optimistic investor—as opposed to a bear.

Capital: A business's cash or property, or an investor's pile of cash.

Capital gain: You bought a stock and later sold it. If you made a profit, that's your capital gain. If you lost money, it's a capital loss.

Certificate of deposit (CD): Not the shiny disk that spews loud music, but a time deposit one makes at the bank or buys from a brokerage or other financial institution. Like a bond, it pays interest at regular intervals or at maturity, at which point the depositor claims the principal, or amount deposited.

Chief executive officer (CEO): The CEO is the highest executive officer in a corporation, sort of like the captain of a ship. He or she is accountable to the company's board of directors and is frequently a member of that board. The CEO participates in setting strategy with the board and other officers and is responsible for the tactics in meeting the corporation's goals.

Churn: Churning is unconscious or conscious overtrading by a broker in a customer's account. Since brokers are most often compensated by the number of transactions made on a customer's behalf, there is temptation to trade too frequently, whether that's in stocks, bonds, or mutual funds with a load.

Cold call: It's cold because the person doesn't know you from a snowdrift. To build a book of business, many new brokers must call people they don't know and sell an investment idea or their services as a broker.

Commission: When a broker makes a transaction for a customer, the customer pays a commission. This part of a brokerage's business makes up a good portion of its revenues, but is not necessarily its most profitable activity. For brokers, however, this is how they make a living.

Compounding: Let's say you're a fifteen-year-old who manages to save a buck a day. In fifty-five years, you'd have $20,000. But if you systematically invested it into a simple and safe investment, like a government bond that returns a locked-in 5 percent annually, after fifty-five years you'd have $102,159.88. How about a conservative annual return of 9 percent? You're looking at $481,795.95. What's happening? Over time, each buck is earning interest on interest. Or, more simply put, the interest you earn becomes a part of your original principal invested. You then go on to earn interest on the interest already accrued.

Correction: A decline, usually short and steep, in the prevailing price of shares traded in the market or an individual stock. Anytime that commentators cannot find a reason for an individual stock or the entire market falling, they call it a correction. Funny, though, they never remember that the stock market corrects upward as well.

Day trader: Day traders are in and out of the market many times during the course of one trading session and often do not hold a position in any stocks overnight. This approach tends to generate a lot of expenses in the form of commissions and denies the day trader the ability to participate in the long-term creation of wealth through compounded growth. It also makes for a lot of time in front of a computer.

Discount broker: Brokers who offer fewer of the "services" championed by full-service brokers but charge lower fees and commissions. Discount brokers are ideal for do-it-yourself investors. (Also see *Broker* and *Full-service broker.*)

Dividend: A distribution from a company to a stockholder in the form of cash, shares of stock, or other assets. The most common kind of dividend is a distribution of earnings. (Also see *Dividend yield.*)

Dividend-reinvestment plan (DRiP): A plan under which cash dividends issued by a corporation are used to purchase additional shares directly from the corporation itself, thereby avoiding commissions.

Dividend yield: The income relative to the current share price that a company will pay out to shareholders on a regular basis, usually expressed in percentage terms.

Dow Jones industrial average: The average is comprised of thirty companies chosen by editors of Dow Jones & Company. These companies are supposed to epitomize the very best American corporations and reflect the landscape of corporate America.

Earnings: The money a company puts in the bank after all of the costs of delivering a product or service have been accounted for. (Also see *Revenues.*)

Earnings per share (EPS): Net income (earnings or profits) divided by the current number of shares of stock outstanding. This is one of the traditional means for valuing stock.

Equities: A name that comes from "equitable claims." Equities are just shares of stock. Because they represent a proportional share in the business, they are equitable claims on the business itself.

Fair value: The theoretical price at which a company is "fairly valued," the price above which it would not be reasonable to assume the shares will rise. Fair value at any given point is derived from a number of qualitative and quantitative aspects of the business.

401(k): A savings vehicle offered by employers that is named after the Internal Revenue Code section in which it appears. Given their tax advantages and the possibility of corporate matching (read: FREE MONEY), 401(k) plans are well worth considering. Nonprofits have the almost identical 403(b) plan, and local and state governments offer the 457 plan. (Also see *Simplified employee pension plan.*)

Front-end load: A sales charge paid when a mutual fund or other investment is purchased. (Also see *Back-end load* and *No-load mutual fund.*)

Full-service broker: Full-service brokers earn commissions for each trade made in a customer's account. They make more money by trading in and out of lots of investments. They are sometimes referred to as "full-price brokers." (Also see *Broker, Discount broker,* and *Stockbroker.*)

Income: See *Earnings.*

Index fund: The only type of mutual fund that makes sense to us. While most mutual funds are actively (mis)managed, index funds are generally computer driven, designed to mimic the performance of a given stock market index such as the S&P 500. During their popularization over the past thirty years, managed funds have consistently underperformed the S&P 500. (Also see *Standard & Poor's 500 Index.*)

Individual retirement account (IRA): One of a group of plans—including Keoghs, SEPs, 401(k) and 403(b) plans—that allow you to put away some of your income into a tax-deferred retirement fund, on which you won't pay taxes until your latter days, when you withdraw your funds. The benefit of an IRA is that the account holder has the ability to invest the money however she likes.

Initial public offering (IPO): A company's first sale of stock to the public. To do an IPO, a company needs to round up an underwriting bank. (Also see *Underwriter.*)

Institutions: Institutional investors include pension funds, insurance funds, mutual funds, hedge funds. These are the big players in the stock market, as they have a lot of money to invest. Although institutions hold only about 40 percent to 50 percent of all stock owned, they account for as much as 90 percent of daily trading volume.

Keogh: A special type of individual retirement account (IRA) that doubles as a pension plan for a self-employed person. The self-employed person can put aside up to $30,000 a year, significantly more than the normal $2,000 cap on an individual IRA. (Also see *Individual retirement account.*)

Life insurance: See *Term insurance* and *Whole-life insurance.*

Liquidity: The easier it is to turn an asset into cash, the more liquid it is. Stocks are very liquid, as they can be sold any weekday at any brokerage. Works of art and homes are not nearly as liquid as stocks.

Load: A fee charged by the salesman who sells you a mutual fund or annuity. (Also see *Back-end load, Front-end load,* and *No-load mutual fund.*)

Margin: (1) To borrow money from your brokerage firm for the purpose of buying securities. "I have margined my account 70 percent" translates to "I have borrowed against 70 percent of the value of my account to purchase more stocks." (2) A measure of profitability of a company, such as profit margin, operating margin, or gross margin.

Market capitalization: The total market value of all of a firm's outstanding shares. Market capitalization is calculated by multiplying a firm's share price by the number of shares outstanding.

Mutual fund: A mutual fund enables you to invest your money, along with thousands of others, in one "fund," in which you all have a "mutual" interest. Presiding over the fund is a manager (or managers) responsible for achieving the fund's stated investment objective. (Also see Index fund.)

Nasdaq Stock Market: A national stock market where trades are made exclusively via computers. The second-largest market in the country, the Nasdaq is home to many high-tech and newer firms.

New York Stock Exchange (NYSE): The largest and oldest stock exchange in the United States, this Wall Street haunt is the one frequently featured on television, with hundreds of traders on the floor staring up at screens and answering phones, ready to trade stocks upon command from their firms.

No-load mutual fund: A mutual fund that is sold directly from the company that manages the fund. Because no active sales force is hawking them, the investor does not pay a commission or sales fee (load). Historically, there is no distinction in performance between no-load funds and ones that charge a load. (Also see *Back-end load* and *Front-end load*.)

Options: Contracts that give a person the right to buy or sell an underlying stock or commodity at a set price within a set amount of time. The majority of options expire worthless.

Price-to-earnings ratio (P/E):   A measure of a stock's price in relation to its trailing twelve months' earnings per share. Oftentimes the higher the sustainable growth rate of a company, the higher its price-to-earnings ratio.

Profits: See *Earnings*.

Public business: As opposed to private companies, a company is public after it issues partial ownership of itself, in the form of stock, to the public.

Quarter: Businesses have four quarters, roughly equal to three months, in every fiscal year, for which they report their financial results. After each quarter, a company is required to file a report with the SEC providing investors with juicy details on how the company is doing.

Revenues (or Sales):   Revenues are money that a company collects from a customer for the sale of a product or service. When you subtract out all costs from revenues, you get profits or earnings. (Also see *Earnings*.)

Secondary offering: When a company offers a large block of stock for sale anytime after its initial public offering, that is called a secondary offering. The stock can come from company officials, institutions with a lot of shares, or the offering company itself in the form of brand-new shares.

Securities: A fancy name for shares of stock or bonds, "securities" is just a blanket way to refer to any kind of financial asset that can be traded.

Securities and Exchange Commission (SEC):   The federal agency charged with ensuring that the U.S. stock market is a free and open market. All companies with stock registered in the United States must comply with SEC rules and regulations, which include filing quarterly reports on how well the company is doing.

Securities Exchange Act of 1934:   Used to plug the holes in the 1933 act, the Securities Exchange Act of 1934 led to the formation of the Securities and Exchange Commission and set the ground rules for companies that wanted their stock to be listed in the United States.

Shareholder: If you buy even one share of stock in a company, you can proudly call yourself a shareholder. As a shareholder you get an invitation to the company's annual meeting, and you have the right to vote on the members of the board of directors and other company matters.

Short-selling: The act of profiting off of shares of stock when the price goes down.

Simplified employee pension (SEP) plan: A special kind of Keogh individual retirement account (IRA). Basically, SEPs were created so that small businesses could set up retirement plans that were a little easier to work than normal pension plans. Both employees and the employer can contribute to a SEP. (Also see *Individual retirement account* and *Keogh*.)

Standard & Poor's 500 Index (S&P 500): An index of five hundred of the biggest and best companies in American industry, selected by an editorial board at Standard & Poor's. The index is often used as a proxy for the overall performance of the stock market and is particularly used as a way to measure how well mutual fund managers and brokers have performed relative to the market.

Stock: A share of stock represents a proportional ownership stake in a corporation. Investors purchase stock as a way to own a part of a publicly traded business.

Stockbroker: An individual who has been licensed by the National Association of Securities Dealers to trade stocks and advise clients on various personal finance issues. These individuals work at full-service brokerages. (Also see *Broker*.)

Stock split: Whenever a company believes that the price per share of its stock has risen to a point where investors may erroneously perceive it as "expensive," the company will split the stock, reducing the price but increasing the number of shares outstanding.

Tax-deferred: When you invest in something like an individual retirement account or an annuity, you are deferring taxes until you withdraw money. This means that you do not have to pay taxes on any gains until you withdraw your funds.

Tax-free: Under certain circumstances you can put money into an individual retirement account or a 401(k) plan on a tax-free basis, which means you do not have to pay income tax on the money that you earned until you withdraw the funds.

Term insurance: A no-nonsense life insurance plan that calls for low annual payments ("premiums") that will increase as you get older. (Also see *Whole-life insurance*.)

Ticker symbol: An abbreviation for a company's name that is used as shorthand by stock-quote reporting services and brokerages.

12b-1 fee: As if management fees on mutual funds were not enough, many funds charge an extra fee. This fee makes current investors pay for the marketing and advertising used to get new investors.

Underwriter/Underwritten: Underwriters are brokerage firms that help a company come public in an initial public offering. They underwrite (vouch for) the stock. When a company has been brought public, the shares have been underwritten.

Valuation: The determination of a fair value for a security.

Wall Street: The main drag in New York City's financial district, although the term is used mostly to refer to the establishment of investing gooroos.

Whole-life insurance: A life insurance product with an investment component. You pay in substantially more money, which your insurance provider will invest for you while taking a porterhouse-sized cut for herself. This essentially turns your insurance into an estate-planning tool—one with embarrassingly low annualized returns.

Yield: See *Dividend yield*.

Acknowledgments

I N THE FAST-PACED world of the Internet, where many quick decisions can, in a year, build or dismantle companies of every ilk, even Fools can sometimes forget to say thank you. Combine writers' deadlines, fact checking, and the occasional necessary jaunt to the beach on top of that and you have a recipe for too much urgency and too little thanks. This book would not have been possible without the help of the following people, to whom we are indebted deeply . . .

Through *The Motley Fool Investment Guide, The Motley Fool Investment Workbook,* and *The Motley Fool You Have More Than You Think,* we've had the great good fortune of working with the same editor, Bob Mecoy. In autumn of 1994, after scouring the online area, he dropped us an introductory e-mail that concluded, in words whose vaguely Oklahoman accent we can now in retrospect recognize, "Hey, guys, I think there's a book here." He found it long before we did. More important, he's made it a distinct pleasure.

We're just as grateful to our ICM agent, Suzanne Gluck, who took Bob's initial interest, flaunted it to the world, and then scored us a significant premium. No one seems so much a pea in the pod to us as Suzanne at her desk overlooking the midtown-Manhattan bustle, coyly smiling into telephone headsets as she juggles multibillion-dollar conglomerates.

We'd also like to give a shout out to Frank Veronsky, our New York City cover photographer; Frank took a day out from his busy schedule to come to Virginia to shoot us Fools.

From New York City, we return to Fool Global Headquarters in Alexandria, Virginia, where thanks go out first to Jeff "Jefe" Fischer, who came with us to rural estates and willingly fed for weeks upon pretzels and Junior Mints as he diligently researched everything from credit unions to trap-door spiders to just who the heck said, "If not now, when?" We are also most thankful to Gabrielle Loperfido for organizing this book, and to Melissa Flaim for organizing our lives. Both mastered the art of rescheduling deadlines as they zinged chapters over the Internet and rushed contracts to couriers.

There would not have been any book without our employees at Fool HQ, who made our sporadic jousts with the muse possible. Day in, day out, Team Fool distinguishes itself in its service to several million readers in over a hundred countries by establishing close relations with some of the greatest businesses on the planet, by losing ten of eleven of our softball games in the summer of 2000, and by making our office into a home, our work into a life. Special thanks go to Selena Maranjian, Alissa Territo, Brian Bauer, Bill Barker, and Mona Sharma, without whose help, pleas, cajoles, threats, and, ultimately, use of physical force, this book would not have been possible.

There would be no Foolishness to speak of without our families. David thanks his beautiful wife, Margaret, and their three perky tots, Katherine, Gabriel, and Zack. Tom thanks his beautiful wife and their dog, neither of whom he has met yet. And we thank together our parents, who raised us in a Chekhovian world teeming with aunts and uncles, godparents and grandparents, cousins, and a sister. We've tried to bring their love of games, of storytelling, of wit and candor and spirit to everything we do. The end result is Folly. Hope that's OK, Mom and Dad.

And finally we thank you, our reader, without whom there is no Folly. So many of you have touched our lives with your stories, your willing offers of aid, your calls for help. We shall work hard to be of the best service to you in the coming decades. We hope you'll fulfill your end of the deal by letting us know whenever you see a way for us to improve our business. To that end, we look forward to hearing from those who haven't yet communicated to us. We can be reached at help@Fool.com.

These six Foolish years have been bewilderingly fun. Neither of us has any idea how this will all end, or if it ever should.

Index

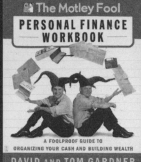

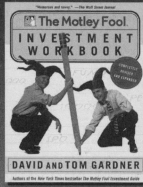

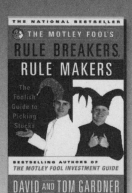